NOT A "BLONDE ESKIMO" BUT THE AUTHOR IN MUK-PI'S PARKA.

ATTIC

Alaska

By
MARY LEE DAVIS

Author of " We Are Alaskans,"
"Alaska, the Great Bear's Cub"

ILLUSTRATED BY AUTHOR'S PHOTOGRAPHS

W. A. WILDE COMPANY

BOSTON   MASSACHUSETTS

Printed in United States of America

To
MARK SULLIVAN
Who urged me to write
o f
OUR TIMES
i n
ALASKA

CONTENTS

vii

Contents

PAGE

ILLUSTRATIONS

Illustrations

Uncle Sam's Attic

I

New Pilgrims for a New Plymouth

THIS Uncle Sam of ours is a trifle old-fashioned, or he would not possess an attic; for modern houses boast only a cupboard or two, and unused space is nowadays considered an extravagance, in such a crowded world.

To have a spacious attic like Alaska and not to use every inch of it, does seem rather shockingly wasteful—especially for an elderly gentleman who talks so very sagely to his nieces and nephews about the virtues of economy! And he himself will admit that rooms downstairs are getting crowded, even though he has given up his former lifelong habit of keeping open house and welcoming all neighbor folk who wished to come and make a home with him.

I happen to be one of Uncle Sam's nieces who has lived for many years in his attic; and I have found it so pleasant a place, both summer and winter, that I wish more people knew of all the treasure hidden here. Although it lies close up under the world's white roof-tree, most people do not know that it is heated to a most agreeable temperature by warm air currents and hot-water heat from below.

High and aloof, reached only through a steep climb up that ladder of the parallels which narrows to the Circle and the Pole, this land of Alaska is

truly a spacious attic, lying above the forty-eight
rooms of state below. Treasures unexplored await a
rainy-day unearthing here. Perhaps a time may
come when Uncle Sam will say: " I need some coal,
and the oil is running low. I have to go to my
neighbors' market for fish and meat, and I'm afraid
I'll have to make a trip soon to the bank, for gold.
I need some copper and a mite of tin, for mending.
Where can I lay hand on them? The neighbors
want to keep their own, and do not like to lend.
There must still be *some* of these things stored about
the old house, somewhere."

When that time comes, we who have poked our
inquisitive noses under the attic eaves and in its
crannies, opened old trunks of tucked-away valu-
ables, and explored dark corners where spare goods
were carelessly piled—back in the prodigal days
when Uncle Sam's great house was builded—we who
know and love the North will say to him: " It is
here, all you are looking for! We who have lived
here long, up under the ridge pole of your house,
have sought out all its treasures for you. Just carry
them down-ladder, and they will run your household for unnumbered years, in peace and plenty."

For Uncle Sam's attic is a place which he, like
many another busy old gentleman, has always
planned to " do something with, some day." But he
has never yet got round to it. He has been so
occupied in running his big hospitable home downstairs, he seldom has occasion to go " up attic " and
explore there for himself. But the time will not be
long, now, when he will be needing extra room, and
here is room a-plenty. A whopping big room this,
larger than any one of his forty-eight below stairs—
one fifth as large as his whole house, twice as large

as his biggest room Texas, five hundred times as large as his smallest room Rhode Island.

Back in 1867 people who knew next to nothing about Alaska declared this attic to be just so much waste space. They called it "Seward's Ice Box" and "Seward's Folly," because it had been Secretary Seward who persuaded Uncle Sam to add the attic to his house, as a protection from strong and then prevailing north winds. They thought this space not worth the price of keeping the roof mended— which is about all that has been spent on it, in all these intervening years! But many of those things are here which you yourself find stored in your own attic—things you don't need just now but which may come in handy some day: all the worn-out and the old-fashioned things you send "up attic," including many well-designed but antique bureaus (some dating back to colonial periods for inspiration, of Jacobean twist, of a George III solidity), whereas one up-to-date, substantial, built-in Cabinet piece would be so much more useful to us who make our homes here!

But those who think there's naught but worthless rubbish stored inside Alaska, are vastly mistaken. Like all attics, it has gathered dust—but ours is yellow dust of gold. And, too, those who search here may find

" Budgets of dream-dust, merchandise of song,
  Wreckage of hope, and packs of ancient wrong,
  Nepenthes gathered from a secret strand,
  Fardels of heart-ache, burdens of old sins,
  Luggage sent down from dim ancestral inns,
  And bales of fantasy from no-man's-land."

Before we go any further, however, I think it only

fair to warn you. By those who do not know the
North, Alaska is considered a very dangerous
country. This is quite true, for she is Circe of most
strange enchantments. But if ever you should come
to know Alaska, you too would love her; for the land
creates a strong and subtle spell. And so, if you are
one of those shy timid souls who only love the warm
hearth-side of home and never stray, even in thought
or mind, then please do not read any further here;
for knowledge of that wide and spacious and all-but-
untenanted attic will bring you only vague uneasiness
and mild unrest.

This is the story of to-day's Frontier as seen by
one who knows the sharp call and yet sharper edge
of life on that Frontier, from own intensive living
there. And the call of The Frontier *is* dangerous—
to the frontier-minded. You never pick up a magazine nowadays, it seems, that somewhere between its
covers you do not read these phrases: " The Frontier
has departed; " " There is no more free land; "
" The limits of the U. S. A. have been reached and
settled; " " The frontier spirit has departed because
the Frontier has departed."

What nonsense are these people talking? Don't
they know any better? Are they really unaware that
in their own Alaska ninety-eight per cent. of the land
is still free land, ownerless, masterless—and so, as
Uncle Sam often growls in his beard, untaxable?
Have they forgotten the very existence of Uncle
Sam's wide attic and all its inviting space, these
witless writers? Or do they have some twisted misconception of our climate so fixed in their minds,
they think that " white folks " cannot, do not, live
here? I wonder, every time I read such statements,
at the closed minds that must lie behind them. I

long to stand out in the market places of the world and shout: "Dolts! Blockheads! Men with the muck-rake ever looking down! Look up! Here is the promised land of this our day."

The American Frontier is not closed to our generation, for Alaska is still gloriously open to us. There is no cold wall here, there is no barrier of an alien soil. The land is ours, in faith, if we but go up to possess it. The wholesome presence of The Frontier, so long a free-blowing wind sweeping away the fumes of a superheated melting pot, need not to-day be lost to our American life. Westward leading, still proceeding, the movement has gone on ever since Roger Williams left behind the first Massachusetts settlements and preferred to face the wilderness and the savage rather than suffer a cramped mind. Here in Alaska, now, as in New England, then, we see the vast extent of a continental mass stretching back from a rock-bound coast—a continent simple in its physical and geographical features, sufficient in time for the growth of an almost unlimited population. In the past the influence upon American ideals of an ever-apparent possibility of growth has been in very truth incalculable, and there is no need to lose this influence now. Although to the rest of the United States the days of the Frontier may seem far away, a thing of different years and of lost ways, here in Alaska they are close at hand and actual, in every thought and deed. Here you can see American colonial history telescoped, drawn near and in the making, now, to-day. The Frontier is not closed. Only climb the attic stairs and you will see for yourselves that this is true.

So I invite you to a look at the north edge of the

map, where travellers draw (according as they themselves are visioned) fabled Chimera—or the Land of Dreams Fulfilled. I invite only those who have a wholesome curiosity to know more about the continent of their birth. I invite only those who care to poke their noses over the world's rim and sniff the savor of what lies beyond. When we ourselves went North we knew we had a deal to learn; but what is learning but adventure? And so, we pushed the great door open to the attic stair. So, we began to climb.

I have written this in memory of that adventure, for I will not tell you of Alaska as one who went there as a tourist; nor did I make a trip to Alaska to gather information for a book. I lived there eight years, in the heart of it. I went there in the wake of a mining-engineer husband, who was sent there by Uncle Sam himself. It was our home, our much-loved home; and I have never called place " home " with such a zest and love as I have felt toward Uncle Sam's own attic.

I cannot tell you all about Alaska, for it is far too big. I'll tell, rather, about one woman's life there. Call it a rainy afternoon's browsing, if you will, under the attic eaves—a few old treasure trunks of memories and hopes glanced into. Nine tenths is my own personal experience, the other tenth the observation of faith-worthy Alaskan friends. The best that I can wish for you, who read, is that you sometime may go " look-see " for yourself, and find there all that I have missed up in that windless country full of deep cisterns of silence. I hope that you may find, as I have done, both the Friendly Arctic and the Social Arctic Circle.

But first, to get to any attic, one must climb—and

so must we.   A very vital part of living in Alaska
is the getting there.   It takes planning, it takes time.
And like the early settlers in New England, one is
always conscious in the new land of all that distance,
that width of waters, lying in between.   The distance is much more than a mere physical fact to be
overcome; it is an abiding mental background.   You
may live a lifetime in Alaska, but you will always
have in the back of your mind the remembrance of
all those miles which separate you in unsurmount-
able time and space from the Old Country, and the
ways and faces of those loved there.

The older Pilgrims had to sail long distance *round*
the globe to find the place of their new colony, but
we must sail long distance *up*.   The slow churn of
the boat's propeller steadily draws us away from all
we ever knew and loved, and brings the equally
steady, slowly dawning consciousness of an approach,
not only to a new world but to a newer way of
thought.   Looking back, I can see now we were indeed like Pilgrims, taking passage on a *Mayflower*
of to-day: leaving behind much that was old, yet
taking with us much, of all that old, which had
been very precious—not only in our personal baggage and in our freight of household goods, but in
our thoughts as well.   For there are memories one
does not easily leave behind in storage warehouse
when shipping on a new adventure.

And, like the *Mayflower* folk and those who followed them, we only guessed in part how much, of
new experience and of hazard, we were to see and
find.   And yet, as they did, we looked eagerly ahead
and with good hope and covenant strained all our
eyes to pluck the landfall of that new horizon, which
so would shape us to new worlds of friendship.

For to live in Alaska to-day is not only a personal adventure, it is an American adventure. American colonists are to-day shaping here for America a new colony of new hope, free and wide and warm with promise—as English colonists of olden days sought out another rock-bound and inclement-called far coast, on which dashed high the beating waves of yet another ocean.

This is the story of our coming to The Great Country, as the Indian word Alaska means. After long years of living here, we too have learned not only to call it so, but truly to know it so: "The Great Country."

II

The Long Gateway

I WISH that I could skip this chapter—as I hope *you* will, if you don't care for scenery! I dread to write it, for I know so well that only a true poet could do true justice to the memorable and haunting loveliness that is so typically the characteristic of our first step into the North.

But if I do not try, at least, to suggest something of the Inside Passage to Alaska—a thousand-mile-long corridor through which we begin to approach the North—then at the very first I shall have played unfair with you. For you can never come to know just what and how the real Alaskans think unless you have some inkling of how they came to think it. And all the true Alaskan " sourdoughs," as the old-timers are called, continually do their thinking with this long stretch of Inside Passage (and all it means to them of separation, delay, removal, barrier) forever tucked away at the back of their memories.

If you live in Alaska, as I have many years, the beauty and the wonder of this gateway to the North will always stay with you; and you'll re-wind the picture in your mind and often run it backwards, like a film of beauty once seen, never to be forgotten. But if you are a settler in Alaska, the Inside Passage will come to mean much more than merely beauty.

Just as the old-time Pilgrims, in their new home, remembered always, so they told, the rough miles of a gray-black winter sea which stretched in menace between them and Mother England, so—when you live within the far Interior of our Alaskan colony, in equal separation—you will find just one thing, no matter when or whence you came, that you must always have in common with all the other white folks living there. For this common memory which you carry, of all the miles you came to get here, is an experience which no true Alaskan can possibly forego; and hence it is a binding factor of incalculable potency in all Alaskan life.

In the long winters you will most recall not the warm color of this so safe and fine a summer passage, but rather that so many miles of leaden pewter-colored sea lie between you and homeland. For in the winter months, when no adventuring tourists seek the North and we Alaskans only travel " Outside " when forced by a necessity to do so, then the waters of the Inside Passage to our North are often treacherous and cruel, and the bones of many a goodly ship have been winter-caught and picked upon these teeth of rock and lie to bleach here. To some who live to-day within Alaska, these miles of distance from the older world are miles of refuge, behind which our pride and isolation shelter. And to yet others, they remain a perpetual barrier. That is why, since recently two friends of mine have made this trip by air and winged it to Alaska, I wonder what differences will come to typical Alaskan thought, for good or ill, when pilgrims of the future have become air-minded and can slash the miles to nothing to hurry to us here, and wipe out mountain chains and rivers as a boy wipes with a sponge the markings on a slate-drawn map!

Another good reason for beginning our story by going to Alaska, instead of starting our story from within, is that truly few people really know where Uncle Sam's attic begins. Do you?

Nineteen out of twenty people whom I meet when I am in the States, will say to me: " So, you are from Alaska? Do you live in Dawson? I had a cousin once who went to the Klondike in '98." And if I answer, as I must, " But Dawson is not in Alaska. It is the very British little capital city of Canadian Yukon Territory. Nor is the Klondike in Alaska, either, for it too lies across the border, within Canada "—they will be either very much surprised or, half the time, will not believe me, but think I'm simply spoofing them! Yet, if you will only look at the map a moment, you will see that both these things are absolutely true. Because it is a fact that by almost any way one chooses to enter American Alaska, one must first make a journey across Canadian waters or Canadian soil, there is therefore a great confusion in people's minds as to the actual bounds and metes of Alaskan territory.

And so I think the only way for us to get Alaska safely pinned down on the map, where it belongs, is for you to go there with me. Our long gateway to the North begins in Seattle, and no small share of that young city's prosperity has been due to the fact that travel to the North and treasure from it both pass through her doors. We'll start our journey there, and try to blaze our trail so we shall not forget the way another time, in back track.

A blazed back trail is an all-important thing. Old-timers tell that the Indian woman, Kate (wife of that lucky Carmack who, with her brothers, first drove stakes on the great Klondike gold fields), went with her husband to San Francisco. Lost in the strange confusion of the city, this woman from the fastness of the Yukon took her own simple method to find the way back to her hotel room. With a fire hatchet snatched from the corridor wall, she slashed and cut a blaze from room to street, all down the varnished baluster windings of the stairs, all along the wooden panels of the halls! But her too-savage and direct method did not appeal to the hotel management, who made the newly rich gold king pay heavily for his squaw's ignorance and indiscretion.

The Inside Passage, opening out from Seattle, extends northward through fringing island-sheltered sea waters—at first along the Canadian coast, where Victoria and Vancouver are the names that remind you of a crossed boundary line, then threading through the clustered islands of Alaska's " panhandle " to Skagway—for a four-day trip of a full thousand miles which the travel-surfeited of all nations have proclaimed the most beautiful long waterway of the world. It is the only easy way to go. Two other, longer, harder ways are more historical than practical, to-day. The old French voyageurs and early scouts of the " Honorable Company of Merchant Adventurers Trading into Hudson Bay " came first into eastern Alaska, years ago, by grilling an unbroken trail of pack and portage across western Canada. And one may sail direct to Nome by sea, and so on up the Yukon into the Interior. If you wish, then go the long ungracious waterway to Nome. But I'll not recommend it. That would be like getting into the attic by dropping down through the sky-light! It can be done—but it's surely not the natural or pleasant approach, whereas the Inside Passage is.

From Seattle's lovely harbor the steamship noses north at once and without hesitation, as though her

AVENUE OF TOTEM POLES IN THE NATIONAL PARK AT SITKA.

THE INSIDE PASSAGE, A TWISTED WAY OF JADE AND SILVER.

Photograph by Pederson Brothers.

TAKU GLACIER SPILLS DOWN LIKE A BLUE ICE-RIVER.

port she knew—out toward the Straits of Juan de
Fuca as the sun drops, gilding on one hand the snow-
folded Selkirks, and flaming on the other against
the calm Olympics. In such a setting a voyage is
well begun. And it's a comfortable and well-
appointed boat we sail out to the north in, to-day—
so comfortable that we forget we're pilgrims in this
real luxury of travel. The first two days you will
be threading through Canadian waters, along the
coast of British Columbia, and all the first day there
will be Vancouver Island lying to the west, until at
Queen Charlotte Sound (if the wind happens to be
sweeping in from the Pacific) you get a two-hour
taste of open water. But soon you duck back of the
sheltering islands, and the way is mill-pond smooth
again.

If you have no love at all for beauty touched with
strangeness, then I advise you to stay away from the
Inside Passage, for beauty's summer home is surely
here. I know that there are many lovelier individual bits throughout the world; but nowhere, that I
know, can you find any picture drawn on so vast a
scale, so day-unto-day in uttering its speech. I've
made this journey many times, in summer, fall, and
winter. But of the summer passage north I've always carried back the same impression—of long and
restful halcyon days full of a continuing sense of
drifting, out and away, above the world, removed
from it—as though afloat on poised gray wings of
snowy-breasted gulls, like those which follow us to-
day in countless gliding escort. You sit before your
cabin door as though upon the top deck of the world,
and on tired minds these dipping ivory wings beat a
slow, sure, withdrawing, wanderer's tempo.

You see, as Kingsley's Argonauts saw, a snow-white peak that, midway between sea and sky, "hangs glittering sharp and bright above the clouds," clean-lined and exquisite as a Japanese sketch. You say: "That's lovely, that is memorable. I'll hold that picture, always."

But there is not one single peak, to be so caught. This vista is not something that a frame will hold, but time is of its essence, continuity. Each day, each hour, brings other crowding pictures. There cannot be a single lovely fugitive glimpse to keep. That's not Alaska's way, for she—this new friend you have come to live with—is a famed prodigal in lavish generosity. She dips her hand into her chest of jewels, and faintly distant snow-patches are million-tinted with caught sun, scintillant as blue-white fine-cut stones, or glow soft rosy pearl of white. Opaline lights turn purple forests or the violet blue of foot-hills into sapphire or to amethyst. The wimpling water sliding past the keel is sheeted silver, till it breaks in jade. She will not rest content that you should keep just one jewelled hour, one day of mother-of-pearl and gold, because she pours her treasure forth unstinted—ten thousand vistas to be caught and kept, when you go sailing to Alaska between the darkly wooded sea-islands and the bright-tipped, mountainy, continental coast. In this, the gateway wears the name-plate of the Friendly Arctic; for when you come to know the true heart of the North, you'll find that both the country and the people are warm of heart and supergenerous in gift. I never saw a niggard in the North!

Very little of all this beauty, though, caught in the memories of those wild frenzied souls who plunged north in the gold rush—crowded three-to-bunk in shifts, on tiny ships that dragged deep-loaded through these then uncharted waters, to an unsensed menace and a nightmare promise. Their eyes were clouded so with dust of gold, they saw no jewelled color here. The brooding summits drifting by in pomp of purple, the far peaks haze-hidden, the margined woods, the lakes of blue and violet, emerald and black, were never told of in that story. In reminiscing of those early days of going north, our dear later-found Alaskan friends tell instead of their still so-vividly-remembered hardships and discomfort.

" I left Seattle in the fall of '97," Jack says, " on a fishing boat built to accommodate a crew of twenty, but carrying two hundred men. Meals were served in wash-tubs, on the dirty decks—if you can call it ' served,' for every man of us dug in and grabbed what we could get, or fight for! If you didn't hog it, you went hungry, that's all. There were no lights or buoys or any sea-marks along the Inside Passage, then. At nights, or in a fog, the captain blew his whistle and listened for the echo. If it sounded ' clean ' and didn't baffle back at him, he ploughed ahead. He didn't know a thing about this coast, any more than we did. We wanted to get North. We'd paid the man big money to dump us, any way or how, at the foot of Chilkoot pass. And ' head North ' was what he did. No decent boat would risk the trip. All we could get, those early days, was a rotten bottom that wouldn't hold two bits' worth of marine insurance. And no one ever saw the Plimsoll mark—if she wore one! It's a miracle that any of us ever got here, with whole skins. But we were young scamps then, and never thought of danger."

" My husband had just died," another Fairbanks friend has told me, " when the *Excelsior* put into

San Francisco. I was desperate, tired, and didn't care. Life seemed pretty much not worth living, anyway. I thought, ' I'll take the little that I have, and gamble. If God wants me to live, He'll let me get to Dawson. I know that I can make a living, once I get there; for where there are a lot of hungry men, they must pay high for food. And God knows I can cook!'

" So I turned into hundred-dollar bills every penny I could lay my hands on, in a hurry. I sewed these bills inside a pair of those stiff high old corsets, the kind we women used to be such fools to wear, and hired me a passage on the first boat going North. That boat was awful—the smells and the crowd. There were five of us in one small stateroom. I was deadly sick, and the steward was good to me; but he thought I was going to die, and so did I. But near dead as I was, I wouldn't let them take my corsets off—or I knew I'd never see that cash again. So every time they tried to make me comfortable by easing them, I yelled my loudest for the Captain! He came, and told them I was crazy, sure, and would be dying soon, so let me be. Well, after six days of it, I got better. Yes, I got to Dawson, but I never struck it rich, like some did."

Then I said, " That must have been in summer, or the early fall. The Inside Passage is so lovely, then. Didn't you see any of it, at all? "

"Lovely!" She almost screamed, and I could well realize why that Captain had come a-running when they tried to take away her stiff and high-boned " bank "! " Lovely! Why, woman, that stretch of time along that Passage has been for thirty years my pet idea of Hades, let *me* tell you! I've never left The North, since, for I've never wanted to face that trip, again. That was quite a-plenty, thank you. Never again—for me!"

And that is why one hunts through all the tales of argonauts and finds no word there of these, to-day, so easily tourist-seen, rose-touched and salmon-tinted, copper skies at dusk; and why one looks in vain for any hint of the slow-dawning thought, such as must come to all who traverse here to-day, that here the heavens are a purer tone, the stars come clearer to the nightly skies, as one drifts North and leaves the smoke-dimmed cities far behind. Mountains seem to shift and wheel, apparently changing their position as the boat twists. One seen astern will pop up dead ahead. You feel that you are turning on your track, and yet you know that you are steadily going North, because the sun stays longer with you. At nine, now, there's no sign of darkness. Then a new moon shows faintly through a deep notch in high hills. Headlands have little lighthouses set on their tips, like tiny flaming cigarettes stuck up on end. The densely wooded islands—so still, so silent, so apparently untenanted—will move aside to let you pass and close in silently again, behind. As though you travelled in a quiet, deep, mountain-cleft canal, these locks built by no human engineer close up their gates and lift you by their quiet even waters, into the promised land.

By the time that you reach Prince Rupert, the terminus of Canada's new transcontinental railroad—and just beyond it the international boundary over into Alaska's south tip, at 54° 40′—you have already climbed seven rungs of the ladder into Uncle Sam's attic, seven degrees of latitude above Seattle. The churning screws purr softly, softly. " Going North!"

III

Fishers of Ice

KETCHIKAN is our first Alaskan "white man's town," but it appears more like a bit of Norway. The mountains hereabouts are high and jagged, saw-toothed, grim, their heads among the clouds, their feet lapped by the summer sea; and countless fishing schooners darting in and out of bays and inlets, straits and sounds, tell every one that we are nearing fishing ground, for Ketchikan is headquarters of the North Pacific fishing fleet.

The whole business part of town is water-front, built out on piles of hemlock. Houses, wharves, the streets and sidewalks reaching back and up, are all alike built out of wood, cut from the Sitka spruce and red and yellow shaggy cedar forests, which crowd in high dense phalanx about the clustering busy town. Ketchikan seems just a wedge of man-cut wood driven into the mountain, and jealously the great trees push upon it from all sides in constant witness to surrounding forest. As our boat swings to dock, the houses seem piled one upon another, so sheer they climb, rising in steep toe-holds upon the planked irregular streets as though they might slide any moment down into Tongass Narrows. The white-railed porches of the wooden cabins look off across a vista of blue water and tight-wooded islands of dark thick-set spruce and hemlock. Pearly patches of high snows flash sun-caught from the

18

pockets of the peaks, and little breezes dusk and shiver the nearer finer green of willows and of birch.

You climb long stairs of logs, moss-carpeted, to reach the perched-up tiny houses that grip to the steep hill. Each house is set in a luxuriant garden, fairly a-drip with flowers. A passionate little mountain stream dashes from hilltops through the heart of town, sputtering and boiling over rocks as a good salmon stream should do. For this is capital of Salmon Land, and the brave home-returning fish of silver red is king here, and canneries are legion where the salmon turn home to spawn in their original waters, and flash and leap and climb to reach that far-sought home again—and die. The air is full of moisture as a tropic sponge, for the warm Kuro Shiwo sweeps in from the wide Pacific along all this coast, and Ketchikan, though tucked inside Alaska's southmost tip, is neither so cold nor yet so hot as Washington, D. C.! The full extremes of temperature here are 94° to 27° Fahrenheit; and I, who have lived many a raw winter and a scalding summer in our great white capital on the Potomac, recommend Ketchikan! I have been here in June and August, and again in October and late February, and found it ever mild and moist and pleasant.

Strong and long sunlight—what time the breath of Japan Current does not catch the hills in drifting rain—makes for a tropic growth of color riotous in flowers, of lichens and of moss that spread a patina of many hues upon the woody surfaces, and ferns and timber richly grow unstunted. The green banks of the stream mass thick with tapestry of overgrowing bushes—enormous pale-pink salmonberry, raspberry and wild black—while the ground dogwood mats the hill.

Down in the heart of business Ketchikan are a concrete department store, porcelain drinking fountains, apartment houses, movie houses, fur shops, several hotels, and even a " Poodle Dog Restaurant " —which sounds so very French to find in this Alaskan Ketchikan! With so much water power at its back door, the town is brilliantly well lighted, in that short hour of summer night through which our steamer tarries here.

This, then, is colonial Alaska!

Beyond Ketchikan, more mountains, higher and wilder mountains, mountains of six to ten thousand feet, rear their stiff sides straight up from narrow sea lanes through the eleven hundred islands of the Alexander Archipelago, where wild cascades are tumbled from the lower hills. The waterway is serpentine, constricted, and you seem headed straight, full tilt, for a good frush into some green-grown mountain side—when suddenly and somehow, as though a great scene-shifter moved a merely painted hill, the silver path reopens. You hope the Captain knows his way! It seems an un-clued labyrinth to one who threads it. How must it seem from air? The pilgrims of to-morrow will peer down from their bird-ships here on dots of darkening green set in a cobalt sea, and, from their godlike swift advantage, may miss some of the mystery, if not the beauty, of this slow-weaving panorama.

Your friendly Captain says: " You'd have a heap sight better sailing, here, if you could lay this crooked channel over on her beam! She's a deal deeper than she's wide, let *me* tell you! "

Next port is Wrangell, with a name that reeks of olden Russian past. It lies at the wide mouth of gold-famed, turgid Stikine River where in old days,

as some still do, the miners outfitted for Teslin Lake
and Pelly River headwaters, and so on to the Yukon.
This was the older route and longer, before White
Pass and Chilkoot were adventured—a hard way—
but all ways were hard, and there was no thought
then of turning back. One of the earliest of colonial
Alaskan settlements, a stockaded post founded back
in 1834 as Redoubt St. Dionysius to resist Hudson
Bay encroachments, the town beside the fort was
named by Russians after their most eminent and distinguished Admiral Baron Ferdinand Petrovich von
Wrangell. But the site had been before that time
an even older town of Stikine Indians, and is famous
now for its old totem poles, fine Indian bead and
basket work, a harbor view of lovely crescent-curv-
ing sea, neat houses set on level land in a most fertile
valley, and everywhere the gardens, flowers. This
Wrangell is the well-remembered old-time gate to
the Canadian interior, long the old Hudson Bay
route; and later, across these grassy Stikine River
meadows, clover grown and scattered with wild
roses—up from the sea into the canyons and the
glacier-covered hills—gold hunters found a way to
Cassiar.

    We know that we are surely drawing north, for
now we read at night till after ten, the soft day
lingering noticeably longer. Why should we ever
go to bed? There seems no end to twilight. From
Wrangell on to Petersburg our way is past Mitkof
and Kupreanof Islands, and it is at the head of
Wrangell Narrows that we see our first Alaska glacier, a blue ice-river spilling down from its top-lofty
home to break in little bergs that tumble off like pup
seals out to play. Here's ice for packing fish—and,
in old days before cold-storage plants were built,

fishermen caught ice here, in the selfsame waters where they caught the fish! 'Twas handy, that.

Petersburg, just within the north entrance of Wrangell Narrows, spells halibut. Quite likely that good halibut steak you ordered yesterday in some eastern hotel was packed in Petersburg in ice self-broken from near-by Le Conte glacier, and so shipped on to Prince Rupert. Petersburg is another very busy American colonial town of the North. It began back in the nineties when good old Peter Bushman set up his Norwegian fish cannery here. It is still Peter's Burg, Port of Prosperity, and thrives lustily to-day on herring, shrimp, salmon, halibut and crab—a " shore dinner " town!

For long the leading merchant here was one Sing Lee who, when a great fire swept the town in 1910, so the old sourdoughs tell, stood in the open street and cried—" Jesus Clist flend to me! He now no burn me down! " The wind changed and the fire stopped dead at Sing Lee's store.

Near by is the long-sought " Lost Locker " placer claim, for which prospectors searched for thirty years. Old-timers grouped around Jim Brennan's " cold stove "—an old-fashioned battery of spittoons within easy speaking distance, the gentle pat of rain outside, a mahogany bar of prehistoric times shining dimly in solemn background splendor—recall that forty years ago a white man was found drifting out in Frederick Sound in a leaky Indian canoe. He was half starved and very nearly crazed, but had with him two fat pokes of a coarse red-yellow gold. Taken to town and cared for, finally he told that he and two others had been a-mining by the margin of a half-moon lake, where they had built a dam of yellow cedar, a crude old-style gold rocker, and a cabin out of stone. Returning to the camp one day, this man had found his two companions cruelly butchered, presumably by Indians. He took the hidden gold that they had washed together, and fled across the mountains. He came at last on tide-water at a small Indian village where, waiting for the dark, he took an old canoe and drifted out—he knew not where or how. He never could be urged by any fear or favor to return, or to attempt return, to the deserted cabin by that half-moon lake, where he had looked too full on mutilated horror. But since that time men ceaselessly have searched the hills for The Lost Rocker claim, and now at last it has been rediscovered.

Along these shores, too, glided years and years ago, in yet another Indian canoe, another white man on a water journey of at least eight hundred miles— looking for glaciers, not gold. This was the famous naturalist, John Muir, who wrote his Scotch-American name upon one of the giants of them, a Goliath among glaciers. With him was S. Hall Young, the veteran Alaskan missionary. I can see myself, a leggy silent child, sitting in my father's study and listening star-eyed to Dr. Young describing the wonders of Alaska and that trip with Muir. He was the first Alaskan I had ever seen, and all he told made pictures. I was to sit again and watch him—an old man now and I a woman grown—while he played countless silent games of chess with my husband before the red hearth of our own Alaskan home.

John Muir had brought with him a geologic eye. And though he spent no time prospecting gold, he wrote on his return that indications about Gastineau Channel, or on the near-by mainland, were favorable to gold deposits. While Captain Beardslee of the

U. S. N. was stationed at Old Sitka, in the early days when Uncle Sam's Navy *was* the government of Alaska, some roving Indians brought to him several chunks of rich gold quartz. Questioned as to whence these specimens had come, they had replied, " From the long water, between the Auke and Taku." Even before this time, however, the half-breed Frenchman Joe Juneau, and his partner Dick Harris, had camped along this channel; and on the tripod facts of their good report of prospects, the Indians' actual quartz, and Muir's keen-sighted scientific prophecy, two men of Sitka grubstaked Juneau and Harris to return to Gastineau and prospect.

On the upper reaches of Gold Creek, three miles from the sea, they found Quartz Gulch, the floor of which was actually paved with glinting flecks and stringers of the virgin gold. Loading themselves with packs of ore, all they could stagger under, they returned to shore; and there, October 4 in 1880, Dick Harris and Joe Juneau sat themselves down on the rocks and laid out upon paper what they called, at first, the Harris Mining District. They also drew up miners' laws to rule what soon they knew would be—when news of this rich strike got out—a wild stampede of prospectors. For although the United States had bought Alaska in '67, it had not as yet extended benefit of any law to the new Territory; and except for the lone naval officer stationed there at Sitka, the land was law-less.

As soon as miners wintering in Sitka and Wrangell heard the good news, every craft in harbor was requisitioned for this new gold rush—nearly twenty years before the tide of fortune seekers streamed into the Klondike. Even the " government," in person of the warship *Jamestown,* hove up anchor and joined in the mad stampede. There being no civil government at all, Commander Rockwell himself administered the oaths of citizenship; and on those early Navy records are to be read to-day the names of many a man well known in later Alaskan history. The pay-roll of the Navy helped to sink the first shafts and tunnels in the flanks of rocky Juneau mountain.

The Auke tribe of Indians, from their settlement ten miles to northward, flocked like crows on the new diggings, to make trade and barter, and camped right down beside the miners' tents and "booze joints" that lined the beach and water-front. On their heels came all the Taku tribe from down the channel! Old miners tell that the combined odor of these two tribes did not commingle in a pleasant Coty nose-tickling bouquet. Indeed, it proved too much for even the not-so-sensitive nostrils of the tough old sourdoughs. So the Indians were per-suaded and subsidized, by gifts of blankets and per-haps by hints of other matters, to move an elbow-room away—the Auke on one side and the Taku on the other!

Rough elements of the raw Territory gathered to these new lode mines, and others came to fatten on their profits, as always happens in new camps, until in 1881 the commander of the *Jamestown* landed his marines and proclaimed martial law. The name of Juneau came later (after the town had been called successively Harrisburg, Rockwell, Fliptown, Plitz-burg) when in '82 the present name was officially adopted. But with old Joe Juneau, as with many another lucky prospector, it was "easy come and easy go." The fortune he had won was swiftly spent, and he was last heard of as running a poor eating-house at Dawson, feeding the lucky strikers of another day and camp.

After the marines withdrew, the lawless element got out of hand and a vigilance committee had to be formed, which held control until a partial territorial form of government was given to " The District of Alaska," in May of '84, and courts and a civil and criminal code were at last provided for, the laws of the state of Oregon being cut down and made over to fit the raw and growing youngster, Alaska. To-day this once so lawless Juneau, where marines and miners " mixed it " on the water-front (engaging in the rough sport of seeing how many of the opposite element of camp could nightly be pitched out upon the tide flats!) is the clean and dignified capitoline Juno of all Alaska, sedate and prim as a Swiss village—where all Alaska's laws are made.

Perhaps because most politicians must forever live under a potential landslide, Juneau the capital city lies beneath the great and towering bulk of a tremendous mountain that rears steep-sided seven thousand feet up from the sea; and sometimes hair-poised masses of white snow that cap and streak it, rush in swift menace of death-giving avalanche down the deep cuts of almost perpendicular gulches, and whelm some house or cluster of her men. But human beings seem to thrive on menace, and Juneau is second only to Ketchikan, the king of all Alaska towns; and both in size and wealth she can queen it over other sections of the Territory. Nearly half the white population of Alaska lives in this First Division, the southern narrow strip of territory through which we've so far passed, although it is but five per cent. of Alaska's total land area. Mills metal and mills political both grind out their work here, for on Gastineau Channel, as I remember well first seeing and *hearing* it, were located a group of great gold-quartz mills that roared and hammered deafeningly, both day and night, in a monotony of continuous thunder.

On May 24, 1881, Pete Erussard, another typical adventurous Frenchman, filed a claim on " Parris Creek " just across the channel on Douglas Island. Handsome, well known, and equally well liked, the grilling labor of the mine was not for him, however; and he sold his claim to carpenter John Treadwell for a song, according to a quit-claim deed recorded September 13 of that very same year. September 13 was a most unlucky day for happy-hearted " French Pete," though; for the great Treadwell mine (which began important output the next year and afterwards extended from the original Glory Hole, ran out in tunnels as deep as half a mile down underneath the channel, and developed into one of the richest lode mines in all the world) produced in its day more than nine times as much gold as Uncle Sam had paid to Russia for the whole territory of Alaska! Once this single mine employed two thousand men and ran the second largest stamp-mill in the world, until flooded in a swift disaster in 1917, when the waters broke through from above and the Pacific claimed again its deep floor of golden rock.

But though the Treadwell has been swallowed by the jealous sea, there is no end to Juneau's rich prosperity. The Alaska-Juneau mine penetrates more than two miles back into the mountain looming in threat over the tidy city, and every four years this mine alone more than pays the original price of Uncle Sam's attic. When President Harding came to Alaska, members of his party rode up an incline railroad pitched at a grade of thirty-seven degrees, and then on an electric train into the depths of rock-hewn mountain tunnel. The ore comes out in ten-ton cars and dumps into the giant tipples, where by gravity it is worked down through the crushers and concentrators until it comes to light again at last in bars that weigh some hundred and sixty pounds of solid gleaming gold. And it is estimated that there are yet a hundred million tons of ore left to mill—enough to operate as now, three shifts, for fifty years to come.

With fish and forests too at her front door and back—forests for trap piles, wharf piles, box shooks, railroad ties, news pulp, commercial lumber—Juneau can rest content under her mountain, smiling at fate. She has her fifteen miles of steep planked city streets, some of them spacious. Not all the tricks of chance end in misfortune, by a deal. The Ice King has played fair with this brave city and supplies her power and light. Fourteen miles of granite-surfaced automobile road—bordered by fluffs of white " Alaska cotton," frostings of blue-tipped spruce— run out to the receding foot of Mendenhall glacier, which once, men say, had licked its tongue of ice to tide-water. From out and under this great ice mass are forced the melting, swift, and powerful streams that feed the dynamos of Nugget Creek, which run the massive engines and the wheels of mines and mills in Juneau.

For even frost and snow must be enmeshed and geared, in our mechanical day of engineering giants.

IV

Family Trees That Make Faces

FROM those three mining towns,—Juneau, Douglas and Treadwell,—close clustered at the head of Gastineau Channel, it is just one hundred miles to Skagway, where we shall leave the narrow seas at last and go " inside " by land, crossing the great Coast Range over into Yukon drainage. So, while we drift north through Lynn Canal, I'd like to gossip about totem poles, the family trees that make faces; for, once across the ranges, we shall never see their like again.

Ever since we passed Vancouver Island we have been in totem country, and even the most supercilious tourist, regarding circumjacent humans with a look—and such a look!—has found his interest turned to wonder here. We began to see these strange sights at Alert Bay, where we saw too our first long, graceful and sharp-pointed Northwest Indian canoes.

A totem pole is a wooden column carved with men or beasts, or both. It may be as high as fifty feet, but is usually about twenty. The incredible brightly-painted beasts, with " jaws that bite, the claws that catch," are carved in deep grotesque relief. The native word for Jabberwock seems to be *Ka-juk*—a fabulous bird who hurls down rocks and looks like a great eagle.

At Alert Bay is a Raven totem crowned with a huge bird head, on which is set a stove-pipe hat! The eyes of this great bird-beast are bright red, the

29

beak an equally bright blue. Below is a queer
hunched-up man-like figure, almost enfolded with
great wings. Beneath this is a richly carven box,
and then another beast's head with a huge protrud-
ing beak that sticks out at least two feet. Still lower
rests another man-like figure, also wrapped in wings;
and on the side of this you see the fiercest-looking
black hawk-head with great green eyes, hooked
beak, and streaks of bright vermilion daubing it.
The whole body of the hawk is patchwork cubist
color. Supporting all this strange congeries of ani-
mated carvings, there squats a crude and horrible
crouched man, holding a spear. He has a leering
mouth, and eyes and nose that also leer in gargoy-
lesque grotesquerie. Every color of the spectrum
has been laid upon this totem, and the images en-
graven here are lurid, memorable, as figures seen in
nightmare.

Other poles are carved in effigies of massive frogs
with hands clasped over their fat bellies, or birds
with fierce projecting beaks, with painted wings outstretched. Great rows of gleaming highly-whitened
teeth are favorite designs, like tooth-paste ads. The
coloring is raw and rigorous, the faces often livid
green, the cheeks high-touched in black. There's
nothing like them elsewhere, so I'm told.

Now "Totem" is a word that has been used in
many senses, and by many scientists; but totems are,
in general, the symbols of an old belief in human
kinship with the animal world, a mystic spiritual
rapport. "The clan," as Frazer says, "sprang from
the totem." All savages, of course, believe in the
human intelligence of animals. Our own fairy
stories show this feeling, for in them the cat speaks,
and the dog, and Siegfried's bird gives warning.

LYNN CANAL FROM TOP "HB" MTN.

"SKAGWAY LIES ON LYNN CANAL, A SOMBRE WAY OF BEAUTY."

"TALL PASSES BACK OF SKAGWAY ONCE DREW MEN LIKE A LOADSTONE."

Thwaites, 52a.   Village Isl. Alaska

Photograph by Thwaites.

"INCREDIBLE BRIGHTLY PAINTED BEASTS ARE
CUT IN GROTESQUE RELIEF."

KETCHIKAN, WHERE HOUSES PILE UPON THE
CLIMBING HILLS

These "savages" believe, just as we when we were children believed, that man and animals are on an even footing, and can interchange ideas. The Indians go still further, and believe that they are actually, not figuratively, akin to beasts. For they say that certain stocks of men in certain tribes are actually descended from or are developed somehow out of certain animals, with which they still can claim familiar kinship. So totem poles to them are family trees or registers. To those who can decipher its crude imageries, the pole erected before a man's house is a plain history to be read, in picture, of the family that lives within. The fabled beasts are no more strange to them than are to us the unicorn and lion that prance upon the British coat-of-arms. These beasts do not seem queer to us, for we have come to know them as a symbol. Yet no real lion ever took the posture this British lion does, nor twirled his tail so crookedly; and no such beast as unicorn exists. So, too, we picture boar and swan heads on our crests. Will Shakespeare had a spear and Washington a group of stars; but these don't strike us strangely, though a man from Mars might ask—"Was Washington a star gazer? And this man Shakespeare—surely he must have been a famous javelin caster."

The strange marks, dexter and sinister here, are no more drawn by chance than are the quarters of heraldic blazonry on fine old family crests of our own yesterday, paraded on the stationery and plate of most distinguished people. It's Indian heraldry of ancient families, these Alaskan forests of totems carved in wood and painted in high color; but we have no wise Herald's College to explain them to us now. The Thlingits are pure totemists; the Haida totem lore has faded into mystic heraldry which they keep but cannot always unriddle. The totems whisper down of old, unhappy, far-off things and battles —for us, but not yet for them—long since won out by human thinking.

For our own savage ancestors, back in the Old World, must have had a very similar belief in "heathen" days; and reputable scientists find traces of this same habit, of naming families from beasts, among the ancient Semitic and Teutonic tribes, as well as among noble Greeks and Romans. Simeon means "hyena-wolf," I'm told; Caleb means "dog," Rachel "an ewe," Leah "wild cow." In Greek myth the swift wind, by certain mares, became the sire of wind-swift steeds, as mentioned in the *Iliad*. To early peoples, sky, sun, wind, and star as well as beasts were not only persons, but savage persons like the makers of the legends' selves, and out of such beliefs they made their fables, when the world was young. Our ancient literatures are rich with this, nor can we well deny that such a fine and flavorsome old English name as Ethelwulf (noble wolf) bears witness to a primitive society that looked with favor on the notion of a certain kinship in character with the gray timber-rover.

Some wise men think that the apparent sanctity and prestige of certain animals, in old mythologies and legends, bear witness that our ancestors (long, long ago, even as the Indians of southeast Alaska, now) thought of themselves as brothers to the beasts. The fancy that the fairy tales of childhood are so full of, these Indian folk really believe; and we can know that they believe it, for they act as though it actually were true. No man will eat the flesh of any animal of which he thinks as kindred. The totem crests define the bonds of consanguinity, and all the children take the *mother's* crest. No man may marry any woman with the same family name (that is, descended from the same common ancestor) ; and he believes not only, as the Haidas do for instance, that whenever a Haida is lost at sea his soul becomes a whale, but also that in dreams his cousin-beasts speak to him of their wisdom, counsel him and guide him.

From the dawn of time man has always been busy explaining this his world in terms of magic, science, or religion. We are constantly about it, trying to answer all the why and how of things. And here we can see, in totem, the nursery tales and legends of a primitive folk, in use and with the living reasons for them, and not as mere tradition or a tale. This savage mythology is the early way of satisfying that great questioning about our human whence and whither. Out of the simple things he knew best, out of beasts and birds and forms of wind and tree and fish, he built up answers to the rudiments of scientific curiosity. He did not build as we have built, chiefly because he did not know what we know.

These weather-beaten, time-worn, weird, strange totems are a sign-post to the past—souvenirs of the days when eagle, wolf and whale spoke the same speech as men, and told their secrets of the sky and sea, far seen. I wonder if perhaps such orders as the Elks and Moose find distant kinship here, in claiming for a group of human beings the noble qualities of animals?

There are many types of totems, as there are many uses for a coat-of-arms. They may be merely family trees set up outside a house, which serve as city directory to Indians. Members of a clan having the same totem name, though living many hundred miles apart and speaking different languages, are still considered blood relations; and, when in a strange village, a southeastern Alaskan Indian will look up at the totem poles outside the houses, until he comes to one that bears the crest of his own phratry, where he knows that he may always enter freely and be received as brother—quite as though he were a "visiting Moose" in a strange city! If not, he'd know himself a stranger and perhaps an enemy, and would pass on. There are totems that mark graves, and totems that are monuments to past events and record happenings. One "story master" totem at Kasaan is quite up to date. An eagle tops it, then comes the head of the Archangel Michael, next a Russian bishop, and at the base a white man's head surmounted by an eagle. This tells to any Indian, well educated in the "literature" of his people, that a chief of the Eagle totem was baptized into the Russian Church—and how, and when, and why.

Like most peoples, the Indians of Alaska tell the story of a great flood, and they say that clam shells which they find upon high hills prove that there was once a flood covering the earth. And this flood scattered people, which accounts for the wide separation of families bearing the same name. When the flood came, the Raven took his mother in his claws, flew up, and stuck his beak into a cloud, hanging there until the flood subsided. But ever since, he's had a beak that's bent! The Raven is one of the important family totems, and, like the great god Horus of old Egypt or the hawk-headed Incan god, is greatly reverenced; but *not* as a "graven image," for the totem has nothing to do with religion. It is distinctively a social symbol, of family caste and prestige, venerated but not worshipped. When the

Indian refers to the Raven as " creator," as he sometimes does, he has no intention of saying that the
Raven is his god, but merely that he was his first
ancestor—his Adam, the progenitor of a human race,
but not his great Jehovah. The only " worship " of
totem poles amongst these people is that very same
pride of family tradition which we ourselves jok-
ingly refer to when we say of some friend of ours:
"He *worships* his family tree!"

Because the crest was so important as a matter of
social identification, every household and personal
possession was marked with it—every utensil and
every treasure, even spoons and dishes. Chests had
the totem carved or painted on them, just as fine old
English pieces from baronial halls have on them to
this day the deeply-carven coats-of-arms of proud and
ancient families. Totem entered intimately into the
fine arts of this people, into their speech and common
industry, into manners and laws, into folk lore and
stories of the spirit world, for Indians believed that
everything had spirits. "There were spirits of the
food you eat, the clothes you wear, the hills, the
mountains, and the trees," they said. "The man who
comes in contact with these spirits is a great man
among his people. The man who speaks with spirits
may become the founder of a new clan."

Open any of our own city directories and what do
you find written there? Such common names as
Crane, Drake, Fish, Fox, Lyon, Wolf are surely but
vestigial totem marks, pointing out a certain distant
kinship of our own with these strange and "out-
landish " painted sign-posts of Alaskan fable. So
these early, savage, almost universal beliefs, brought
down to our own day in fairy tales of Grimm and
Æsop, in werewolf stories, and the myth of Leda's

swan, stand carven here in the long gateway to the North for any wandering tourist eye to see, but not perhaps to understand.

"Man has a soul," these painted gate-posts tell, "which is connected some way with his breath, and can be separated from him, some way, out of the material body—temporarily in sleep, permanently in death. The animals, and even wind and sky and sea, have souls too, and wear our human powers and passions, emotions, voice, intelligence." So the poets of a long-gone day translated into human thought the voices of the universe. So the totems read. So sing they, say they, tell they the tale of ancient guess-work into the mysterious realm of metaphysical arcana. . . . "The savage, too, from forth the loftiest fashion of his sleep, guesses at heaven."

But just as Pilgrims of old days, on their long way to a new home, might well have stopped en route at Greenland and seen and found there much of stranger ways, unlike to anything or anybody on the continent to which they went or whence they came, but could not tarry there and must go hurrying on, for they were bound for a new land still further on beyond; so we, though we perhaps should like to live amongst these stranger people and learn at first hand more of all the "why" back of these totem poles,—we too must hurry on.

Perhaps we could not ever learn the secret, for perhaps it is already lost. The totems stand, like Stonehenge, only to remind us of a past that was, but is not.

V

Soapy Smith and Mother Pullen

I AM going to confess right here that I am *not* about to take you into the far-lying heart of Alaska by the shortest way!

There are two reasons for this—no, there are three. You may sail from Juneau to-day out through Icy Strait, past the mouth of Glacier Bay, past Cape and Mount Fairweather, and across the wide Gulf of Alaska, straight to Cordova, Valdez, Seward, or Anchorage, on the south coast of the mainland of Alaska (as you will see by glancing at the map) ; and thence, from any one of these four towns, by various overland routes, you may turn straight north into the center of The Great Country and Fairbanks.

But when we first came to Alaska, the Government Railroad from Anchorage over Broad Pass had not yet been built, the automobile road from Chitina back of Cordova was not well developed, the trail through Keystone Canyon behind Valdez was in bad repair, and the Seward terminus was as yet in process of adjustment. To-day you can reach Fairbanks in the summer months by any one of these four ways, in pleasure and in comfort, and by the railroad all the winter months. But when we first came north, the one most feasible approach to the interior was via Skagway, the Upper Yukon, and Dawson.

It is a fact, and yet a fact not always given due consideration, that very much of the past history of Fairbanks and of other Alaskan towns lies buried in

Canadian Dawson, for us to find and understand, if
we can—just as, in equal measure, the past history of
little New England colonial settlements lay rooted
in old English shires, or the roots of our great
Middle West migration ran back to and drew
nourishment from the soil of Virginia or Connecticut, whence it was pioneered. So, since the
Skagway route is the trail the Argonauts of '98 took
chiefly to the Klondike; and since we shall again
come back, "Outside," by other routes and ways, if
you are patient; and because, too, I have always
been so glad I came myself into the mainland
country *first* by the Great River and the road of history, instead of by the newer, shorter, easier ways:
if you'll agree, I'll take you with me into the Interior by that longer and older waterpath, which
twists back through Canadian hinterland, to come
again, by side ways of an eastern-facing window,
into the bulky center of Uncle Sam's attic. For
the thin Alaskan strip from Ketchikan, we have so
far been traversing, is never more than ten marine
leagues wide at any place, back to the summit of
the Coast Range all along to eastward. And behind
that range lies Canadian British Columbia; and up
on top of " B. C." lies "Y. T.," for Yukon Territory bounds the mainland of Alaska in a meridian
line straight north from great Mt. St. Elias near
the coast along west longitude 141° "dans son
prolongement jusqu'à la mer glaciale," as the early
treaty reads.

Tourists who are attracted only by the lazy beauty
of the Inside Passage, the merely curious or the
ease-loving traveller who avoids a possible discomfort or delay, will take the short, unusual, railroad
day-trip up over White Pass summit, or perhaps

spend a few days at the tourist paradise of Canadian Lake Atlin, and think they've seen Alaska. But they have not, and should not fool themselves into thinking so. They've seen but five per cent. of Alaska's land area, so far, and all the mighty bulk of the Great Country lies beyond and yet unguessed. Even if they do cross by rail over the White Pass and on by boat to Lake Atlin, they've traversed only fifteen miles air-line of actual Alaskan territory. Those with a genuine desire to see the High North, and to know what calls *behind* the ranges, will never be content with such a compromise.

Skagway was once the wild, bad, boom town of The North, a bustling cosmopolitan community of many thousand gold-crazed men en route to Klondike, unloading here their outfits from the over-crowded boats in preparation for the Trail of '98. It was the home of fevered hope, of mad despair, of cruelty, greed and hate. To-day the " Flower City " lies asleep upon the sands at tip of Lynn Canal, dreaming, alive but in its yesterdays.

Strangely, perhaps you'll think, the guardian spirit of the quiet town's hectic past, curator of its memories, and the most enterprising of its present citizens, is a woman! No one knows Skagway who does not know Harriet Pullen. For years she has *been* Skagway, to all who stop and linger there to hear from her own vigorous dramatic lips the tale of Skagway's tarnished day of glory.

This tall, all-competent, adventuring soul dropped into Skagway first with the first Klondike trailers—a widow with her brood of little boys a-clinging to her calico skirts, and seven dollars in her pocket. She drove a four-horse freighting outfit up the wild and ragged gulch by day; and though the stiff brakes on the terrible inclines near broke the body, they could not cut the grit of this near-Amazon of women. By night she stood beside an oven in a tent, and baked dried-apple pies and cakes, that sold for fabulous sums to hungry men intent on golden-fleece adventure. She made her pans by hammering out tin cans. She manufactured drinking glasses from discarded beer bottles, with the true pioneering woman's ingenuity. Would you know how? She'll tell you. You tie a stout string dipped in coal oil round the widest part, then touch a match to the string and dash the bottle in cold water—which cuts the neck away, as with a knife. And then you grind the sharp edge in the sand and have a perfect drinking glass. She nursed a local Indian chief, who gave her a rich ceremonial coat of ermine, decked in beadwork, which she will show you. She is a member in blood brothership of many local tribes, and speaks the several Indian dialects of the coast. One son was drowned at Juneau, one was the first Alaskan boy ever to enter West Point. There this upstanding red-head, six-foot-three-in-socks Alaskan played right tackle on the team for four years, and lovingly was dubbed "the Eskimo" by fellow classmen—though very probably he had never even seen an Eskimo! In the Great War this Colonel Pullen won the Distinguished Service Cross and, with his brother, Captain Royal Pullen of the Engineers, made for the name of that brave mother such rare reputation that General Pershing has been quoted saying, "I wish I had a *regiment* of Pullens!" Here is colonial America to date, as bred and raised at Skagway, atop the attic stairs.

To-day is Mrs. Pullen's, too, for she's not one to live back in her yesterdays. The Pullen House is

the hotel of Skagway, and, with its bungalow surrounding cottages, rests in a stream-cut lawn and
massed in flowers. Here you may have a room with
bath, or in her banquet hall you may gather with a
hundred and fifty others to feast on Mother Pullen's
good things from an especially designed fine set of
Haviland, and eat with solid silver service of her
own device. And when you sit before your breakfast cereal and coffee, you will be fetched an individual blue-enamelled pan of unskimmed milk,
with skimmer of your own, to dip the cream and
take to your heart's fill! For just across the bay at
old Dyea, once the foot of perpendicular Chilkoot
Pass where so many met their deaths, Harriet Pullen runs a ranch and herd of Jerseys and of Holstein,
providing unlimited fresh milk and butter. "Out
of the strong, out of the strong," your memory sings
in hearing her rich laugh ring out, all hours, all
times. Out of the strong surely the honey of this
world has come—both yesterday and now.

She opens for you her wide treasure room of
curios—a piled-up place where one may browse for
days and read Alaska's history in fingering these
relics of her past. Hand-hammered copper of the
Russian days, and silver candlesticks from Baranof's
castle over at old Sitka; great strings of purple-blue
rare Russian beads, made of Bohemian glass especially for the early fur trade; the first newspaper of
the great Dawson strike, with Klondike news in
large gold letters, and a picture on it of George
Carmack, who first struck it rich there, surrounded
with large daubs of gilt to represent huge nuggets;
Soapy Smith's gambling table-round, of two-pieced
oak in which is a slight slit (he called it " the accom-
modator ") whence, by a quick flick of the hand, an

ace could be extracted; as well as his fine crap table, roulette wheels, and " knuckle dusters " for a use best guessed!

You will unearth here, too, a medicine man's mask, long bead-strings made of jade or amethyst or wampum, tobacco pouches formed of white swan's feet, and bags of cedar bark; moose robes and coats are here, soft-tanned as clean and smooth as woolens. And then, drawing herself up to her full height, Harriet Pullen tells you of the days of Soapy Smith.

Jefferson Smith was one of the world's truly notorious bad men, and for years he and his gang of outlaws terrorized both Wrangell (where the Teslin-Telegraph Creek trail led also to the new Eldorado) and Skagway and Dyea, the side-by-side step-offs for White Pass and the Chilkoot ladder-way. Yet " Soapy " looked the gentleman, as a true villain should to qualify in expert bunco-steering; and so suave was his manner and so affable and kind his ministerial-looking face,—like Tito of George Eliot's " Romola,"—the inner rottenness would never be suspected from a look at him; for he was tall and slim and handsome, polite and gay. His nickname came from earlier days of rather simple forms of mild chicane, when at county fairs and in plain sight he folded crisp five-dollar bills about a cake of soap and sold them for a dollar to unsuspecting yokels. Needless to say, unwrapped, there was no bill there! " The hand is quicker than the eye," you know. And Soapy's hand was of an unguessed swift dexterity, either in drawing cards from " solid " oaken tables—or drawing shooting irons!

At Skagway gathered hordes of Klondike seekers, going in with funds, and going out with well-filled pokes of precious dust. It was the time, too, of the

Spanish war, you will remember. Smith opened a
" recruiting office " for the U. S. Army. Hundreds
of men, discouraged by the hard back-packing over
the steep passes, which rose so straight up from the
sea they seemed from below to lean over backwards
—or discouraged by mere sight of the stiff climb and
all they heard of danger further on—decided to join
the army. Entering Smith's " recruiting office," they
were told to strip for physical examination. In an
adjoining room another member of the gang, made
up to look and act like an army surgeon, stalled at
conducting this examination while Soapy's crowd
went through the luckless fellow's clothes and outfit.
They left him only the least desirable of his clothes,
in which he might peacefully sneak out by a back
way, a whipped and broken man—or, if he showed
a fight, his body later would be found afloat and
bullet-riddled in the bay. Shots were so constant
and so frequent no one paid attention. There was
no law, and as fast as one crowd had been " cleaned,"
other innocents were arriving; and so the merry
sport went on. Another form of the same game was
the Information Bureau, where strangers newly
landed, eager for knowledge of the fabled trail
beyond, crowded in like flies to a spider's trap, and
only left when stripped.

Yet Soapy " played the game " in his own way,
was loyal to his followers and, strange to say, gave
liberally to the Union Church. An old-timer of
those days, who landed here in '97 and was a trustee
of this church, tells with a chuckle now of those
strange days, when " contributions came from all
sects and from no sects. Liberal contributors included gamblers, Soapy Smithites, and all other
kinds of sports—a strange complex of saints, skeptics,

infidels, atheists, and all other kinds of publicans and
sinners. Every denomination represented in Skagway was asked to suggest a trustee, at a first public
meeting held under the blue sky. Any minister who
happened to be located in Skagway would have been
made pastor of that unique fraternal flock. The
one chosen was Rev. J. Hickey, a young Canadian
Congregationalist who was there waiting for the ice
in the Yukon River to go out, so he could continue
on to Dawson. All Skagway grieved when he departed. His was the truest expression of Jesusanity
it was ever my good fortune to know."

While Soapy Smith was one of the most generous
givers to the church, he had a rob-Peter-pay-Paul
sort of creed, I'm afraid. On one occasion he
helped most warmly, giving personally much time
to collect a fund for churchly charity, and himself
handed this sum over, with a Chesterfieldian bow, to
the hard-working conscientious pastor. That night
one of Soapy's cohorts crawled beneath a tent and
stole the money!

But there came a time when even lawless Skagway
turned against this King of Terror, as they called
him. The town got a bad name all up and down
the coast, of course, and fame of Soapy's terroriz-
ing gang dimmed the bright glitter of the gold fields
beyond. Vigilance committees formed, and a meeting of the decent element was called—upon the
wharf, for two reasons: No house was large enough
to hold the conscientious objectors to the high hand
of un-law; and too, out on the wharf's end, ways
and means could be discussed without an overhear-
ing. Frank Reid, an engineer and a man of known
courage and determination, was stationed at the
land end of the wharf to keep out eavesdroppers and

spies—or any known member of the gang, such as
Fatty Green, Yank Fewclothes, or Kid Jimmy
Fresh, who might come to rough-house.

Soapy heard of these preparations, of course, for
his spies were everywhere. " I'll end this," he's reported to have said, and single-handed started for
the pier. Reid challenged him, and both men drew
and fired in the same fraction of a second. The
gangster dropped, killed instantly, but the gallant
Reid, though fatally shot, lingered on for two
weeks, before they heaped his grave under the hill,
within that little, now deserted, green enclosed acre
up the canyon—beneath a granite shaft inscribed, if
you will hunt it out to-day:

Frank H. Reid
Died July 20, 1898
He gave his life for the honor of Skagway

Then, as Mrs. Pullen says, " Soapy's gang jumped
like jackrabbits for the hills," but fifteen of the
desperadoes were captured by determined, hardened
groups of miners. Attempts at lynching were most
vigorously put down, the better element and saner
council wisely prevailed, and the captured crew
were taken on to Juneau and were legally tried and
convicted there for sins against "the honor of
Skagway." The quiet town lies a-sunning now
under those tall passes, which once drew men to it
in riot and in glory like a lodestone. The trails are
grass grown, and the footprints of the pioneers have
hardened into stone.

VI

They Called It "The Worst Trail This Side of Hell"

TO-DAY you leave Skagway for the summit, and the headwaters of the Yukon just beyond the divide, in a modern observation coach of the White Pass and Yukon Railroad. The train draws slowly through the more-than-half-deserted town, up Broadway now flower-reclaimed to its old natural beauty by the ambitious women living there. In place of thousands of a quarter century ago, there are now only a few hundred souls. But thirty-five women have converted one of the famous, fabulously-equipped, old ex-saloons into a charming woman's club, as fine as any in a fair-sized town anywhere in U. S. A. On the ground floor they house a well-stocked library, and upstairs are club-rooms. The whole is a community center for the common use and pleasure of the people; and so, you see, the friendly coöperative spirit of the old-time "Union Church" has not departed from the "honor of Skagway."

Through these amazing women's efforts, unsightly, vacant, and dilapidated shacks remaining from the stampede days, and now long time unused, have been torn down; and on the razed sites in the early summer mornings you see great digging going on, and work of spade and trowel. No spectres these of men a-seek for gold, but women turning earth to create beauty! Soon the abandoned spot is massed in blossoms, and the raw wound covered with an unbelievable growth of flowers. The people wave to the slow-drawing train in friendly salute—they come to doorways and shade hand to eye—and call a message of good luck to you, in memory of those other days when starting for The Pass and "the big dizzy mountains that screen it" was full of dangerous death-defying meaning.

But we are seated in deep wicker armchairs, on cushions of green plush, within an airy well-electric-lighted and plate-glass-enclosed observation car; and from our outside seats will only glance out and look down from quiet perusal of a magazine, and now and then recall that where these marvelous hundred and eleven miles of railroad now zigzag up through the snaggy mountains, looping themselves to Alpine toe-holds and spidery bridges, to snake and wind up to the impending summit, once thousands of human pack-mules struggled up the grade, on aching backs and scarified shoulders bearing their burdens over the heart-breaking trail, and horses died by thousands in this canyon still unforgetably named "Dead Horse." Men said no railroad could be built here, by any means whatever. But it was built, although surveyors had to be dropped down from cliffs on ropes to run the preliminary line, and its construction cost not only many millions cash but many lives as well. Men worked all summer, day and night, to build this railroad. The first train brought out $2,000,000 worth of gold.

The green-white water glints far down below, as you look out and down from a car-side that overhangs the precipice. Dizzy, you turn to face the blankness of the mountain wall in preference. The deep death-like valley there below is too sheer, too awful, and too full of fierce hot memories. I don't like roads with only one side to them! The Indians always said there was a curse on all who passed here. For years they kept all from this way, if you could call it so, to the Interior. Thlingits told that every time a white man crossed those jagged peaks —too steeply pitched for snow to catch and lie there—the warm breath of Chinook would melt the snow and bring swift white death hurtling down on him. On the Chilkoot, in '98, when pack-laden white men in thousands were climbing that thirty-five hundred feet of steep trail, Chinook winds brought an avalanche that crushed out more than seventy and wounded many more. Chilkats and their half-brother Chilkoots passing below look up and pause to pray, in terror of that sleepless Destiny inhabiting the peaks: " O Skagua, Home of North Wind, have mercy upon us! "

Only mad men would essay those trails, yet the psychology of a stampede is the psychology of mad men, full of irreconcilable incongruities, of frenzies and obsessions and mad energies. The finding of any new or unguessed gold deposit is a " strike," and the congregation of great numbers to one place is called a " rush." A new strike usually attracts only the prospectors or miners of the neighborhood or near-by camps, to whom the news is told, and in whose names the finders stake out claims. But when the news of a strike, for some reason, excites the imagination or passions of outsiders, of tenderfeet, of " cheechakos " (as they say in Alaska, green-horns, people unused to the North and its ways) then we have a " stampede." It was this tenderfoot, un-trained, inexperienced element which made for tragedy and hardship on the Chilkoot and White

Pass, and on beyond in the white waters of the roaring canyon. To old-timers, to experienced miners, this Klondike strike was just another gold rush, and they had been on hundreds and knew all the ropes and ways. The unprepared in body, mind and outfit, who joined by thousands in the rush, were those who made a wild stampede of it, who suffered and were often broken by it. A stampede is a frenzy and a stampede is a laboratory of mob psychology. Many of our Fairbanks neighbors and good friends were men who once had taken this long trail, and later came to Fairbanks; and so our winter evenings there were full of the dramatic, tragic, foolish tales of it—the wastes, the unpreparedness, the cruelties, the absurdities.

Don't you remember Charmian London's rare description of how her famous husband, twenty-one and full of the passion for adventure, crossed the Chilkoot, " the worst trail this side of hell " ? He set out from the beach at Dyea—" a shouting bedlam of gold-rushers amid an apparent inextricable dump of ten thousand tons of luggage ——" and took the up trail to Happy Camp, Sheep Creek, the terrible sheer " Scales," the treacherous swamp beyond sardonically called " Pleasant Valley." London had brought along " fur-lined coats, fur caps, heavy high boots, thick mittens, and red flannel shirts and drawers of the warmest quality—so warm that Jack had to shed his outer garments when packing Chilkoot Pass and blossom against the snow a scarlet admiration to Indians and Squaws! " And so Jack London out-skinned the noble redskin on his own home grounds. This was but one of many thousand classic absurdities upon the " lunatic trail."

In the sense in which Alaskans, and, as far as I

know, mining people in general use the word,
Charles Chaplin's great film of "The Gold Rush,"
following the tragi-comic misadventures of a misfit
hero, would have been a fraction more truly named
if it had been called "The Stampede." But to most
people the word "stampede" connotes cattle, though
it refers of course to *any* sudden, confused, impulsive
mob movement. A stampede is a movement of
people who don't know what they are about—and
this certainly applies to that master creation of
Chaplin's genius. The run of the plot is negligible
and it is heightened, of course, by screaming gro-
tesqueries. When the film was shown in Fairbanks,
our local paper advertised it thus: "Sourdoughs
. . . You'll Learn About Mining From Him
. . . And How!" But, as Gilbert Seldes so perfectly has said, "for the major scenes and for the
minor detail I am positively fanatical. . . . Nowhere have I witnessed such a moving presentation
of loneliness. The fugitive, the wanderer, the lonely
man—he is Chaplin's hero, and close to tragedy."
In this incomparable character study—for as such
it most appeals to us who know the misfits of the
North, physically unequipped, unborn to victory—
Chaplin *is* all the quintessence of that wistful futile
search and foolish labor which drew so thin a line
between the comic and the tragic masks. I will
confess I went night after night to see this film, seeking some possible flaw in its perfection and finding
none. And I was constantly amazed that even a
creative genius of the mime's art, such as the later
Chaplin, could have caught so subtly all that dear
futility, so alien to the usual brute tales of the North.
The film is a deep insight into the hearts of those
who *don't* fit in.

If you would feel vicariously the thin edge of reality upon which those mad men danced, then feast your eye upon " The Gold Rush," where in the filmy shadow-show this master clown will surely touch your heart to understanding of the inefficient, the insufficient, flotsam of fate and chance who formed a large part, an insoluble part, of the great stampede days, and who, by the cruel sifting processes of the North, were rocked and washed and finally spilled over the rough edge of her great pan —as miners sift their placer gold and ruthlessly discard the black and garnet sands, with all the lesser values, by the inexorable test of gravity.

To those prepared or unprepared such a mass movement is a great sifting process. " Multitudes, multitudes, in the Valley of Decision." At every turn were choices, and by every choice men stood or fell, and all their future carried the deep mark of that decision. The moment a gold seeker landed at Skagway he was faced with immediate need of choice. Should he go up the Chilkoot towering above Dyea, a strip of almost perpendicular icy ladder up which precarious climbers went—ofttimes by night lest any ray of sun touch off those trigger-fingered snows—on hands and knees, laying hold of stunted juniper and spruce roots, where a misstep would hurl them down the mountain side? Or should he take the slightly longer climb, beginning four miles nearer, not quite so sheer and steep at first, up to White Pass?

" It's hard to tell which one was worse," the sour-doughs say to-day. " Both were so bad, and I went both ways, often. The last pack into Lindeman was only three miles, which I back-tripped four times in one day, carrying better than a hundred-pound pack. Not much? Well, try it then—above the ankles of your shoepacs in mud, along that chain of lakes, or in the tundra, or on sharp broken shale! And mind you, no one was allowed to enter Y. T. without full 700 pounds of grub. The Northwest Mounted Police at the foot of Lake Marsh turned you back unless you brought at least that much with you. For they knew from what happened the year before that, if they didn't, famine was before the inexperienced misfits who didn't savvy living off the country."

Later came a hundred other choices, necessary, swiftly made, or all was lost. In the Box Canyon— should one portage outfits round it, at cost of days and days of agonizing toil, playing safe and sure for life and limb but perhaps being caught beyond in the impending freeze-up; or shoot the rapids in a few death-defying seconds, and, in a fragile boat whipped from raw logs, dare fate and death, and all, on one cast of the loaded dice? Two minutes or two days? Decisions—from which men never afterwards escaped, and which have marked our breed of men who won at last beyond the ranges, with a brand of rare individualism and self-confidence unparalleled, to my knowledge.

You climb White Pass to-day without need of decisions, on slipping rails that eat up greedy miles— eight miles of circling road to get ahead one mile! Below are constant signs of the old trail, foot-worn, now overgrown. There are the stone-piles into which are set the now bent willow sticks which mark the graves of those who broke and fainted here. And in some places stone piles and willow sticks crowd very close together.

streets that are an unforgetable memory in minds of
men who walked them in the gold-fever-racked days
of '98. You cannot know the one without the other,
and to us who are Alaskans Dawson is even more.
Although not in Alaska proper, but just across the
border, Dawson City contains the background and
the reason for both Nome and Fairbanks, for Dawson comes before the other camps of the North, in
every meaning of the phrase. This was the hard
school where our early sourdoughs learned their
first-grade lessons in the wisdom of the High North,
passed her severe examination, and graduated to be
termed her Pioneers.

To-day her enemies call Dawson " an old man's
home for decayed politicians and remittance men."
Those who wear a pessimistic monocle can cite a
basis for such finding in any generation-old frontier
town, any British colonial city. But if you see only
this aspect here, then you have not seen the reality
of Dawson.

The town of Dawson lies on widely sloping ground
at the edge of a valley, and stretches along the river
bank for two and a half miles. Like Juneau, The
Dome rises back and above it, with high hills opposite. The great mushroom town of other days,
when Dawson housed its nearly thirty thousand
people and boats were tied ten deep along its
water-front, has settled down to orderly and unevent-
ful middle age after its flaming youth. Here are
schools and churches, a hospital, a library, pleasant
residences, all the resources of a modern town, in
spite of the fact that it is " built upon a frozen peat
bog." The streets are wide, the vistas always open
to the river, which is the town's great highway.
Even though many buildings are deserted, Dawson

keeps something of a big-town manner still. The comfy houses have flowers in every window box, hanging baskets of growing vines droop from the small porches, hothouses and vegetable gardens seem to be attached to each cottage. No people could appear more cheerful than the smiling cottagers; and yet, walking the streets of Dawson after eleven, though it is daylight still, I find them haunted streets.

In this cabin, at the foot of this big slide back of St. Mary's, a lad of twenty-one once spent a winter. Here he saw such sights and lived such nights, his mind forever after kept the impress. American red-blooded literature is rich by many treasures because Jack London walked the streets of Dawson with his pal "Swiftwater Bill," and formed here that strange, shuddering, unbreakable, Quixotic attachment for The North of Paradox which another lad, also a Dawson ghost, truly called "The Spell of the Yukon." The hot youth of these now quiet streets is unforgetable, because these two youths once had lived here.

Robert Service was a British boy who had been to Glasgow University, and came out to Canada when he was only twenty. He was clerk in a Dawson bank—and in the early days of Dawson a bank was an old trunk set in a tent! "Very quiet, very shy," my Fairbanks friends describe him; and I know a score of men who lived for years in Dawson, saw him almost daily, and knew, as well as any one could ever know, this most retiring man. The editor of our Fairbanks paper, who once published here in Dawson, claimed to be the first person Robert Service asked to consider his poems for publication; and I have often heard "W. F." speak of the thrilling real sense of a "find" he felt, greater than that

JUNEAU, QUEEN CITY OF ALASKA, LIES BENEATH A
TOWERING MOUNTAIN.

Chilkoot Pass, Alaska, in 1898.

Photograph by Hegg. Codova.

CHILKOOT PASS IN '98, A PERPENDICULAR ICY LADDER.

ROBERT SERVICE'S CABIN, HAUNTED BY GHOSTS OF AN OLDER DAWSON.

THE YUKON, THAT GREAT RIVER OF THE NORTH. RESTLESSLY
ROLLS TO SEA

of any gold strike, when reading those first poems of an unusual genius. The finest tribute we of the North can pay to Robert Service is to state this true and solemn fact: it really takes a desperate effort—is indeed almost impossible—to speak or write anything about the real heart and the spirit of The North and *not* to quote him. He has said incomparably well so many things the rest of us have thought and felt and know, but find so hard to phrase.

This quiet retiring bank clerk—in the great rush, not of it—watched the whole pageant of the great stampede unfold, observed and heard, and in the silence of his little cabin at the end of one of Dawson's streets, where the steepening grade decides to quit in favor of the hillside, Service caught and wrote down the intimate spirit of the thing. No one of those actually in the stampede ever did this, for London dealt in concrete phases, not in overtones. But as an outsider, listener at an observation post, young Service saw most of the game. From his counter in the banking house he watched with an unusually understanding eye all that hectic life as it slipped past—its bitter and its cruel, its humor, its generosity, its chilled enthusiasms, its breaking and its making of men.

At nights, up in this little one-room cabin, he put his thoughts to paper, and wove a spell of Klondike which cannot ever die. Here came to birth the soiled and pretty lady "known as Lou," the crazy grimness of a Sam McGee. The rustic cabin is empty to-day but for these ghosts. Moose antlers overhang the door, wild roses crowd the little yard. The unstripped poles which rail that small porch of a mighty view, are peeling off and weather-beaten;

the steps of log by which you may approach and enter, have not for many years felt any master's footfall.

What he observed and heard, from this secluded cabin on the hill, was quite another Dawson from the one we see to-day. The Royal Alexandria, where we house, was once a famous dance hall, where (so my old friends tell me) " box rushers swarmed, men got plum crazy, and tilted pokes of dust out on the bar. Nuggets were rained on favorite girls, women sold their favor for their own actual weight in gold, men smeared themselves all over the place, and got so drunk they drank from the spittoons! Yet there was little theft and little murder, thanks to the Northwest Mounted Police, who had a well-deserved rep for handling the mob, and got an order out of chaos, somehow. At the border they kept a list of everybody setting out for Dawson, and we all had to register again as soon as we got in there. Any man who got himself convicted for a crack of any law was introduced to ' Corbett and Fitzsimmons.' That was the city wood-pile of a thousand fat logs and a brace of heavy cross-cut saws! Those slick gun-toters of Skagway and Dyea took one good look at that big wood-pile, and didn't like the picture! Cracking law *here* meant just ten hours a day on the business end of that saw, with an iron ball and chain stuck to your foot. And there would be a ' mountie ' standing by, neat and nonchalant in his big stetson, scarlet coat, tight breeches and high shiny boots, with a crack and a snap to that voice of his that made a man jump worse than a six-shooter! You know that it gets cold in Dawson of a winter—colder than Fairbanks, I'd say, though it's not so far north.

The old winds sometimes howl around The Dome, and Dawson's so shut by hills, she gets less winter light than we do. Well, when she's dropped to fifty minus, and a fellow is put to the wood-pile, you *saw* for dear life, pretty vigorous! In thirteen years Dawson had only twelve murders, as I remember; and every blessed one of those twelve murderers got convicted and bumped off to the good Queen's taste —except one fellow, who fooled the majesty of law by dying before they'd time to settle with him!

" Those were the good old days—when we paid a double eagle just for a place in line at Post Office. And why not? Your time was precious when there were millions just underneath the grass roots. In one night a man I knew spent $750 for cigars and $3,000 for drinks, blowing it in. She was a high, wide, handsome town, old Dawson—plenty of booze and gambling. But orderly, mind you,—no rough stuff, like Dyea and Skagway. The 'mounties' saw to that."

Out on the creeks beyond Dawson, whence the gold came, to-day a great ditch brings down a terrific force of water, which is eating up the very last grain of what once seemed inexhaustible treasure. And even though my husband is a mining engineer, I must say that this type of mining by dredge and hydraulic certainly spoils the look of a country! You drive out on a good auto road up the Klondike River, now almost blocked with tailings, to Bonanza Creek, where the black-nosed hungry nozzles are tearing down the hills and leaving desolation. It is hard to realize that so short a time has elapsed since George Washington Carmack, out fishing with his Indian squaw, panned the first high-grade gravel on Bonanza Creek.

Some say it was on the 17th of August, 1896, that Kate Carmack herself, washing in the creek eight or ten miles from the present Dawson, noticed yellow pebbles in the water and carried them to show her husband and her brothers—Skookum Jim and Tagish Charlie. Alas, poor Kate, her life was one of sordid tragedy! The Indian woman as a millionaire's wife was unhappy. Carmack left her to shift for herself, and she returned to her own people in Carcross where, after years of poverty, she died. Some say it was Carmack himself, out hunting with his Indian brother-in-law,—or, in another version, "fishing for salmon beside the old birch tree,"—who first saw tell-tale coarse colors on Bonanza. Others claim that Robert Henderson preceded him in the discovery, had sluiced and taken out about $750 in gold here, earlier in the summer of '96, but that Carmack was the first to stake. At any rate, a " quiet rush " began at once among the knowing ones already mining in the neighborhood; for McQuesten, " the father of the Yukon," had come into this country back in '73, by the Mackenzie and the Porcupine, and he had built a trading post at Fort Reliance, six and a half miles below the present site of Dawson; while the Hudson Bay had established fur outposts in the section long before that. So there was a group of about two hundred well-established pioneering white men already on the ground, to take advantage of Carmack's strike. David Mackay, Daniel McGillivray, and Harry Waugh were among the first to start actual mining, and each of these men made a fortune. Ladue staked out a townsite at the mouth of the Klondike (the Ton-dac river of the Indians) and in partnership with Walter Harper, another old-timer, in-

duced Ogilvie, the Dominion surveyor, to lay out
streets and lots. This he did, naming the town
" Dawson " in honor of his superior, the Director of
the Canadian Geological Survey.

Information of the strike did not reach the Outside, however, until mail from this section came
through in January, and by then all the best ground
had, of course, been staked. But in the spring some
fifteen hundred persons set out from the States, a
few going the long boat route by St. Michael and
up the Yukon, and the remainder over the passes.
So far the news had caused only a flurry of interest,
for gold rushes were " old stuff " on the Pacific
Coast, and had been since '49. But on July 14, 1897,
the Alaska Commercial Company's steamer *Excelsior* swung in through Golden Gate like a Spanish
galleon of old, and landed at the foot of Market
Street a vagabondish crew who staggered ashore
bearing three quarters of a million dollars' worth of
pure gold. In Seattle, on the 18th, docked the
North American Transportation and Trading Company's ship, *The Portland,* bringing an even larger
cargo of gold and confirming news of the strike.
The greatest gold stampede in history was on.

The Bryan campaign of '96 had bruited the word
" gold." The Midwest sweltered in a phenomenal
heat wave, that summer of '97, and the " ice-bound
North " of tradition sounded very alluring. Times
were hard, and placer mining is an occupation in
which any poor man may engage, for it requires little
capital and yields (theoretically!) great returns.
This new strike appealed to the imagination of
men; it seemed to be an open door of hope for the
unfortunate. But those unfortunates who came to
Dawson with the stampede, at the end of '97 or in

the spring of '98, found that they were too late to take up ground, and they must either take a "lay" on a claim or work for wages. The Klondike was not a large region but a very small one, only thirty miles square; and of this, only small portions of the creek beds were available for mining. There was room for 2,500 claims, at most, and all of these had been taken up in the "quiet rush," before the great stampede ever began. This was another of the real tragedies of '98, for it was a fact entirely overlooked by the crowds that soon swarmed into the country.

"Wherever the procession halted, to make a transfer or a portage," men tell, "there sprang up a town. The summer season in Alaska, though intense, of course is short, and closes in on winter with amazing quickness. Soon the rains descended, making quagmires of the trails, drenching everything and everybody, and the oncoming snows put a stop to everything. The hardier ones pushed on undaunted to the goal. But these belonged to the great minority. Their fellows, inexperienced and soft, beat a hasty retreat to Skagway. The original miners worked their claims for a few years, and then, having skimmed off the cream, as it were, they sold out to the Yukon Gold Company, a Guggenheim corporation." So the years have passed since Carmack's sensational discovery brought a human tidal wave rolling into this Canadian territory, to lap its spray and roll on over into adjacent Alaskan territory, and make the name of Klondike a household word in all the world.

The weak and the indolent, the sons of Mary, the sons of rest, tarried only a little while. Martha's sons of toil remained, attracted by the strange spell of the North. The climax of gold production came in 1900, when in one year $22,000,000 was taken from this little district; while in all, $200,000,000 has been mined, to date.   By 1910 the richest gravels were worked out, and most of the population had left—many stepping over just next door into Alaska. For the result of the discovery of the Klondike was the subsequent development of mining at Nome, Fairbanks, the Iditarod, Ruby, the Koyokuk and many other gold fields—all in Uncle Sam's Alaska. Only an imaginary, near, and man-made boundary line divides Alaska here from " Y. T." ; and the two territories are alike in history, opportunity and geography.   There's nothing Service says of the Yukon that can't be said also of Alaska, except the Northwest Mounted Police—so picturesque and useful—whom, alas, we Americans do not have. Almost all the later Alaskan gold discoveries were made by prospectors who got their early schooling on the creeks back of Dawson—those creeks with golden-sounding names such as Bonanza, Eldorado, Gold Hill, King Solomon, Gold Run, Monte Cristo, Ready Bullion—and plain flat names, too, such as Irish, French, Sourdough, and Cheechako.

Here, with the terrible callousness to life natural where so much had been risked and where there was so much to gain, " Swedes were cheaper than mine timbers. "   Gold stood around in old cans on the shelf, next to the sugar, or in old rubber boots stuck into a corner.   " There was no time to wash," one old man recollects. Another—" We cooked our food on the same shovels we dug with.   It's an easy way. We liked it."   One woman friend of mine in Fairbanks told me that she made more money baking bread for miners, on Hunker Creek, than her husband ever took out of his claim there!

For the greatest enemy these creek miners knew, in those early years, was not the cold of Dawson winters, nor the mad frenzy of the gold rush, nor yet man's greed or hate or jealousy, but scurvy. And scurvy is entirely a matter of diet. It's not the climate of the North which makes for scurvy, as so many people falsely think. Stefansson, exploring for many years upon the Arctic ice, never had scurvy, for he understood its cause; but sailors in the far South Seas, whole armies in the Tropics, have died of scurvy if they had unbalanced diets lacking the foods containing that mysterious and elusive new-found something the scientists call "vitamine C." Death from scurvy can happen in any place where you don't eat either fresh vegetables or fresh meats. There are plenty of the former in the Tropics, and plenty of the latter in the farthest Arctic regions. So ignorance is the only excuse to-day for any sufferer from this disease, once so dreaded by all who went down to the sea in ships.

I know a Fairbanks man who spent a winter on one of the Dawson creeks, in a cabin with one partner. My friend was a Yorkshireman, " sot in his ways," and he'd a notion that " a white man should take a bath and three meals every day, eat plenty of meat that's rather underdone, vegetables if you can get them—and fruit, even if you have to filch it!" His partner did not hold to such " finnicky " ways, and so, though bunking and rooming in the same tiny cabin, for all that long winter they kept separate grub piles and did their separate cooking. My friend kept solemnly to his fixed English schedule, at the cost of extra time off for hunting, fabulous sums for dried apricots and prunes, and the jeers of his companion when, in frigid temperatures, he stripped and bathed.

The other ate one ravenously hearty meal of
" beans and sow-belly " per diem, never touched
fresh meat or fruit, and never bathed. Toward
spring he developed gums that were swollen and
purple, his teeth came loose, and he grew gloomy
and depressed. His joints were an agony of pain
from hemorrhages and changes of the bone marrow.
" You could press your finger in his arm, or the calf
of his leg," George says, " and the dent *stayed* there,
like putty. It was horrible! " Before the summer
came, the partner died, whereas my friend is still a
husky chap and tells to-day with glee how, with true
Yorkshire stubbornness, he rationed out his lonely
prunes and half-raw caribou steaks, and, although
jeered at, saved himself from a like tragedy.

The greatest feat of that great Captain Cook—
who, in his long eighteenth-century sailing trips,
touched and named so many points on our own
Alaskan Coast—was not, I think, his far discoveries,
nor yet his brave death in the South Seas, but rather
the fact that he was the very first to make a conquest
of scurvy by feeding liberal rations of " sweet wort "
and sauerkraut to his men. To-day any intelligent
person knows the anti-scorbutic supplements to diet,
but back in '98 men with red bleeding gums and
loosened teeth they spat like cherry stones, crowded
the Dawson river bank as the first scows of freight
arrived that spring, and paid " two bits " a piece for
lemons, apples, oranges, potatoes, or onions!

The lucky ones who thus checked the scurvy in
time, before it had gone too far in its inroads,
showed improvement in two or three days and were
cured in a month. The others lie within the slopes
of those same gold-washed Klondike hills they came
so hopefully to conquer.

VIII

Scraping the Arctic Circle

I F you leave Dawson about ten in the evening, on the much larger river boat which is to see you through to Fairbanks, the streets will still be light as day. Fortymile will be the first stop, and the last upon Canadian Yukon, for the International Boundary just beyond is crossed in the night. Fortymile is one of the very oldest gold camps in the far North, if not the oldest, and here the local methods of mining frozen ground were first effectively worked out way back in '87. It is likely that you will wake up next morning in " Eagle City," the first port of call in Interior Alaska; and as you look out you will see the Stars and Stripes flying from store, customs house, and several small cabins which—as you will probably notice—are roofed with the hammered-out tin of five-gallon gasoline cans!

Eagle is an old camp, far antedating Dawson, for here French traders, trappers and voyageurs made old Belle Isle their winter rendezvous. To-day perhaps a hundred white people live near Eagle, but at one time it was a rallying point for swarms of destitute miners—either coming down from Dawson " broke," or on their way " inside " by the Copper River Valley route, reaching the Yukon at this point in an unbelievably tattered and exhausted condition. Those were days of defeat and bitterness, which men who suffered them are never likely to forget.

But tiny " Eagle City " had one day of triumph

and such news as no proud town of all the world has
ever known. If I could have a wish, I'd choose to
be in Eagle City not as now, in midsummer, but
rather on a cold and memorable day in February,
1906. Why? I'll tell you, for the story has to do
with one of the most courageous men, both in his
life and death, our present century knows. He wrote
his Viking name upon a long-drawn chapter of world
history and geography, and signed the " finis " in the
little telegraph office here in Eagle, at the end of
the U. S. Signal Corps telegraph line.

If you had been in Eagle on that February day
in 1906, you might have seen a tall gaunt figure of
a man, blond-bearded to the very eyes, frost-coated,
mush into the quiet town behind a team of dog-tired
huskies, who dropped down in their tracks and
curled immediately to sleep when their unknown
driver entered the Company Store and began hur-
riedly to purchase a short list of medicines, tobacco
and provisions. Men gathered here around the
warm stove took him for just another " Big Swede "
prospector in from the hills and began to question
about " the diggings," in the usual friendly, leisurely,
inquisitive, Alaskan gossipy way.

But the big man, frost dripping from his pushed-
back parka hood, was most laconic and seemed
strangely hurried. He told them, shortly, that he
had been " cruising in a little sloop, up north; the
vessel is in winter quarters at the mouth of the
Mackenzie; one of my associates is sick, we are all
out of tobacco, and so I've come (a mere matter of
a little more than a thousand miles it was—on foot—
over an unbroken trail!) to secure what's needed."
" He might have been talking of having ridden for
a few miles to a country store, so far as appearing

to regard his journey as anything unusual was concerned "—comments Jack Underwood, who talked
with him. "Alone, save for the company of his
dogs, he had made a tremendous journey in the dead-
black sub-arctic winter, through a country he had
never seen before, and was prepared to start back "—
now, almost at once.

By accident he happened to see a sign over the
little log cabin which was the end of the telegraph
line, and, as though in afterthought, the big blond
" Swede " stepped in and sent a message which was
to be heard clear round the world. Between puffs
on a newly-filled pipe he dictated to the man in
khaki at the telegraph key a terse wire, addressed to
" Haakon, Christiania, Norway "—and signed it
" Amundsen."

Almost before the close-mouthed stranger had left
the little telegraph station the town of Eagle began
fairly to bulge with excitement! The sloop in winter quarters at the Mackenzie had reached there
from the east—not from the Pacific, but, as no other
vessel had ever done before in the history of man,
from the Atlantic! The Northwest Passage, which
explorers from the day of Columbus had sought so
long, so vainly, had been adventured, won—a dream
turned to reality—by this shabby, quiet-eyed stranger
who was even now, after tending his dogs, starting
back over the long trail into the never-never land of
the still farther North, with the needed medicines
for a sick sailor and friendly tobacco for his ice-
bound companions. The little office was soon piled
high with messages addressed to Roald Amundsen—
messages from kings and presidents and emperors,
from editors frantic to get the great navigator's story.
But the man who had won the ages-sought prize of

the Northwest Passage, who was later to win the
prize of the South Pole, who crossed the North Pole
in the *Norge* with Nobile, and later lost his life in
greater-love-hath-no-man gift of footless searching
for that same vainly lost Nobile—Roald Amundsen
had faded out into the North again and made no
answer.

I wish that I had been in Eagle that day in February, and seen the greatest Viking of our generation
come, send that laconic message, and return again in
modesty and mercy. I think it must have been one
of those moments when a listening angel, setting
down earth's story, paused in his record of our usual
trivial happenings, to smile and underscore one
word. Here was a *man*. And yet, the North is full
of similar men with the hearts of Vikings, and every
little town boasts sourdough heroes who have gifts
of physical endurance and stiff courage, almost
equally remarkable.

That word "sourdough" is a term one hears the
moment one steps foot on an Alaska-headed boat. It
sounds so silly, yet it is overgrown with meaning.
As soon as you learn how it's spoken, and what the
inner meaning is, you too wish to become a sourdough and not be called with ill-concealed Alaskan
pity a "cheechako"—a tenderfoot, jackaroo,
johnny-raw.

For "Sourdough" is The North's synonym for
"Pioneer." The early miners always kept, in a
closed crock or pot, a portion of the yeasty batter
dough from pancakes or from bannocks. There
were no handy fresh yeast cakes in those days, you
know, whereas a sour dough is living and continuing
ferment. It was a similar sour dough my own
pioneer grandmother in the woods of Michigan

(and yours, perhaps) made first from her potato yeast and kept to raise to-morrow's " flannel cakes." From the new batter she would take a fraction out, to-day, and put it on the shelf in a warm place. To-morrow it became the little leaven which leaveneth the lump for to-morrow's " raised flaps." And this is what Alaska's pioneers did, too; only it was so cold in winter that, to keep the friendly yeast from freezing, they often took the crock to bed with them to warm it under blankets with their own body heat!

To be without their sour dough was real depriva-tion, and men would walk days' journey to secure some. It was the last thing put upon the pack-horse or the sled of mornings, the first thing taken off at night. One old prospector tells me how, having lost his pack-mule because a snowslide rolled it down the mountain slope, he painfully climbed down and quickly scraped into his empty tobacco tin some of the sour dough which had broken from the pot and smeared all over the poor dead beast's nose! In a vest pocket next his body he kept this warm till night and camp. Perhaps the story's true—for stranger things have happened in the North.

So you can see that Sourdough has a meaning. It means the yeast of life, primarily—a synonym for all the daily bread of man. It means that one has lived alone, long years, and sought the unblazed trails behind the grim dark hills. It means the smell of birch fires burning in the dark at countless hard-won camps. It means that you have lived with silence as companion, in partnership with space, and out of freedom and the farness have now new vista and new creed, in knowledge of resources alive to your two hands and your own soul. If you are newly come to Nordland, you soon catch the rich symbol and high honor which lie behind this lightly-spoken word. And you, too, yearn to enter into the spiritual, deep, Arctic brotherhood of these self-reliant men.

The sourdoughs on our steamer are full of talk of "going out" and "coming in," for all beyond Alaska is forever "the Outside," and it's here you first begin to learn the real Alaskan view-point. Our fellow passengers are sourdoughs mostly, although in all there are some fifty of us. There is a sergeant of the Northwest "Mounties," too, to lend us color. He is to disembark at the mouth of an almost unknown river that flows down to the Yukon from the north. Following that river—the only route—up to its source again in Canada, single-handed he is to bring back to the court of justice a native who committed murder. And he will do it, too. You can tell that, without a second look. This man is a particular pal and partner of Jim Fairborn, one of our dearest Alaskan friends; and, as Jim said to me not long ago, "If you've read 'The Silent Force,' you'll know him!" When Sergeant D—— leaves us, the men call out to him as Alaskans always do in parting—"May our trails cross soon!"—"Here's to the next crossing of the trail, old-timer!" For it's another language these men speak, of trails and strikes and pans and dust and dogs—with mixture of a strange vocabulary.

Whenever our sourdoughs leave us, at various camps along the Yukon, we learn what the Alaskan gentleman affects in summer headgear! The movement of the boat is usually sufficient to keep mosquitoes at a respectful distance; but the moment we stop to "wood up" or let off freight or passengers, their humming of an orchestra begins. "If there were more, they'd just have to be smaller," the mate

imprecates. So, as our sourdough passengers alight,
they tie about their broad-brimmed hats great rec-
tangles of black (or sometimes highly colored) net
or chiffon, which have attached strings at the lower
corners to tie beneath the arms. Thus the whole
head and neck will be protected. Otherwise, on inland excursions such as our sourdoughs make during
these midsummer weeks, in boggy places and by the
marshy rims of lakes, the pests would be quite un-
endurable, for here they rise in dense swarms.
Haven't you read "The Barrier"? The name of
Barrier is a play on words for Rampart, a town
where Rex Beach himself once lived, and which lies
on this section of the Yukon. If you have read that
story then I know you will recall the not exaggerated
episode in which a torment of Yukon mosquitoes
figures so dramatically.

Below Dawson we have been noting signs of
muskrat and of otter. Our first Alaskan moose is
a sight not soon forgotten, for the great brown
awkward-looking creature comes plunging through
the willow bank, palmated antlers upthrust and
curious. Then some one cries "Caribou!" and
verybody rushes to the boat side to see five caribou
swimming the river. They run along the bank,
within a few yards of us. We have more calls of
"caribou" later, and take pictures of them swimming across our bow—pictures taken at nine P. M.,
for we are nearly at the Arctic Circle now and the
light is strong. Circle City is our next morning's
stop, though Circle City belies its name and is not
yet inside the Circle; but McQuesten and the men
who named it thought so, when they built here in
'96 what called itself "the largest log-cabin town in
the world." To-day there is an excellent and scenic

road stretching across country from Circle City to Fairbanks, just completed, and one may take a motor here and drive the hundred and sixty-four miles in seven hours or less, and avoid several slow days of summer river travel, or a full week's old-time mushing.

The Yukon flats begin where the channel splits and subdivides and the river spreads itself out over a sometimes ten-mile-wide island-strewn bed, where the native Indian pilot marks the daily shifting channel by tin cans set on the tops of stakes. For the next two hundred miles we shall be running through level country, with mountains still in sight but as far away as the eye can reach, pale blue and indistinct as in mirage. Trees along the bank are being pulled into the river as the undercut soil of the sun-melted bank gives way. They hang head-down, as dangerous "sweepers," until next spring's high water will work them loose and float them on and down the river, to be a boon to treeless Eskimo villages far beyond, out in the west. It's Sunday, and a Deaconess of the Episcopal Church, coming back to her long Indian missionary work in Stephens Village, leads a service and we all join voices in old hymns. The day is bright and warm. A large brown bear with two black cubs is walking on the low bank, hunting a salmon catch, and the captain swings the boat inshore so we may take a picture. Though time does not seem much to matter here, we ask him curiously how long it takes to get to Fairbanks, and he says: "Five days from Dawson, if we're lucky. It may be less—but yet again it may be a lot more if the river is too low, for we have lots of freight."

Our river captain is descended from one of the

very earliest explorers of the great Oregon tract, and so he has inherited his wandering foot. And he will tell you that an uncle once was master of a racing packet on the Mississippi, the one on which Mark Twain travelled and of which he wrote. Here we find a similar great river and a similar river tradition and conditions. Our river boat is a large stern-wheeler and a direct copy of old Mississippi packets, even to her high stacks and to the man with sounding pole out on the freight barges which we push ahead downstream—the man who calls back in his high-pitched, musical, monotonous voice the marks so meaningful to all who " read the river."

For the lore of The Great River—and so the word " Yukon " is interpreted—is another fascinating chapter in Alaskan history and experience. Those who graduate from this good school are weather-beaten, wise and keen, with wrinkled crow's-feet at the eye corners which pucker swiftly into fun or whimsy at the slightest provocation. All those who read the river's shift of depth and shallow, constantly, are quick to read the equally mysterious human shallows, too; and rivers breed their type of men as true as mountains do, or seas.

IX

Sons of the Midnight Sun

IN 1883 Lieutenant Schwatka U. S. A. constructed a raft on that Lake Lindeman which he had named, and navigated the Yukon River to its mouth. As in his reconnaissance he neared this middle section of The Great River of Alaska, where it throws a league-long half hitch up over the Arctic Circle and returns again, he wrote in his journal: " The 29th of July was a hot sweltering day, with the sun and its thousand reflections sending their blistering heat into our faces. In fact, our greatest inconvenience near the short Arctic strip of the stream was the tropical heat. . . . We drifted down the hot river, by low banks that needed nothing but a few breech-clouted negroes to convince us that we were on the Congo." One surely does not enter through any icy portal, to reach these flattened polar areas! In fact, temperatures of 110° and 115° in the sun have been recorded here.

The only town on the supra-arctic twist of the Yukon is old Fort Yukon, directly on the Circle and about halfway of the river's total length. It is the oldest English-speaking settlement of this region, and has been a hunters' and trappers' trading post of importance ever since established in 1847 by Mac-Murray of the Hudson Bay Company. I am wondering if you have noticed, as I have, how many names of these earliest pioneers are Scotch and Scotch-Irish names? McQuesten, Duncan, Harper,

Mackenzie, Stewart, MacMillan, Ogilvie, Mac-
Gregor, Campbell, Muir, MacMurray—these sound
like a roll-call of the clans, and these are the names
first-comers wrote upon our northern maps, to set
their broad Scotch stamp upon the country like a
covering plaid. Fort Yukon lies at the inflow of the
Porcupine, which rises in Canada and comes down
from the north and east. On the upper Porcupine
is the now famous Hudson Bay outpost, Rampart
House.

The Hudson Bay had held Fort Yukon for so long
that, when Uncle Sam bought Alaska, they refused
to move from this post, professing to believe that it
lay well within Canadian territory and not in " Russian America " at all. Now Russia and Great
Britain had agreed long ago that the 141st meridian
should be the western boundary of British territory
and trading concessions; and Uncle Sam, in buying
his attic, had taken over these treaty rights, too. But
the Hudson Bay people at Fort Yukon insisted that
the 141st meridian still lay well to the west of them,
instead of more than a hundred miles to the east—as
it is air line, or nearly two hundred miles as the
crooked river runs!

Maybe the Hudson Bay factors knew the truth.
Maybe it was a colossal bluff. But what this great
semi-official British fur monopoly said, in effect,
was: "You may have bought what you call
'Alaska' from Russia, with all the rights and privileges appertaining thereunto; but we are here, we
have been here, and here we stay!" And yet the
Hudson Bay did move this fur post, and moved it
twice—until it finally did reach British territory. A
small detachment of the U. S. Army was needed to
start that move, however, for "The Great Com-

pany " had rather run things in its own high-handed way, in northwest Canada, and saw no reason why it should not continue to do so here.

Uncle Sam felt differently, however. You see, he had a fur company of his own, now, which wanted to " make trade and barter " in Alaska, and so of course would like to have no rivals. The Alaska Commercial Company, a San Francisco firm, was organized about the time of Alaska's purchase and took over many of the old Russian trading posts and concessions, which had been included in the bargaining. They also took a twenty-year lease on the rich fur-seal rookeries of the Pribilof Islands. Later, the Alaska Commercial Company changed its name to the Northern Commercial Company; but under whatever name it operated, it was and meant to colonial Alaska very much the same thing that the Hudson Bay meant in early Canadian days.

Unhappily, though, the Commercial Company took over as a liability (whether they were aware of it or not) much of that bitter hate the Indians felt for the cruelties and injustices of the old Russian fur company. The Tsars used to send fighters to their Russia-in-America, to protect their fur interests; but Uncle Sam didn't do that, and the Indians consequently murdered in cold blood some of the earliest American traders, both on the coast and in the Interior. Mrs. Bean, wife of the first fur trader on the lower Tánana, was cruelly killed and her death went unavenged for many years. There was no justice in the land, there was no form of government, there was no hand of law in all of this enormous inland region during that unhappy twenty-year interregnum between the going of the Russians and the final coming of Uncle Sam's men. Slavery of war

captives still continued, and old hates, old fears, and
old distrusts, bred by malpractices of Russians, per-
sisted here until very late in the nineteenth century.
This is a phase of things almost forgotten now, but
once it was a very terrible reality. The early story
of the "N. C. Company" contains a mort of rigorous
drama!

But to-day the old N. C. Company is again reorgan-
ized, to meet the new conditions in the North; and
now there's not a town in all this section of Alaska,
to my knowledge, which does not have a "Company
Store," and "company" always means the N. C.
Every one of these little river settlements is domi-
nated by its N. C. warehouse and shop; for as The
Company grew it spread, reaching from Unalaska
and Kodiak up the Susitna with its trading posts,
north to Saint Michael, and eventually up the Yukon
to the very gates of Dawson. It bought out the Hudson Bay post at Fort Yukon—when the British company was finally persuaded that it was trespassing
considerably beyond its own national bounds. Captain Raymond of the Engineers, U. S. A., himself
ascended the Yukon and in August of '69 determined,
under the skeptical British eyes and noses, the actual
longitude of this post.

The old N. C. was the owner and operator of several ocean-going vessels, too, and long before the
famous Klondike stampede it had placed a river fleet
on the Yukon, for the use of miners and its own
traders. These boats were on hand to transport the
stampeders and their outfits when, in 1902, gold was
discovered in the Tánana Valley near Fairbanks.
But in the early days, and before Uncle Sam officially
came to the North, it was the Hudson Bay Company
which built and held Fort Yukon.

In 1862 Archdeacon McDonald had set up an Indian mission here, under the Church of England, and translated the Bible and the Book of Common Prayer into the Indian dialect. His was indeed a good work—the oldest, except for Russian missions on the lower Yukon—a work still continued in the hospital of Fort Yukon, by the Episcopal Church under the direction of our friend Dr. Grafton Burke. This far northern hospital in America is a gracious building made of log, with many windows from which, on this warm summer day in which we see it, flutter innumerable white curtains in the open July air. For, as Schwatka found back in the eighties, this willow-grown and poplar-lined flat stretch of the Yukon can be really hot at times, all through the sun-drenched summer.

These fluttering-curtained hospital windows are situated within the Arctic Zone, but look south across our imaginary Circle into the North Temperate Zone. After five years exploring in the Arctic, Vilhjalmur Stefansson spent three months under this friendly roof as the guest of another famous explorer —Archdeacon Stuck, who first ascended " Denali." Stefansson had been stricken at Herschel Island with typhoid, and then with pneumonia and two attacks of pleurisy. His life was despaired of by his friends; in April, 1918, they brought him overland to St. Stephen's, where he was finally nursed back to health through the care of a dear Fairbanks friend of my own who was then one of the mission staff at the hospital.

At Fort Yukon you may truly see the midnight sun, if you are here near summer-solstice time. At midnight the sun will be low, and touch the horizon *in the north.* Yet it will not sink below that line, but will swing up, without disappearing, and continue its northern circle. You can read newsprint here at midnight, as readily as at noon.

Though we arrive at these little river towns at the most impossible hours, it makes no difference to the people; for the summer nights are white nights, and more comfortable than day because the low sun is a refuge from the heat. As the packet swings in sight around the river bend, and the long blast echoes and re-echoes back into the drowsing heather-colored hills, the whole town wakes and rushes to the bank—a bank of gelid mud, but turned ethereal pastel color by the long flattering northern light. The cry of " Ste-e-e-e-am boat " (a long-drawn-out rising inflection on the first word, a short drop on the second) sounds all along the waking town, ashore.

With splashes and with puffs, with creakings down inside of her, and clanging bells that echo from below, our boat which seems so clumsy turns slowly, heads upstream, quarters the current, rounds to, drifts back, and edges in toward the steepening bank. The caught lines thrown ashore may sing like harpstrings, but they must hold. The high bank is the only landing place, and this The River, as is the wilful way of great rivers, is constantly re-shaping to suit its own shifting whimsy so that each landing of each voyage is a new, separate problem. No wonder there are seaman's wrinkles about the pilot's eyes, for he must read those channel changes constantly. New bars are forming, and the sounding poles out on the foremost barge are continually awork and flashing down, and up. Old beds, hidden snags, surface ripples, undercurrents—all these the pilot reads, subconsciously. He knows, but cannot for the life of him tell *how* he knows!

But more than people come to meet the midnight landing of our boat at tiny villages. The huskies hear the slow chug of the steamboat's labored breathing long before the white folk or the Indians do, and their long howl of a delighted greeting is usually the first note of warning we are here, and antedates even the cry of "steamboat." At some small fish camps where the boat does not tie up, the dogs who pull Alaska's winter sleds are being boarded for the summer. Chained to old packing-boxes on the gravel bars, lying on the flat box roofs, mosquito stung, hot in their furry winter coats, they howl a long-drawn protest as we pass. In winter they are needed and are busy, but in the summer they are boarded out wherever fish is plenty, and must fight the flies and fleas and other pests, in doggy boredom. Their wolf howl is a declamation against the whole new scheme of things. Some one has said that if Alaskan dogs had known the trouble George Carmack was to make for them, they surely would have bitten him to death!

At places where we stop, the dogs are waiting for us on the high banks, yapping, snarling, fighting fiercely for position; for they know they will be thrown the food scraps from the boat, and they are almost crazy with excitement. Sometimes they run so fast to reach the bank, they can't stop at the edge and tumble in. The most amusing sight I know along this length of river is the crowd of huskies, with their solemn, wolf-wise faces, crowding the bank, their anxious tongues adrip with expectation, lined up like company upon parade, with eyes glued to the porthole of the cook's galley. And they are never disappointed.

Some of our longest stops are merely "wooding

up," for Yukon steamers feed upon the country. All winter long "The Company's" woodchoppers have been busy in the silent woods, and great stacks of cut logs are neatly piled at stated intervals along the river banks. At Gibbon there's a pile—or used to be—of 6,000 cords! Going downstream we burn a cord an hour. Going up (as soon we must do, when we swing into the Tánana, and push our heavy barges) we shall be burning four or five an hour. The boat is run in close to high cut-bank, and gangplanks are thrown out. The purser goes ashore with a long notched pole and measures up the wood on hand, as he will later measure and report the cordage taken. Instantly there is great business and commotion below deck. Gangs of Indian stevedores seem to spring from nowhere, down in the hold, and begin to rush ashore with hand trucks and rush back with loads of logs, like ants at work upon an ant pile— fast and furious—taking on fifteen to twenty-five cords of spruce at each such landing. We passengers don't mind these delays at all, for we can go ashore and prowl about, exploring, coming back with plenty of flowers and berries—and mosquito bites, if we forget our sourdough nets!

Below the Yukon flats the river narrows between high hills again, and here is Rampart City, founded in '97 during the Klondike stampede, when gold was discovered near here by the half-breed Russian, Joe Minook. It is at Rampart-on-the-Yukon (not Rampart House upon the Porcupine, as some have thought) that Rex Beach lived one time for several months. His cabin will be pointed out to you, if you care to walk to it past the long streamline of buildings. Many of these are now deserted, for Rampart was a "boom" mining town and the Beach cabin is

at the farther end. "W. F." has told with great
gusto how, on the day of his arrival at Rampart,
Rex Beach mixed up a batch of scrambled eggs in
his new "outside" derby hat, for his first meal here!
This really happened, and the sight must certainly
have been quite as ridiculous as any of Chaplin's
delicious foolishness in "The Gold Rush." In a
letter to a Fairbanks friend of mine, dated January
5, 1917, Beach tells that the reason he "left that roof
and sought another was because Annie, my sourdough associate's helpmate, insisted upon boiling
frozen fish-heads in a tomato can and eating the eyes,
while we college boys were at our meals. It was not
appetizing to try to eat while those fish craniums
were being vacuum-cleaned!"

When we reach old Fort Gibbon, where we leave
the Yukon to turn into the Tánana River, the pilot
puts off in a small boat to explore the channel. For
the Tánana silts up its two-mile-wide mouth so constantly, the bars are most uncertain and a channel
must be hunted every trip to find a way through.
And we are pushing two heavy freight barges, one
balanced on the nose of the other, so to speak. These
are attached to us and to each other by lines and
winches, that must constantly be let out and adjusted
as we "jackknife" around the sharp river bends or
swing inshore to make our landings. There is no
sleep for captain, or for pilot, on the Missouri-like
muddy Tánana, with its "quicks" and boiling sand-
spits. Every time we hit a bar we must back off, if
back we can, and try again. The river trail is a
slow primitive way, but this is the manner in which
new lands are always opened, and I am glad I saw
the true North first by tracing this slow, patient,
natural artery up into her very heart. And though

the upstream going is now so slow, why should we hurry? It's warm—so warm we never wear a coat. We take long walks out on the big freight barges, and we have had our first heavenly sight of Mt. McKinley,—the " Denali " or " Most High " of the Indians,—the topmost peak in all of North America. Although it lies more than a hundred miles to southward, the mountain top hangs in a glow of rosy opal above the low trees of our wide river flat, and appears to be unbelievably close and near.

The Tánana carries vast quantities of water down from the snow-peaks to the southward, but for the most part it is so wide a stream that its channels are not deep, even for these river boats which draw but four or five feet. Its valley is one of the most richly fertile in all the North, containing more than half a million acres, it is estimated, of agricultural land; and rye, oats, wheat and barley are being grown by farmers here and dairymen, in ever-increasing volume. Tánana means River of the Mountains, the -na, -no or -nu ending (as variously pronounced in central Alaskan native tongues) denoting always " river " or " water."

Fairbanks is located about three hundred miles from the junction of the Tánana with the Yukon, and at about one third of the river's total length. But first we pass the mouths of the Kantishna, Tolována and Nenána rivers, and at Nenána is a smart new town of green-and-white buildings, made to order for our Uncle Sam. Here the government-built Alaska Railroad, running in from the Pacific coast at Anchorage and Seward, now crosses the river on a fine high bridge. And here, to-day, you leave the boat and go by rail the forty miles to Fairbanks. But when I first came to the North there was no railroad

built here and one went on by boat, up twisted
sloughs, past Whiskey Island and innumerable fish
wheels turning in the current, spilling their sluggish
salmon catch—to Fairbanks and a new home there.
The rail way is the easier and swifter, but the water
way was lovelier.

I never can forget my first sight of Alaska's Golden
Heart, as Fairbanks has been called in love by those
who know her best. The spindle of the wireless
tower, the three great stacks of N. C. power plant,
thrust up into the soft-hazed, low-sunned, midnight
hour and broke across a dome of fathomless sapphire.
To the left, against a slope of low prone hills, the
waves of shadow rustled on green fields of the wide
outspread Government Farm. An arching mesh of
iron dead ahead marked the new road-bridge across
the river, setting a limit to navigation here and connecting Fairbanks with its clustered suburb, Garden
Island. Spreading for a mile along its serpentine of
river bank, the spacious town stretched out as far as
eye could see, and looked a real metropolis in contrast to the tiny camps or mock Norwegian villages
we had been seeing ever since we left Dawson.

Older log cabins had their roofs earth-covered, on
which grew flowers and bright and lovely weeds,—
"Arctic roof gardens," we came to call them. Here
were the docks, the spires of churches, big buildings
which I later came to know as The Company's store
and warehouses, and the square, clean, three-storied,
large, gray-painted edifice they told me was Saint
Joseph's hospital. The slow boat pushed her way,
with slackened pulse and almost noiseless whispered
low breath now, up through the narrowing channel
and between the rows of houses, as though she drew
through a canal of Venice. The cabins crowded

close upon the right, so I could look into their tiny yards and spy the faces of the friends whom I was soon to come to know: hear husky Scotch-burred voices call a greeting to returning sourdoughs, from the street, or warm and fun-packed Irish voices thrown from shore to those aboard come home again —until, in my remembering of these moments, now, it seems as though the boat was slowly pulled to dock by those caught words, those outstretched hands of greeting which tugged so at our stranger heart-strings.

This rambling green-roofed cottage on a corner, set in its yard of rose and berry bushes, will be my first home for the next two years. The graceful tiny church of logs next door, with its toy belfry topped with golden-glinting cross caught in the north sun's light, is our soon-to-be-loved Saint Matthew's, as built by that Archdeacon Stuck of grateful and well-famous memory. This square-verandahed log house, lined in a mass of pansy boxes, is the town's library of which I one day shall become director. The white frame building next, so fresh and clean, against which the geranium boxes flame in color, is Dr. Sutherland's—he who will be the hero of our memorable flu panic. And on the N. C. dock, the window boxes filled with massed nasturtiums are red-gold orange blobs of color, unforgetable, to symbolize forever to my eye this Gold Heart of the North.

A first impression is a treasure, and I for one can never lose my first, rich, warm impression of this far sub-arctic town. Beauty and friendliness and cheer were here. It seemed a place where comfort and good living met, and nothing in my years of taking root have ever made a change of that opinion.

Photograph by Cann. Fairbanks.

THE FIRST LOCOMOTIVE TO COME TO FAIRBANKS, NOW A CURIOSITY.

Photograph by Cann. Fairbanks.

FAIRBANKS LIES IN A WIDE VALLEY WITH GOLD-WASHED HILLS
TO THE NORTH.

Photograph by Cann. Fairbanks.

THE MIDNIGHT SUN AS SEEN NEAR SUMMER SOLSTICE ON THE YUKON.

Photograph by Cann. Fairbanks.

ST. MATTHEW'S IS OUR TINY CHURCH OF LOGS WITH A TOY BELFRY.

X

Alaska's Golden Heart

NINE out of ten stories of Alaska towns begin with a dance hall and end with a dance hall. That seems to be the accepted and ready-made formula. To the person who has learned Alaskan life only from film and fiction, Alaska's past, present and future are all contained within the walls of a dance hall; and perhaps all through our own long journey into this far country you have been wondering why I have overlooked giving you a lurid description of an up-and-doing, open-full-blast dance hall. The simple reason is, I've never seen one.

Quite recently a moving-picture corporation was formed to film typical Alaskan stories, in Alaska: an innovation, for before this time " Alaska " films had always been " shot " in California. This film was indeed taken here, and well taken, and we greatly enjoyed the experience of meeting and entertaining many of the actors and helping them to get authentic Alaskan background for their sets. But the very first step was to reconstruct a dance hall, painstakingly and from the memories of oldest inhabitants. The director said he " had to have a dance hall, for people in the States always expect a dance hall in Alaskan stories." But the dance hall had to be re-constructed. Many of my older neighbors and acquaintances in Fairbanks, it is true, could tell us vividly of those days and scenes—though usually they don't. Some loved the garish day and

87

hark back with a real regret to the old times; but many more wish permanently to forget them, press forward now, remember not past years. It's better so.

But never in all my own Alaska travel all over the Territory have I myself as much as seen a dance hall or heard in passing the blare of its music, for all this is part of the distant past. In its day the dance hall filled a need long since drifted into the limbo of things forgotten. Do not come to Fairbanks expecting to see dance halls. You won't. You will see farms and mines, many healthy children, 600 motors for 2,400 people so that all may ride who will, and more airplanes and more landing fields per capita than in any other section of the world to-day. But nary a dance hall! Nor is there a glacier within a hundred miles of Fairbanks, so I found, but there are at least a hundred hothouses. There's not a totem pole in sight—nor ever has been—but there are scores of telephone and electric-light poles! Most people here have never seen an Eskimo, any more than do you in your own home town, except upon the silver screen at our fine, new, and " Farthest North Thea-tre," seating 700 people and with an excellent built-in pipe organ. And there are not as many Indians to be met with on our streets as one might find in many a Western town to-day. For Fairbanks is a new and white man's town, and never was an Indian or a Russian village.

What I found here instead, to my amazement, was a library, a hospital, a school, a kindergarten, churches, hotels, banks, stores, club-houses, restau-rants, laundries, electric lights, telephones, tele-graph, a bus service to " the creeks," busy boats and launches, and a railroad terminus; for even before

Uncle Sam constructed his railroad from the coast
to Fairbanks, enterprising local citizens had built
a narrow-gauge road to the creek mines, the Tánana
Valley R. R., since taken over and operated by the
Government as a feeder to the " big road." " Going
to the Creeks " or " living on the Creeks " does not
mean, in Alaskan parlance, a picnic. Far from it!
The creeks are the gold-bearing placers, radiating
and ten to thirty miles from the central town which
is the commercial, transportational, financial and
social center. When a man goes " back to the
Creeks " from town, he is going back to work, hard
work. For any one who thinks of either lode or
placer gold mining as a " snap job " is a person
strangely ignorant of fact.

Fairbanks very much resembles a Western cattle
town in its physical appearance. The majority of
the older cabins are built of log, and locally there
is sharp distinction made here: a " cabin " is a log
building, while a frame dwelling is a " house." The
newer houses are of frame, and all—both log and
frame—are very substantially and warmly built.
Then, too, Fairbanks is not itself a mining town, but
is the feeder for a score of mining settlements near-
abouts, and it is also the commercial center, transportation head, and outfitting point for the whole
enormous interior of Alaska, north to the Arctic
Ocean. Commercially it stands to the Middle North
to-day very much as Westport Landing (that was later
to become Kansas City) stood in the early development of the Middle West—the place where one
type of transportation ended and another more primitive type, for further-going pioneers, began. Hence
Fairbanks has a commerce far exceeding that which
you might expect from the size of its population,

and has, too, a very real financial and geographical importance; for like another Kansas City it is located in almost the exact center of the main land bulk of the country. It is a very bustling town, just as up-to-date as it knows how to be: quite as much so, indeed, as the sub-arctic conditions of climate and its far isolation from civilization, in time and space, permit.

Whereas Dawson is, roughly, 190 miles south of the Circle and Nome 140, Fairbanks is but 120 miles below the actual Circle. However, the winters in both Nome and Dawson, so I am told, are far more windy than in Fairbanks, because with us, as cold weather comes on, the air becomes phenomenally quiet and still, the atmosphere almost breathless in its keen, clear, poised intensity. If you have ever lived where it is both cold and windy, you will readily appreciate this difference. Any mid-winter picture taken in Nome shows cabins covered to the roof in drifts of snow through which, as Nome friends tell me, they often tunnel from one house to another. A typical Fairbanks winter experience, in the " deep cold," is that our thin light snow will lie for weeks piled up on picket fences like high-domed caps of marshmallow; or, even more a test of quiet, the snow will hang in unshaken white ribbons two inches high, on weighted loops of telephone line—undisturbed, untouched by any faintest breath of wind, for weeks! This I have seen from my own windows, not once but many times, in our afar hyperborean home " back of the North Wind."

Fairbanks was the last great gold camp of the North, but the men who founded it were *not* stampeders. They were graduates from the rough, hazing, sophomoric days of Juneau, Skagway, Dyea,

Dawson, Nome. In the great sifting process the
weaklings and the tin-horns had, for most part, been
discarded, dropped over the North's rim—and so
lost to it, good fortunately, forever. The men who
remained had already sowed their untamed youthful
oats in untamed youthful camps, had seen greed and
sin and lawlessness in their unlovely end-products,
and tasted dregs of bitter Dead Sea fruitage. Often
in lonely cabins of a blizzard-blown winter night
they had talked of how they loved the North, esteeming her good in spite of all her sternness and caprice.
They had talked of how they wished some way, some
how, a man could really live here with this loved
Alaska as a white man should—lawfully, and not, as
Robert Service even then was writing, up in his
lonely Dawson cabin: "Rape her riches, and curse
her, and go away."

These seasoned Alaskans were fit, were tried, were
sure of themselves and of the land. They wished to
see a town rise in the North some day that would not
be a Port of Missing Men, "a city wicked, wonderful, short-lived." They wished, and they wished
hard, for a good place to settle in, to colonize, to
work honestly and loyally for: a place of permanent
human habitation and of possible future development, and not a mere treasure house to pillage
quickly. They wished to find a place where men
might penetrate below the mere surface of life,
where men might have a chance to reach down to
life's bed-rock pay of all-enduring richest values.
These "old Alaskans" were tired of wandering,
tired of a rootless tumbleweed existence, tired of saying, "Lo, here! Lo, there!" They had in them,
as Service with his keen perception saw and wrote,
a very real hunger:

" A hunger not of the belly kind, that's banished with
    bacon and beans,
But the gnawing hunger of lonely men, for home, and
    all that it means."

Then, at the psychologic moment, the " Tánana
camp " came in. To it there came not a mad rush
of frenzied cheechakos, but a group of determined
sourdoughs who knew just what they wanted and
were fully determined to make the pot of gold and
rainbow end actually coalesce this time. That secret
wish must have been lying dormant long, in minds of
many men, in many places. From Klondike creeks,
Nome beaches, from Gastineau lode mines and the
green-stained Copper Mountains of the Southern
Coast, old-timers rallied to the clan call. Men who
had met before on many a hard-won trail and tried
their common mettle, met again here in the very
heart of The Great Country to build an all-Alaskan
town. This was to be that ideal " no mean city," for
which in lonely scattered dreaming they had been,
unconcertedly, so long devising.

The site was limitless in possibility of ultimate
expansion, set in a gravid width of valley, upon a
navigable river, with worlds of coal and wood at the
back door. Here they could build as they wished,
from the ground up, and build as they had learned
to wish to build—permanently. Here there would
be no cruel Russian past to undo, no superstitious
Indian past to haunt, no bad-town past to wipe away.
This town would not be set upon the sea edge so
that a man might be, at certain itch-foot times,
tempted to skip away to Seattle on any boat that
passed; nor was there any threat of towering mountain hanging over it. Here there should be a settle-

ment of actual, factual colonists, of men who were already pioneers, acclimated, prepared, knowing the odds—a law-abiding town to which they could fetch gladly and with quiet assurance the women of their serious choice from older soils, a town in which they could shape for them many happy homes.

For the very first time in the North, home-making women were considered in the founding of a gold camp. Fairbanks is and was, and I think long will be, a place of home-dwelling people. Other Alaska towns have been, in time and with an effort of good citizenry, re-worked from camps of struggling lawless men to settlements of home makers, which now they surely are. The real distinction of Alaska's Golden Heart is, that almost its first conscious throb began with the steady pulse-beat of actual home-seeking colonists.

It seems to me that this determined spirit of a permanent founding, so characteristic of Fairbanks at its best, was bravely shown in 1905 when the infant settlement, not yet on firm financial feet, in one year fell victim to the shock of two major disasters, from which it rallied with rare courage. A great flood in the river caused a loss of $50,000, a heavy blow to the struggling three-year-old village; and then, in less than a year and when all the flood damage had scarcely been repaired, there came a great fire which in forty terrifying minutes swept and destroyed the whole business center of our town. But—before the fire had stopped burning and while men were yet hard at work fighting it—contracts for rebuilding were being made at the very fire nozzles; and townspeople were at work, clearing away wreckage and preparing for new buildings, before the very ashes of disaster were even cold!

XI

"The North That Never Was"

THE Frost King built himself a palace long ago, so men said. He walled it all about three sides with topless peaks, with snow perpetual, and on the fourth he placed a sea of ice which melted only when, one time each year, he waved a Merlin wand upon it, then swiftly closed again.

No white-skinned mortal knew the vast extent of all that lay enclosed there. A few had peeped in fear over the eastern wall, where the Great River cut a gate. A few had peered in from the frozen sea-side, in those short open months of summer. And one or two, seeing the river path stretch through the Frost King's garden, had taken lives within their hands (or so they thought) and scampered through from east to west, like frightened boys that race fear-speeded, in dare-devilment, through a dark graveyard—as I believe they thought this inside of Alaska truly was. But from the highmost southern wall, most fearsome and most grizzly, no white man ever had looked down at any time upon what lay enclosed there. Men spoke of that which lay within as frozen, lifeless, cold, and without loveliness or good repute—a desolation. The only sound, they said, was crack of grinding icebergs; the only sight was static forms of life. Here all things, as within the Garden of the Sleeping Princess, were frozen in a waiting stillness, as of death. . . . They

94

spoke of what they feared and they imagined, and *not* of what they knew.

There never was a garden walled—unfelt, unheard, unseen—but there grew up false stories of it, based on mere peeping or on wildest rumor. There never was a garden walled, wherein a Sleeping Princess lay imprisoned, but one day there has come the handsome prince of romance, predestined to break that spell. The age-old lies about the Frost King's palace were forever shattered when, back in 1885, a very young and greatly daring Lieutenant of the Second U. S. Cavalry broached and broke the southern wall of Alaska, and for the first time in recorded history a white man looked north from that great divide and saw with truthful eyes the fertile summer-blooming reaches of our upper Tánana Valley, stretching away to join the greater Yukon—entered and brought back his good report.

I wish I might have looked north with Lieutenant Allen, at one-thirty of that June morning from his new-found pass within the mountains just above Suslota Lake. After two months' adventuring up the Copper River from the Pacific, at first by sled and then by cordelle with a moose-hide boat dragged on a tow-line against the tug of swift back-pulling current—after almost nameless hardships, due to misunderstanding and hostility of natives, to his own unpreparedness for climate and for country, as well as " that last great enemy of all explorers, hunger " —he had at last, almost by chance, reached the divide between the Copper and the Tánana waters.

I have found in the archives of the State Department a worn old record of that journey, a record no Alaskan can read without a quickening heart; for this was the first white man to reach into the Frost

King's ill-reputed inner place—over that high south wall which had been previously described as " one Mt. Hood piled on another." His exploit was to open to white colonization a region with the boundaries of an empire.

" Fatigue and heat," that yellowed journal reads, " prevented a start . . . until 5 P. M. . . . At 1:30 A. M. after the steepest ascent made by the expedition, we were on a very short and narrow ' divide,' 4,500 feet above the sea level, with bold, barren bluffs on each side. From this *the most grateful sight it has ever been my fortune to witness* was presented. The sun was rising, but not in the east, in fact just 2 points east of north. We had nearly reached the ' land of the midnight sun,' to find in our front the ' promised land.' The views in advance and in rear were both grand; the former showing the extensive Tánana Valley with numerous lakes, and the low unbroken range of mountains between the Tánana and Yukon Rivers. On this pass, with both white and yellow buttercups around me and snow within a few feet, I sat proud of the grand sight which no visitor save an Atnatána or Tananátana had ever seen."

This is the moment that I wish I might have shared, when, like Balboa on his peak in Darien, the halls of gold were opened and new worlds of empire swam into his ken. The wide valley of the Tánana stretched out below, luxuriant in growth of June-blown wild rose and grassy meadow, spinneys of birch and cottonwood, streams soon to be found aleap with salmon and with grayling, lakes rich in pickerel and whitefish. The Sleeping Princess of the Frost King's Palace woke to life and to the love of man that early morning. The fairest daughter of the old North Gods shook from her magic sleep and, hero-won, submitted from that moment to a mortal's conquest. The fabled ice walls crumbled, the leaping fire-music died away, the beauty of a truth replaced a grizzly legend.

I think it no wonder that people living in Interior Alaska have, even to this day, a place feeling noticeably different from that of people living on Alaska's coast, just as in the States there has always been a difference between dwellers in long-settled portions and those on the newer western borders. Sometimes our pioneer superiority complex takes amusing and extravagant angles, it is true, and I have sometimes caught myself indulging in it, and smiled to think, " I've caught it." But you can't very well help this, if you live here long within this inner valley, amidst the men who first won to it through real tests of the long-stretching trails. Later colonists who come to-day across those coast passes, by then-undreamed-of luxury of train or on to-morrow's wings of flight, cannot even imagine the groundwork for this feeling. But we who came into the North within the middle period and caught the ending of the older day as well as the beginning of the new, hold in our memory at least the basic facts which made the winning of the Middle North so real and vital an adventure.

A certain sifting process determined which of Alaska's future citizens should live upon the coast close to the open highway-sea and which should dwell " inside," behind the ranges. Some people are not happy far from the sea, while to others the sea means unrest. Only those ventured through the smoking peaks and up the white-foamed canyons who were not appalled by the unthinkable vastness, were not afraid of being caught alone in awful avalanche, and did not know a vestige of that particular form of self-distrust which makes most men avoid great spaces and great silences.

The all-togetherness of " the Interior spirit " is an accepted symbol and an accepted fact. I have heard Coast people complain, in envy: " You Interiorites get more than your share of good things because you always pull together, in a gang. You beat us *to* things. You jump in and snatch at any bone with meat on it, like a pack of malemutes! "

That isn't meant to be a compliment, but actually it is. We *do* work together, for people who have known the common experience of such trails have learned the unforgetable lesson of Arctic brotherhood: swift decision, followed by immediate, direct, effective, concerted action. It has become a quality ingrained and inescapable. When the people of Fairbanks decided a few years ago that a railroad to tide-water was an absolute necessity—if Interior Alaska was ever to be developed as a land of white and permanent colonization, like that great West which it so closely resembles—then the Interiorites got together and gave their views publicity throughout the entire U. S. A. In due time the railroad was an accomplished fact. Like the Western railroads built after the Civil War, this one has more than justified its creation ever since, and will continue to do so even more, in years to come. The Iron Horse took the trail which the feet of pioneers had broken.

" W. F." says, " As with other towns, so with Our Town—there are numerous things which need fixing. But it's seldom we holler for help! "

Toward those who are content to live in the more populous, easier-reached, and milder-climated Coast towns, the old Interiorites in turn show sometimes

something of a scorn. The very same feeling used
to exist in the Far West, in the old days of the cattle
ranges. I'll never forget my own first summer in the
northwest tip of Colorado—I, a city-bred girl,
dropped down a bride with a surveyor husband into
that corner which was then the farthest from a railroad of any section of the States. I felt and knew
at once that the old-timers there were sorry for me!
I was so green, so tenderfoot, I had so much to learn.
My very speech betrayed the easy ways of cities and
dependence. It hurt—that feeling which grew in on
me, of being different, lesser, and un-tried in resource.

One memorable day, well in my second Western
year—a day I never can forget, for every item of that
look and scene is fixed in memory as a flashlight shot
—a chance cow-puncher with whom I was riding a
mile or so on trail said casually, in speaking of himself and myself: " We Westerners! " The swift reac-
tion was so great, instinctively I jerked my horse to
standstill and the man wheeled round to face me,
startled—and was more startled when he saw (I
could not help his seeing, though I'd have given
much to hide it) the tears of a great, sudden, unex-
pected joy that filled my eyes.

" Great hat! " he cried. " And what have I said
now? "

" It's nothing—nothing," I explained in haste.
" Only—I am so happy! You've just said one of the
nicest things any one ever told me. And though we'll
never likely meet again, I'm never going to forget
it! "

I left him, mystified and more than ever con-
vinced, I have no doubt, that women are queer creatures! But I was as exalted as though I had received

the stroke of knightly accolade, after long vigil and long test. He meant by "Western," you see, very much the same thing our Interior Alaskans mean by "Sourdough." And that is why I quickly understood the intense feeling our Interior sourdoughs have about their own hard-won land, even when they sometimes carry it to amusing extremes. Theirs is a generation that is swiftly passing, and one day this precious matrix of loyalty to their own inner land, in those who early came, will all be lost if it is not passed on in a tradition; and so it is perhaps well worth recording, now.

I've heard men often say, in speaking of Coast folk, "They never crossed the ranges." Among ourselves that is indictment! Or, as our "W. F." would often editorialize, in the old days, when irritated because citizens of Juneau or of Anchorage would not see eye to eye with us of the Interior: "They're beachcombers!" Or, as yet another said, so graphically: "Sure, I know the body of Alaska was like a slab of critter-meat the Roosians and John Bull had bargained for and butchered, in betwixt them. They'd cut it like a T-bone steak, a juicy mouthful of good meat, but with a stringy tail of fat and gristle that no man likes to set atween his teeth, if he can have the good loin next the bone, or knows the better taste of! Sure, I know. The cut was all long made, and Uncle Sam had just to take it all, or leave it all. But a man don't have to *live* where he don't want to!"

The town of Fairbanks was located when and where it is by a trick of fate or luck or chance, even as most other gold camps have been located. It is on the right bank of Chena Slough of the Tánana because one man got stuck near here, another man got lost near here, and a cook went for a long ride! It doesn't sound probable, I know, but it is true; and it is also true that Italian, French and Japanese names are all tangled up in the original settlement of Fairbanks: Pedro, Barnette, and Wada.

As Joe Ulmer (who is a Past Grand President of the Pioneers of Alaska) tells the story, Felix Pedro was born in Italy in 1859, emigrated to America as a young man, and after working in the mines of many Western states for several years, decided to try his luck in Alaska. Here he prospected the Fortymile, and it was here that the late Alfred H. Brooks of the U. S. Geological Survey met Pedro and engaged his help in a reconnaissance of what is now the Fairbanks country. While near Piledriver Slough on the Tánana, Pedro found gold prospects in several places, but returned that year to Circle City. Once in the winter of 1900 he tried to find again those likely prospects, but could not. In the summer of 1901, however, he took a pack-horse called Old Pete and in company with some other experienced prospectors wandered over from the Chatanika River into the Little Chena. But Pedro was very evidently lost, and this country—coming upon it as he now did from such a different angle—all seemed totally different and unfamiliar. His comrades were angry that he had led them into such a wild-goose chase, as it seemed, and they would have lynched him, so the story goes, if Jack Kinally had not intervened. That winter was spent in desultory prospecting, but in July of 1902 Pedro himself at last found pay on the creek that now bears his name, Tom Gilmore washed some good discovery pans on the present Gilmore Creek, and others staked on Cleary and Goldstream. During the summer more prospectors from the Circle country drifted in, and soon a dozen near-by creeks were staked and named.

In the meantime Captain Barnette had started up the Yukon from Saint Michael with a small steamboat, the *Lavelle Young,* and a barge loaded with supplies which he planned to use in founding an Indian trading post where the Delta runs into the upper Tánana. Coming up Chena Slough, probably thinking it a short cut and misled by his native pilot, he ran aground near here, due to low fall water, and was compelled to tie up his barge and winter. As he could get no further at that time, he decided to make a virtue of necessity and, since there was an Indian village only twelve miles below, this island seemed as good a place as any for a permanent trading post. So he settled here, built a big log house for his store, and his coming proved a boon indeed to the hungry prospectors wintering near by on Pedro's creek. In fact, every pound of his outfit was sold out by March, even though (as George MacQuarrie, one of the first comers, tells me) flour sold at $65 a hundred weight, bacon at $1.25 a pound and oatmeal at a dollar! It was this post established by Barnette which determined the present site of Fairbanks, for the ground he laid out as a town-site lot was later bought by the N. C. Company, and their present stores and warehouses are now built upon it.

News of Pedro's gold strike spread rapidly to Circle, Dawson, Rampart and Nome, word being carried by Wada, a Japanese boy from Barnette's stranded boat. As MacQuarrie says, " He went up-river to Dawson that fall, and all the way along, when folks asked him about what was doing over on the Tánana, he kept his mouth shut and looked mysterious, the very best way in the world to start a rush,

and there sure was one." It was not many weeks
before the sourdoughs began pouring in, from all
the old camps of Alaska, and in four years these
Fairbanks creeks became Alaska's greatest gold producers.

When I first came to Fairbanks I lived on Front
Street facing the river, in a rambling six-room log
house, the older part of which had been one of the
town's original cabins. Just the other day, in looking over some forgotten papers, I happened on a
letter which I had written from that house, during
my first winter. Perhaps if I let you read it, in that
way you will get my very first impression of housekeeping in Alaska's Golden Heart, far better than
I could rebuild it for you, now:

Do not think of us as freezing, please, or as living in
an Eskimo snow igloo! One of the many paradoxical
things about Alaska that I have already discovered is the
fact that people are more comfortable here in winter than
they are in many places " outside." This is because the
houses are of heavy logs, and solidly constructed, and
well and newly chinked each fall with clay, so that all
preparations are made beforehand for a severe winter;
whereas so often in the States, because cold comes infre-
quently, the houses are not really built to withstand cold
at all. We have a most modern bathroom, which is
quite a rarity in Fairbanks for there are only six of them
in town; and I find it a great treat to my new friends and
neighbors here, to ask them to " come over and take a
bath!" You see, otherwise they have to go to one of
the public bath-houses, but it is much pleasanter to bathe
in a porcelain tub here, and, when the thermometer
stands at forty below, to sit about and visit afterwards
and have a hot cup of coffee before bundling up and
scurrying home through the frost-teeming electric-lighted
early-afternoon streets.

We also have a big kitchen with a modern range and plumbing, and many double-glassed windows that face the south—where such sun as we now have is to be seen peeping over the mountains for just an hour or so at noon each day. People tell us that we have an old domestic tragedy to thank for our many unusual conveniences to-day in this really very comfortable house. For to me, coming from our three years at the radium mine in Colorado and living in a tent there on a mountain top, this house is the epitome of comfort. They tell me that one of the old-timers of this camp built our original house and lived here, with his wife and children. But one day he fell in with a crowd of his old pals from early Skagway days, and forgot about his present domestic ties so far that he disappeared for nearly two weeks, on a prolonged drinking party! When he got back he was so ashamed of himself that he promised, if his wife would "forget it," not only to add a much-needed wing to the original cabin, but also to install the "finest kitchen and bathroom in the North." From such strange springs do the warm waters of our present domestic comfort arise!

We have also to thank this little tragi-comedy for our big furnace (which eats up incredible cords of wood, in logs that I just can lift, and that's all) and our own well, located in the cellar just under the furnace so that it never freezes even when, as yesterday, the thermometer on our front porch hit the amazing point of sixty-eight below zero. There is an electric pump attached to this well, and it fills up a tank located in the attic. The house is hung with burlap in soft warm brown tones, instead of being papered; for they tell me that there is too much expansion and contraction of the walls, in the extremes of temperature here, for plaster to hold tight. The burlap is very satisfactory and indeed most artistic, making a neutral background like a studio wall, and it tones amazingly well with the old pieces of furniture we have brought from home—the grandpa clock, the old Nantucket desk, great-grandmother's four-poster and the other things—as well as with our oriental rugs. And

don't think these things incongruous here. These rugs
of Orient are far more near to Asia now than ever they
have been since knotted in Saruk! And the old grandpa
clock that once was made in Perth, has much more
chance to catch again a Perthshire cadence here than in
Nantucket or in Denver. They seem content, these old
things. They seem to say: "Ah, yes, we understand.
Another colony, and we are your true colonials. We feel
quite comfortably at home here, thank you."

And so, you see, although the spirit thermometer outside says " deep cold " (and mercury will freeze at minus
forty, so they cannot use it here), our house inside says
" home and comfort." I wrote you last August, after
we got here, of the unbelievable beauty of the gardens
and the wonder and the mystery of sun-filled summer midnight dusks. Do you know, I think I'm going to like the
winters just as well? I like the contrasts here—the land
is like the serpent of old Nile, bewitching because of her
infinite variety. I'm keen about it all. Most of the
people living here consider this the finest climate on earth,
and I'm beginning to believe it, myself.

Aside from our joy in the pieces themselves, I'm glad
I brought our old furniture. It's so suggestive, all the
time, of that New England past and those other colonists
who brought with them *their* treasures from *their* homeland overseas, when setting up *their* new colonial home—
to help to keep their hearts from home-sickening, and as
a symbol that their minds were solemn-set to root here
and make the place a pledge of faith to all the past. For,
you see, we feel ourselves already as a part of this great
new American adventure, but moving in the pattern of
those old colonial home-makers, carrying forward the
customs—and even the furniture—of an older world into
the new soil. And these worn pieces of a glowing warm
mahogany help us each day to keep in mind that other
picture. Men back in England thought New England
was a barren cruel land, and felt a misplaced sympathy
for friends who went to live there in the wilderness, very
like the sympathy expressed by you in your last letter to

us here! Don't waste such thoughts on us, my dear, for the old-timers here who know it best, call it "God's Pocket." Isn't that a phrase of faith and wealth and all security? These sourdoughs, as they call themselves, though they are very far from being saints, yet have most of the qualities we think of saints as made of, seems to me—high courage, faith, and gripping everlastingly to an ideal they've set their hearts upon. "And what is else, not to be overcome?"

Outside, our house is a sort of coffee-and-cream color, with a dull-sage painted roof of corrugated iron over the wood—all covered now with a soft blanket of a foot or more of close-packed snow, which helps to keep us warm and cozy. And as the logs of the house are newly daubed outside with white-gray limey stripes of chinking, we present in our exterior phase a winter symphony of pleasant white and brown, really very lovely. Here is indeed good architecture, for it so squarely fits the purposes for which it was designed, and is so truly adapted to the environment in which it is set and out of which it roots and grows. Our little brown home in the North is in perfect focus with the climate, with the social customs of the community, with the history of the camp's development and with good sane common sense! What more can you ask of architecture?

I have only two faults to find, and they are so minor I'm almost ashamed to mention them. The other day, the day of the first "deep cold," I looked up from my sewing and saw some little white spots on the wall. I knew they had not been there that morning, for I had freshly swept and garnished the big square living-room, expecting guests that afternoon for "sewing and coffee," as the telephone invitations are usually given. At last, my woman's curiosity was too much, and in the middle of a sentence I got up, walked across the room, and tried to pick off one of those white dots. I guess that my look of amazement was open enough, for the ladies of our sewing bee, who had been watching, burst into a delighted laughter at my look of consternation! The white dots were the heads of nails, in door jamb and window frames uncovered by the burlap; and the deep cold penetrating the walls had followed along the iron and condensed the moisture in the warm room into a frost, covering the nails' heads so tightly and completely it could not be scraped off. My new friends have been kidding me ever since about "seeing spots."

Yesterday when I took a bath, I was luxuriating in the warm steaming tub—especially luxurious to tall me because it is an extra large and extra deep tub, an " over size " to fit the huge body of that once old-timer who, as I told you, built this house for his own comfort. Well, steaming there and thinking with amusement of your letter of polite sympathy about the cold we must be suffering here, I happened to look up and saw three irregular white streaks running across the blue-gray " sanitas " of the bathroom wall, just above the tub.

I had learned my lesson about spots, but streaks seemed to be a different matter. Besides, I argued, frost would be impossible just above that tub of steam. Gingerly I reached up and scratched with a finger nail, and—sure enough—a great blob of white frost fell down and splashed into the tub!

Upon investigation, I realized that the bathroom had been built in the jog formed by the corner of the house's new ell, and hence that one of its inner walls over the tub was really an old outside wall. The frost of this deep cold spell we are having just now had followed in along the logs, which stuck their ends outside, and the heat of the room had brought the frost out all along the chinks. I could feel the bulge of the logs under the sanitas.

My other objection, aside from dots and streaks, is that our house isn't " on the level." Nothing is on the level here! Mind you, I say "thing," not people, for the people are the squarest and truest I've ever known, and are a lot like the best of those in the West. But our living-room floor is so wavy it almost makes me seasick to walk across it; for it has an oceana roll! You see, all of this town is built on deeply-frozen gravels of an island in the big river. Except for a small cellar big enough to hold the furnace and not much else, the house is built right on the ground, on mud-sills of logs. Especially because we are so close to the river bank, which forms a sort of fault,—and which is itself contracting and snapping from cold, with cracks like rifle shots,—the ground is forever moving and adjusting and heaving, and so the floors heave and move, too. But all the other housekeepers have wavy floors, so we never notice it any more.

You weren't sorry for me about the right things! You never thought of spots and streaks and wavy floors, I'll wager. And I can add one more Alaskan rarity that I'm very sure you've never guessed: Last week we were sitting here playing a quiet hand of bridge when suddenly there rose such a clatter that I thought the roof was caving in. Then I located the noise in the kitchen and rushed out there, only to see the dishes on the shelf dancing up and down as though the ghosties had them—and the bulb of light on a cord was swaying back and forth in a big arc, as though possessed. Allen, too, had jumped up and was rushing about to see what was the matter. But our guests called to us—" Come on back and finish out the hand. It's nothing. Just another earthquake. Katmai is turning over, that's all. You'll soon get used to that. It happens every month or so. When you have seen the ice come and go, then you'll begin to be a sourdough too, and you'll never notice a little thing like earthquakes. It's your lead."

Now what a Land of Paradox this is, I ask you? Frost one day, and an earthquake the next! A woman said to me at church last Sunday: " You'll like Alaska. It's the land where anything might happen—and most generally it does! "

I guess that she was about right. I *do* like Alaska, and things *do* happen!

XII

Who Said, "A Cold Wall"?

MOST people imagine Uncle Sam's attic as completely surrounded by a wall of cold, making it not only hard to reach but almost impossible to live within. But those who live here know of no cold wall.

The Southern and Maritime Provinces of Alaska are in direct contact with the main line of one of Earth's great central heating systems; and our Interior Province is well and completely sheltered on three sides. Even that farthest quarter of Alaska which lies on the exposed Arctic Slope is not uninhabited by "white folks," and splinters of the very North Pole's self, so to speak, have been brought home to us by Amundsen, Wilkins and Ben Eielson. No; the attic is well built, is very self-contained, and, like the houses of our town of Fairbanks, is quite evidently intended by its Architect for comfortable and all-year-round occupancy. And yet Alaska's climate—the one thing all Alaskans are most united in loving and praising—is just the very thing about which outsiders are most skeptical.

What are the factors which make for a cold climate? Most people think of only one: high latitude or nearness to the Poles, and that we surely have, in some parts of Alaska. But there are many other equally determining causes of cold. When you've taken them all into consideration, you'll see why most of Alaska, most of the time, has, as Jim

Fairborn puts it, " just the kind of climate California wants to have—cool enough in summer and comfortable enough in winter!"

The first moment you put on your thinking cap you will hit upon the second cold-determining factor —altitude. "How high up" on mountain or plateau is quite as important as "how high up" on the curve of the globe. When, as people have since Ptolemy, we read of snow-clad peaks, ice caps and genuine glaciers existing in the alpine highlands of those Mountains of the Moon that lie right down under the earth's equator, in the very heart of "hottest Africa," then surely we realize that altitude alone may be enough to neutralize the ordinary effects of latitude. And Fairbanks, though only a little below the Circle, is only a little above sea-level. Wind currents and icy drafts that mountain ranges draw down into valleys, or shut off, are other items in toting up the sum of any possible cold. Whosoever live in mountain country know this, and Fairbanks is windless in deep winter.

But one of the very most essential factors in determining whether or not a country is really cold, is that complicated matter of ocean currents and their modifying influence on the climate of any land-mass lying in their track. Nearness to or distance from the sea, then, and the temperature and direction of the prevailing currents flowing through that sea, are concluding and intensely powerful matters that must be looked into, before we can say whether any specific part of Alaska is or is not "very cold."

Alaska lies, as we know, contiguous to continental America on its east side, but thrusting out into the North Pacific in a tremendous jut, which carries both its southwest Aleutian arm and its northwest tip

at Bering Strait, westward until they all but inter-
lock with Asia. The whole southeastern, southern,
and southwestern coasts (the major portion of
Alaska's twenty-six thousand miles of highly in-
dented shore line) lie open to whatever forces are
at work in the North Pacific.

Down at the broad equator line of the Pacific
Ocean the revolution of the earth upon her axis from
west to east, endlessly spinning, deflects westward a
draft of heated air which, in its turn, produces
equatorial currents. Upon striking the Asiatic
coast, just east of the Philippines, this sun-warmed
water splits in two parts, one branch deflecting
sharply north off the coast of Japan. Swinging over
to the right and sweeping along past the Aleutian
Islands toward the American continent, the " Japan
Current " warms and moistens the entire south coast
of Alaska and, following with its drift circulation
the swirling winds of North Pacific, flows down
along the Panhandle. This great Kuro Shiwo or
" Black Stream " is analogous in the Pacific Ocean
to the Gulf Stream of the Atlantic and is the hot-
water-heating system of Uncle Sam's attic.

At the time of Alaska's purchase, lack of accurate
information about its climate led to bitter and most
unjust criticism of the far-minded statesmen who
effected the transfer of title deed from Russia to the
United States. People referred to it as Seward's
Ice Box, Icebergia, Walrussia. Perhaps this association of Alaska with the word " Russia " is what
first set the cold notion in people's minds; for most
of us do falsely think of all Russia as cold, whereas
it is far too big a place to be lumped under any one
category—as also is Alaska! And even at present,
to most of those United States citizens who own our

Territory but have never yet set eyes upon it, Alaska seems another Greenland or Labrador or Siberia. Precious few connect its climate in their minds with the climate of Norway or the British Isles, which is the true comparison.

After years of all-season living in that part of Alaska which is actually the winter-coldest, and which has a greater yearly variation in temperature than has the very Arctic Slope itself, I must truthfully say that I have never suffered any hardship directly attributable to cold, nor have I ever known a day when mere cold made me uncomfortable or necessarily kept me within doors. I have felt very much *colder* at plus 30 degrees, in wet snow which penetrated clothing, than at clear dry minus 50 in a fur parka. I have had accidents and adventures, yes; but many of the adventures were due solely to my own ignorance, and accidents will happen in the best-regulated and mildest localities. In the short " deep cold " spells of interior Alaskan mid-winter one either stays in the house or goes out only for routine marketing, business or school. One doesn't travel long distances unless it is absolutely necessary, when it is colder than forty below (the point at which " deep cold " sets in and a very definite change is noted in the atmosphere) ; and above this point the trails are not dangerous or at all unpleasant, if one keeps moving. In fact, from fifteen to twenty-five below we think the most ideal mushing weather, and I myself have driven with dogs, for sheer pleasure, on days when the thermometer read minus twenty-five and thirty. Old prospectors on trail often used to carry a little bottle of mercury, and when this froze, as it does at minus forty, they simply did not travel but " holed in."

In considering *any* Alaskan problem, the fact that it is indeed " The Great Country " must always be kept in mind. You have already travelled through Alaska's southeast strip of territory, and have seen that there, at least, the air is always warmed and moist (from one hundred to two hundred inches of annual rainfall being characteristic of that section), due to the in-sweep of the blessed Kuro Shiwo, which makes the complete circuit of our southern coast line. As these waters are open and navigable the year round, the only difficulties to winter transportation from Alaska's many fine ports are being removed gradually with each added year, by the setting up of new lighthouses and buoys and channel markings to make plain the twisted inland waterway that winds its sheltered trail to Seattle. All along this coast, equator-warmed ocean winds and currents, as well as the sea-level location of all the southeastern Alaskan towns, more than counteract the fact that these ports are farther-north colonial settlements.

England lies in the latitude of Labrador; but England is not sterile, because it has the Gulf Stream. Indeed, its southern counties have very much the same climate as the coast of South Carolina! In the same way, Alaska's old Russian capital of Sitka, lying at 57° N., has very nearly the same year-round average of temperature as Halifax at 44° 39'; and records kept at Sitka for twelve years prove that " there has never been a week *in winter* when the temperature was as cold as at New York City, Washington, D. C., or Berlin, Germany; nor has there been a week in summer when the temperature was as high as at any of the three places mentioned." Sitka in mid-January often has exactly the same temperature as San Francisco, in "sunny California." It lies in about the same north latitude as does Edinburgh, and their climates are very similar since both are at sea level and both are influenced by similar ocean-warming streams. Sitka has a far milder climate than either of the Scandinavian countries, yet no one ever thinks of Edinburgh or Halifax or Scandinavia as uninhabitable.

Fact is, three fourths of Alaska is not an Arctic province at all, but lies well within the North Temperate Zone; and the climate of Uncle Sam's attic as a whole shows just about as much variation as may be found within the walls of the forty-eight states below stairs. Official thermometers in Montana have dropped as low as anything we ever see even in mid-Alaska, and parts of Alabama experience lower temperatures than do sections of Alaska's southern coast.

This matter of Alaska's great size is almost unrealizable to those who have not in person taken its long trails. To say that Alaska stretches from Hyder at 130° W. longitude to Attu Island beyond 173° E., or that it contains a total area of nearly 600,000 square miles (about ten times the land area of New England), means less from the climate point of view than to say that its north and south reach is, by 200 miles, greater than the distance from New Orleans to Duluth! And as it would be a very thoughtless person who expected to find identical climates in New Orleans and Duluth, so too we must be very foolish to expect the same climate upon Amatignac (the southernmost Aleutian island) and at northernmost Point Barrow. Yet Point Barrow, because it is a sandspit lying upon the sea and subject to sea changes, is not the very coldest place in all Alaska, by any means. With our north-south borders as far apart as the Mexican border is from Canada, why on earth should people expect one uniform temperature for Alaska? We have plenty of elbow room here, you see, for many peculiar diversities and differences, for each one of Alaska's four great divisions has a climate in which the four elements of altitude, latitude, windy-ness and sea influence are differently blended.

Archdeacon Stuck, who built our Fairbanks church and spent many useful years at Fort Yukon, used to lecture a great deal to Mission Circles in the States, and was often questioned by ladies who came up afterwards to ask, " How *do* you endure the bitter cold in Alaska? " He always replied, in his crisp English manner: " Madam, a person of good sense does not *endure* the cold. He protects himself from it." And that is one great advantage we humans have, in dealing with mere cold rather than with heat. We *can* protect ourselves from cold; and, too, in time the " arctician becomes arcticized." That is, a protective blood-change is said to take place, which helps to keep us warm.

The Arctic Sea is full of life, and, as Stefansson has so well demonstrated, abounds with living creatures which have made the necessary adjustments to its conditions. Domestic animals brought to our Alaskan North begin at once to become arcticians and to arcticize. Plymouth Rock hens, during their second winter in Fairbanks, often grow warm feathers, like gray ragged trousers, all down to their toes; and Monte, our beloved Airedale that we brought from Seattle, became a veritable fur-bearing animal with each added year of northern exposure. I believe his soft wool grew to be fully four inches

long, though he was of the crisp-haired and wiry
type originally. All short-haired dogs develop here
a heavy coating of furry material underneath their
scant normal hair, for nature seems to be old-
fashioned and believes in her creatures wearing
heavy woolens in winter! Her wild things do not
"endure" Arctic cold; they protect themselves from
it. And so do we.

In all but two ways, conditions in Alaska to-day
are similar to conditions in New England when it
too was being colonized. Gæa the old Earth
Mother is the same, stirring her great currents in
the ocean bowls. The same sky overhangs us here;
beast, bird, and fish are just the same, and human
nature hasn't changed one bit. But in some ways
we're better fitted now to colonize a so-called difficult land than were the folk of yesterday, because
we have to-day our modern handy tools of both
applied and social science. Each new discovery of
a natural law has meant just one more lever in the
hand of man, to lift his world of comfortable living
a possible hitch further into the North. Civilization's self is drawing surely north, and has been ever
since it first arose in those warm river valleys of
nearly prehistoric days. *North*ward the course of
empire takes its way—and has, for some time past.

It may be a shade less romantic to live just under
the Arctic Circle in a steam-heated house, electric-
lighted, telephone-equipped, listening to music of an
orchestra playing in San Francisco, or jumping in
a plane and flying off on errands of our banking,
merchandise or mines; but these new toys and tools
have not only speeded up man's ancient business of
carving out new provinces from the raw materials
of geography, but they have helped to make of us

colonists a happier-spirited lot in the doing of this chore. On reaching here, the Cold Wall proves to be no wall at all; for with increased control over heat sources and light sources we can now live with comfort in places once considered 'way beyond the pale of civilization. Indeed, if one but gives a glance back over history, one can't help noticing that this very ability to devise ways and means of resisting cold has become the real measure and de-fining quality of Human Race's adaptability, and hence of Civilization's possibility. The stimulus of cold and the challenge of cold have developed mental powers in man and made a *homo sapiens* out of him, willy-nilly. The race has learned to live outside of Eden and yet to make an Eden even there, beyond the cold walls.

Think of all that cold has done for us! It stimu-lated men to dare the fine adventure of fabricating and controlling fire. Cold devised clothing for us, constructed shelters, and made us lay up food against a foreseen day and need. Cold the inexorable, push-ing close at his heels and nagging forever at the ease-loving brute that lurks in nature, caused him to remember, forced him to foresee, eventually made a true man of the Eden outcast, and forced the con-tented cave-dweller first to create some wits inside his slant-browed pate—and next to use them! It seems to me we owe a very generous debt to cold.

But what is " cold " ? I've come to think that there is no such thing as " cold " at all, but only " colder than " ; for I doubt very much if any two who happen to read here will absolutely agree on a definition of what " really cold " really is! Where does true cold begin? Some people feel " cold " in a room that's 60°. Some people think it is cold when the thermometer drops to freezing; others are willing to admit that it is cold when down to minus 40°; but others still, who have been brought up in the North and to whom it is a natural habitat both by race and personal adaptation, say: " Shucks! What *is* cold, anyway? It's nothing—and never hurts people who use a little common sense about it." Or, as I overheard one of our old-timers say, inelegantly but with much truth: " Cold don't ride to no tune of facts or figgers. It's *feelins* make cold. A man's own gizzard is his best thermometer. You feel all scrunched, or you ain't. That's all as is to this ' cold ' proposition."

My own guess is that the matter of Alaska's purely relative cold is answered best of all, perhaps, in Yankee fashion by, " What do *you* mean by cold? " An Italian and a Japanese helped to found Fairbanks, and both were old-timers and loved the North —yet Italians and Japanese are supposedly fond of soft climates. I know of many negroes in the North, good happy citizens here; and Stefansson tells a delightful story of his friend Jim Fiji the Samoan, who lived for many years in the very farthest north of Alaska and liked it so very much he never would go home. The great major portion of our colonists, who are one hundred per cent. " Nordic," live in the North by preference because we dearly love the climate here and, above all other factors of Alaskan life, honestly prefer and actually exult in the invigorating pep of it. Ours is not a penal colony. No one is indentured to live and labor here! We have come and we remain solely because we find in our Alaska " the makings " for interesting, wholesome, and useful living.

The oft-recurring questions of " how cold " and

" how do you stand the cold " are not so much, perhaps, a matter of solving great geographic equations of north parallels and degrees, of latitudes and altitudes, thermal ocean currents or prevailing winds. They are purely a matter of one's personal chemistry. You either like a certain amount of cold mixed in your annual diet, or you don't. It's a question of the adjustment of your personal carburetor, a question of whether your own human engine works at best efficiency and highest rating with an intake of warm or cool atmosphere. Only those turn north happily for all-year living, to whom the mere word " cold " has no terrors and who have experienced in their own persons the healthful stimulant of certain amounts of cold.

Stefansson again and again reminds us that if we are to think of the Arctic region truly, we must think of it as part of a sphere, and not as the flat and inaccessible top of a cylinder cut off from the rest of life by a sharp unclimbable rim. There is no edge off which one drops into the Never-Never, sailing north. There is no Cold Wall beginning at the Arctic Circle, or near it; and neither is there a Cold Wall extending about Alaska's southern rim. That rim is washed by the same waters that warm Hawaii, directly south of the Aleutians, where Cook and Vancouver wintered and provisioned when they were first exploring Alaska's coast. To these clear-sighted navigators Hawaii and Alaska were all a part of one job. They sailed the great circles and saw the globe as a whole, not as a cylinder with an unuseful and unapproachable top.

The barrier of Alaska's " cold " is a purely imaginary line, crossable by all who do not shiver at the mere sound of shivery words.

XIII

The Attic Is a Summer Playhouse

ALASKA'S way, in our great valley of the Middle North, is to drop her children straight from winter into summer. We're used to that, and though we sometimes miss the slower coming of green Aprils and soft Mays that usher in the less intensive summers of more temperate zones, because we *are* Alaskan sourdoughs we have learned both to expect and to enjoy her startling, paradoxical, swift, temperamental shifts.

In the Coast towns there's sometimes very little and a but gradual change between the relatively warm moist winters and relatively cool moist summers, due to the automatic well-regulated control of that year-round heating system with which they are equipped. But in the Interior, where we are shut off from that warm-water system by the highest peaks that rise on the North American continent, the seasonal changes are very marked. These ranges are a southern wall which shut off Kuro Shiwo and catch all its warm moisture on their slopes in winter snow and summer rain, so that in Fairbanks we are apt to have a warm dry summer and a cold dry winter. At White Pass the snowfall may be 25 to 30 feet, and Ketchikan may have 235 rainy days in the year—or as one of our Scots described it: "A blink of sun and a downpour, a blink of sun and a downpour. *Sundry* weather!" But at Fairbanks the annual precipitation is only from ten to fifteen inches, making for almost continuous clear days, and an all-rainy day is almost unknown. In some years we actually do not get enough snow for good sledding, until quite late in the winter. Indeed, there are many times when we'd be grateful for much more snow, to make winter trapping and hauling more easy, as well as next spring's mining. I have lived in many places in the States where the winter snow lies much deeper than it has ever been known to in our Middle North.

Very high mountains extend all along our south, and there are also mountains to the east and north, so that we are exposed to winds only on the west, where lies a shallow and relatively narrow sea—not large enough or active enough to set up its own climate whorls or cause any great disturbance from that quarter. That's why I say we dwell like happy pre-Homeric hyperboreans "back of the North Wind " ; for the Endicott Range shuts off any blasts from the north and makes central Alaska, though lying further up the globe than central Russia, a considerably warmer place in winter. Those who explore or whale, and therefore " winter " on the unsheltered Arctic coast north of the Endicotts, observe such a difference beween our climate and theirs that they are apt to speak of us with the very same superiority we use in speaking of the mild Alaskan south coast! Stefansson writes very condescendingly indeed of those " sheltered forest trails of the Yukon Valley, where the thermometer may drop very low but the wind seldom rises very high." For we are truly sheltered, both from the blue winds of the sea and the white winds of the peaks.

Spring of the year begins officially—as reckoned by astronomers and as reckoned also by our swiftly-reducing electric-light bills—at exactly the same time it begins in all other places in the northern hemisphere: that is, March 21, the vernal equinox. For of course you realize that old Sol, our great central lighting system, does not play any favorites in this matter of illumination. We of the North are not cheated in our amount of natural light, as summed up throughout the year, for the sun does not play any tricks with the *total* amount of sunlight granted to various portions of his satellite Earth. There are no " favored climes " in the matter of sunlight— or if there are, we in the North really are the favored ones, for we have a shade *more* total apparent sunlight. Because refraction shows the low-swinging summer sun above the horizon after it has actually gone down, we really have a longer time of looking at it than do more-centrally-located places. To our near-Arctic village, as to the Tropics, the same total amount of sunlight is meted out, year round—the old earth tilting on her axis and exposing now this pole, now that, like an eccentric roast revolving on its spit before a fire. Our sunlight comes in larger chunks, that's all. The sun is longer absent on his apparent southern winter journey from us, but in compensation he stays with us more continuously during his three months' summer visit. We do not sit in year-round darkness here, hatching a vain empire, but all the work-time summer long we have enduring sunlight. That's a fine thing to remember when you are tempted to be sorry for the " sunless North! "

These weeks just after the equinox are the time when people here have to be very careful about snow blindness, for the land is all a dazzling winter white as yet; and though we have a superabundant light, the sun has not yet warmed us up enough to create a melting heat. Even at work inside the house, these weeks, I've often worn snow glasses in the middle of the day; for if I didn't and happened to glance out toward our big south-facing dining-room windows, I was literally blinded by the glare of brilliant sun on brilliant snow, and everything turned black. Old-timers call it " Black Sun Time," because they've all known its danger. As late as May eighteenth I've seen advertisements in our local newspaper for "Optical Goods of All Kinds—Snow Glasses." Eskimos have shown me their wooden eye-protectors made to wear at this season—carved goggles which fit the eye and have a narrow slit in them: " Very good, make walk in him. No good, make hunt in him," so Tuk-tuk told me. Sometimes they make them out of whalebone, too, he said.

Snow blindness is a very real possible disaster of the North—not a tragedy due to cold, but to the sun, you see, by another of Alaska's paradoxes. You feel as though your eyes were full of sand, and it's as painful as an earache—one of those intimate pains you can't escape from. Your eyes continually water, and though you are not " blind " in a strict literal sense, you cannot see at all without such agony and effort that you might as well be actually sightless.

This is one reason why we're very glad that spring, in the North, is short and not a long-drawn-out season. Another reason is the River. It opens in late April or early May, and during and just after that time there is a period of intense drama for every town upon the Yukon drainage, while the glacier and snow-glutted streams sweep down from the mountains and cause great uncertainty and commotion, at best. When at their worst, they flood the towns with backed-up icy water and make "the break-up " a time to wish well past. This flooding does not happen very often—I think in Fairbanks it has happened only once in my eight years. But when the broken ice jams on a river curve and water backs up swiftly, then it must be released with generous charges of miner's blasting powder. Every one breathes a sigh of relief when the River has at last broken its ice-bonds and starts on its open way again, to sea. Now we can begin our summer business without fear of interruption.

One day your roof and lawn are covered with, apparently, an undiminished blanket spread of snow. Then—as by magic—somehow—swiftly—the snow has gone. Some time that week you're startled by great, shrieking, long-continued blasts of the fire whistles and a mad ringing of the church bells. School is instantly dismissed—it has to be! For no one not bedridden will miss this greatest spectacle of all the North. You and all the neighbors pile out of houses as fast as you can scamper and run to the river bank to watch fascinated—no matter how often before you may have seen it—that terrifying and tremendous spring opening of nature's piled-up winter forces. Great cakes of blue-white glistening ice are rushed along or tossed like chips or piled up high in toppling masses that grind and splinter and roar in passage like the day-long reverberations of massive near-by gun fire. And neighbor shouts to neighbor, above the din and clamor—" Summer's here!"

There is no April spring of a "soft tripping maiden, o'er the lea," such as the lyric poets love to sing. Our only touch of spring is shock and dynamite, the spring of giant forces turned to mammoth play. We have no spring as of the south, with ivory tint of dogwood or the cream-flesh-pink of wild azaleas, honeysuckle, laurel. Alaska does things differently, and stages in the spring her greatest dramas.

That lawn which yesterday was white, to-day is green—except where a stray winter-loose neighbor horse walked across it; and there, wherever the hoof marks broke through the sheltering warmth of snow, the grass is dead and must be sowed again. Memorial Day is garden-planting day with us. Celery and cauliflower, already started in our hothouses, are now set out; and pansy beds are made. We have been relishing local hothouse lettuce, radishes and tiny onions since Easter, and we gladly pay a dollar a pound for the first tomatoes or four-bits each for cucumbers. We plant our ninety-foot all-round-the-house nasturtium beds, knowing that in an unbelievably short time they will be up and blooming, for by June first there is continuous daylight. And we townspeople take a great delight and pride in our flowers, and mass our summer cabins with them. I've seen sweet peas grow in profusion, twelve feet high, completely smothering tiny cabins that were so short a time before snow-covered.

I think it is this deep-grained Alaskan love of contrast and of swift dramatic volte-face, which makes us glory so in green of gardens, the dramatic shift from our town's winter white of ermine hoods and snowy capes of overhang, to summer dress of flower-strewn Joseph-coated color. There's nothing I can say will make you realize how much we Fairbanks people love our flowers, or what a startled hymn of praise they always win us from any wandering summer tourist! I've watched these tourists stand agape and stare at Delia Dunham's unmatched cup-sized pansies, and overheard them chuckle, " So *this* is the Frozen North, eh? "

About this time, too, our deep well which never even thinks of freezing in winter, must be watched and surely used each day or, in midsummer and with temperatures sometimes in the nineties, it may freeze solid! Why? Just another Alaskan paradox, though this time it is a quite familiar magic— the same phenomenon that freezes your ice-cream. That is, the melting frost inside the winter-frozen earth is being pulled up now by the warm and continuing sun, and, because it is a moving and not a static frost, it will congeal the water in your well-pipe if you don't watch out. In winter your furnace dries and warms the well area, but in summer the cellar is cool and moist from this underlying frost.

Dr. Burke tells me that four miles within the Arctic Circle, at Fort Yukon, a mark of 100° has been recorded at the official and carefully read Weather Bureau station there. We Interior Alaskans insist that we have Scripture proof that our summer climate is truly " heavenly," for we not only have no night here then, but moth and rust do not corrupt! One of the first things I discovered on coming to the Interior was that moths (as well as snakes) were unknown here; and it is so dry a climate, year round, that housekeepers notice little opportunity for rust to form, in this semi-arid atmosphere with no more sky moisture than has Southern California.

Do not let the " semi-arid " I just wrote mislead you. Though there is little rainfall, we do not miss the rain in summer since our crops have a natural and ideal sub-irrigation, most favorable to gardeners and farmers. This is quite an advantage over Southern California's irrigation projects, for ours is given us by Nature, and costs us nothing. Wherever ground has been turned, the long warm sun draws up moisture from substrata of long-frozen gravels through the rich surface soils, all the twenty-four hour day. Storage moisture, in the form of snows let loose and slowly seeping in the spring, add to the sum of released ground frost and make for plant growth of almost tropical luxuriance. Although we do not have to worry much about our garden water, neither do we have to worry over possible rainy days or " spells," when planning summer outings, since the light rainfall makes dull weather a thing unknown.

Quite naturally, with such unusual actions of our sun round which the normal human day revolves, there is no ordinary routine business or social life here during the summer months. Miners work their claims all twenty-four hours of the day, and the growing plants are not observing union hours at all, but flowers hurry out and speed up their fruiting and seeding. Mining plants on the creeks do their three shifts as well, not to be outdone. And so, although the placers can be worked only about one hundred days, a full year's energy is concentrated into these three hectic months when all the gold-bearing gravels mined in winter underground have to be " cleaned up." As long as the spring water lasts, what would in the States be vacation-time is hardest work-time here for many. And we in town feel that we too want to spend every waking moment in the open, as long as friendly sun is visiting us as guest. The twisting roads spread out through a pattern of silver birch and blue spruce—roads now, but only a few years ago the hunting trails of Indians and of trappers.

Many people prefer to sleep through the warm noon hours and work or play in that cooler part of day, which would otherwise be called "night," but cannot be called night here, if that word means a time marked off by darkness. Picnics and ball-games are often scheduled to begin at ten or eleven' P. M. for that's the time midsummer days are loveliest. Not only are there few mosquitoes abroad then, but the air is coolest and the sun colors softest upon the cloud-like, blue, mauve hills afar. In the intensely clear and dazzling air there are few summer days when the massive mountains (Hayes, a hundred miles by air; Denali, a hundred and fifty) do not cut sharply on the palpitant sky line, piled high and rosy where the sun slants on them, rising above the garish light and lush heat of a sea-level valley floor. There is interval of but an hour or so between the sun's going and coming, and even when the sun has dipped below the north hills for a moment, it is hiding only just beneath the horizon and is already preparing to swing up again. It has not dropped away and down with that swift plumb drop of the Tropics. It is still shining there, just back of that mauve and purple hill, and in the short interval the upper sky is tremendously aglow with ultramarine light; so that the very darkest midnight in the valley is only a mid-dusk of lighted shade and shadowy light, shot with a mingling sun-set and sun-rise. At midsummer we can read the finest print all through the night, and we often begin a tennis set at eleven or twelve, when the level lights are loveliest and the courts back of our house are opaline in color.

For there is no glare on midsummer eves, only an unearthly and unreal amethystine atmosphere a-quiver upon differently sun-radiating surfaces; twilight and dawn melt into one another gently, without any intervening period of darkness. For long midnight hours the sun is either just above or just below the horizon, and I remember Stefansson saying: "One would think that only extraordinary carelessness would make you lose track of time so far that you are in doubt which of the twelve-hour periods you are in, but it happens frequently. . . . When there is no darkness, one's irregular habits become extraordinary. We may not feel any special inconvenience from staying awake twenty or thirty hours, and we are equally likely to sleep fifteen to eighteen hours." I have myself, when alone in the house in summer, wakened from a sleep and had no notion whether the clock's " three " meant afternoon or early morning. I've called up Central, not to ask the time, but to ascertain ante or post meridian! And old Dawsonites tell that in the early scarcity of clocks they used to know whether it was summer day or summer night only by the bartenders on shift! We ourselves so often read straight through the summer night, without realizing it, that we actually had to set an alarm clock to know when to go to bed! Many are so disturbed by the necessity of sleeping in bright daylight, they wear little eye-masks of silk or velvet to simulate darkness.

The white nights are a problem, too, for parents, since the children of the North quite naturally do not " want to go to bed by day; " and yet they, unlike the plants, cannot grow rapidly for three months and then sleep all winter. So we have a town curfew, ringing at ten in summer, to warn all children unattended by grown-ups to be off the streets and home. It's really very necessary, for otherwise our children may drift in at two A. M., and say to frantic mothers: " But, I didn't *know* it was late. We've been berry picking, on the hills. I watched the sun but it never went down at all. Honest, Mother! " And that's quite true. We are so close to the Arctic Circle that, from the near-by hilltops, the sun does not ever set upon midsummer night.

A friend has collected and listed seventy-six wild flowers which are native to the Fairbanks district, and almost before the snow is off, the Yukon crocus or *Anemone patens* is up; then the iris and briar rose are out, the Iceland poppies, bluebells, and uncrumpling ferns. Forget-me-nots and blue and yellow violets, buttercups, daisies, magenta masses of decorative fireweed, and hosts of berry blossoms come crowding on the hills. It's then we hear the high crackling laughter of the gulls (what time the first boats come), and purple-blue lupin also returns, which seems to me the loveliest of all our northern flowering. Against all this, white birch and quaking asp form background in which warm summer airs play leafy tunes; and the gray poplar, silver green, and the dark green of larch and spruce lend color to that Northland summer symphony which Service felt and saw and caught:

> " The summer—no sweeter was ever,
> The sunshiny woods all athrill,
> The grayling asleep in the river,
> The big-horn asleep on the hill."

XIV

The Dust That Lies in God's Pocket

PRECIOUS-METAL mining districts are the most fascinating places in the world to live, if one is interested in either human nature or Mother Nature. Here you see her at a work that's always going on, for this earth we build so solidly upon is not by any means a dead thing. Its hardened crust-cakes are most like a pavement built of stone setts, always tilting, grinding, shifting, eroding, settling here and rising there—as the miner who works below ground best knows of all Earth's children, for he is most earth wise. That's what geo-logy means!

Here in Alaska we have not only to watch the daily everywhere miracle of sterile granite mountains being transformed by soft rainfall and scratching frost fingers into the mantle of earth; but here the prospector, like Ariel, has come "To do me business in the veins o' the earth, when it is baked with frost." The Alaskan prospector is a partner of geologic pasts; he thinks in their terms and tries his best to trace the meaning of their ancient landwritings. Only thus his pot of fortune *may* be found, for there is always the element of chance and uncertainty about any mining. Any day the vein or pocket may peter out; but on the other hand, any day one may strike a bonanza! Each hole sunk to bedrock, each adit in the hill, is just another chance shot to a fortune: a hundred-to-one shot, perhaps, but worth the work and taking.

131

Whole libraries of books have been written about gold mining in Alaska, books of every stripe and color—true, untrue, and partly true. Some have been written by men who've never been north of Seattle, and some by men who have devoted the best years of their lives, in Uncle Sam's Geological Survey and Bureau of Mines, to scientific study of Alaska's truly vast mineral resources. From one point of view, then, it seems utterly foolish to add even the sketchiest chapter to a subject which has been so thoroughly covered, while from another point of view it seems equally foolish to attempt to press into any small space any adequate suggestion of that great industry which has stamped Alaska as one of its richest producers.

I have to beware, too, because mining is the "why" of our coming to Alaska. In fact, most early Alaskans came here for the very same reasons that brought Captain John Smith to New England in the spring of 1614: "To Take Whales and make tryalls of a Myne of Gold and Copper"! Mining is my husband's chosen profession and my own long-ridden hobby. "Much have I travelled in the realms of Gold." And so it will prove a real test of self-control if I can confine my hobby-riding here to the short course of one lone chapter. If mining terms and thought in mining cast pop up all over through this Alaskan journey of ours, please do forgive me. For we all have our bents, and you have seen by now, I know, that mine are turned to mining and its ways. What we attend to, shapes us, and all Alaska's past and present are golden stamped in pattern.

Our own approach to Alaska as a mining field was both peculiarly impersonal and personal, as I think

I should explain to make the background clear. We were not interested in any one district or any one mine, because Uncle Sam had sent my husband here to establish a Bureau of Mines Station for *all* Alaska, and, by the rules of our Department, no one in its civil service may own or operate or exploit a mine on which he may have occasion to advise or report. For us, that meant every mine and prospect hole in all Alaska; and therefore, although many opportunities of course offered, it was always necessary to keep the general and impersonal view-point. In this we had a unique outlook and one which was fortunate in many ways. Personal interest did not pull us to look more favorably on one section than another; and because we were "outsiders," for that very reason I think we often saw more of the game, as outsiders sometimes do. Then, too, we had both of us lived long in other mining districts of many types, from coal to radium ore, and so we knew other ways and methods and could come here without golden dust in our eyes, to study Alaska's special problems with freshness and perspective. For this reason we especially appreciated the racy and peculiar qualities of Alaska's pioneer sourdough prospectors, whom we soon found to be the cream and essence of the early population. And so I think I'd like to speak here of the human side of mining, instead of its mechanical or economic phases. In that way I'll indeed be speaking of a thing that's very near my heart.

In his problem of gold finding the prospector has two unknown quantities to resolve—unless he goes by mere dead luck or other people's say-so. But most old prospectors are far too keen and too individualistic to think of doing that, for most are either amateur geologists or—having learned in a long, hard, practical school—are very observant and "figurin'" in their calculations of likely prospects. A prospector knows that he must answer two questions in his mind: "Where does gold come from, and how?" If he can do this, he has a very fair chance of success.

Gold is an "old" metal, old in earth time and old in value in the eyes of men. It has long been sought, because it possesses properties of such great usefulness. It is not affected by dry or moist atmosphere and so "doth not rust nor corrupt"; it is extremely ductile, the most malleable of all metals when pure, and hence one of the most workable and sought in manufacture, so that from earliest days artisans have joyed in its use and shaping. It has a permanent and very lovely color and lustre, so that it does not tarnish, even though it may lie for centuries buried in Egyptian tombs or lava-bedded cities of antiquity; and it can be welded cold, a practical side of its quality which the worker in gold best appreciates. Also, no other metal lends itself so beautifully and fittingly to processes of coinage; all of which, together with its relative rarity, have made of gold a symbol of the highest purity and value and the world's standard of exchange among civilized nations. No wonder men for years have sought it, and that few tangible things are "more to be desired than gold . . . than much fine gold."

The mother goose who lays this golden egg is the Mother Lode—metal from the hot primal core of earth forced by the constant earth shifts and long successive æons of geologic changes, up through the veins of rocky flesh to show as fine flecks on her surface, in rare places. "Quartz," "hard rock," "lode," "reef," or "banket" mining is a search for and a laborious digging out of these "veins in

place." One man found such a place near Nuka
Bay not long ago, where a vein of gold-bearing
quartz, many inches wide on the surface, fairly glit-
tered with the precious metal. This was found by
pure chance, while burning off the ground for other
purposes, and it lies in block slate formation similar
to the deep Mother Lode mines of California. This
native gold is well sealed within the granite hills,
however, and is usually to be found only after long
and most tedious labor. "Hard rock" means hard
work and takes hard money to finance, for the mountains must be disemboweled to make them fruitful,
and "spots sticking out as big as a horse-blanket,"
such as the old prospectors joy to speak of, are about
as findable as roc eggs within the bossy beaten work
of mountains. The great mines about Juneau are
quartz or "hard rock propositions" of this nature,
requiring vast expenditures of capital to develop at
their peak efficiency but yielding golden returns
when so organized. The truly remarkable thing
about the Alaska-Juneau mine, for instance, is
not its rich outflowing of gold but the fact that,
through expert organization and technical efficiency
in concentrating methods, ore worth less than ninety
cents a ton is mined and milled and made to pay a
handsome profit. This is *real* engineering skill.

Placer mines such as those of the Klondike, Nome
and Fairbanks districts are of a different type entirely. The word "placer" comes through the Spanish *plaza* and means: a "place" where surface de-
position is washed for valuable minerals, as gold.
The *a* in placer is short and is pronounced like the *a*
in fat; it is not the long *a* of ape, as so many who
are unfamiliar with mining technology or old California tradition insist upon mispronouncing it.

Through a succession of years too numerous to
reckon as men count, tiny streams slipping through
the fingers of Time have pulled and worn at old
and highly-mineralized metal-impregnated hills.
Through epochs back of history, great Nature herself has been slowly rocking this peninsula of Alaska
like a titanic miners' cradle, with infinite patience
washing out the gold values from the rocks of a vast
district and concentrating them into small " placers "
or places: at the bottoms of favored creek beds, on
the floors of gulches, on gravel bars in rivers, on
sandy sea beaches, below the sodden tundras, or on
high benches that mark the streamline of most
ancient water courses—according to " the formation " that can be read by knowing ones. The poor-
est man, with only his two hands, a miner's pan, a
slab of bacon and a sack of flour for grubstake with
his sourdough crock, may if he's wise—or merely
lucky—strike a bonanza, *i. e.* a surface placer gold
deposit, rich and workable " from the grass roots
down." This alluring possibility has made placer
gold the lure of ages. The cleverest geologist can
do no more than say, " This place is favorable." No
one can say with certainty, " It's here—it's there."
As the old miners' saw goes, " Gold is just where you
find it ! " For no human eye has watched the founda-
tions of the world being laid, or seen the mountains
rear their shapeless bulk from sea-bed, in the hiss
and flame of that great forge-room.

The source of Klondike gold seems to have been
the small stringers of quartz in the schists which form
the bed-rock there. No important quartz veins have
been discovered near, so that (unlike most other
noted placer regions, such as the California gold
fields) there was no present source or Mother Lode

to work back to and unearth, after the first rich gravel washings had been made. That's why, to-day, after the golden fleece of Argonauts has been carried off and great dredges and hydraulic nozzles have been at work for years, there is now no further Klondike development, and some of the massive " gold boats," as the dredges are called, have already been shipped on to the Malay States—to dig up tin there! This move is typical of the world-thinking of great mining companies, who are the true internationalists of our present all-metal age.

Fairbanks is more fortunate than her older sister in that she has several lode mines now developing near by; so that when the placers are exhausted and the present big companies at work dredging the entire creeks (and not just the " high spots," as was done by hand methods) have finished their work, as dredges always do in time, then there will still be the hill mineral sources left, even though no new placers or other minerals are meanwhile discovered. Also we have here all our wide and fertile valley, with agricultural and grazing lands to fall back on, just as California found her real richness *after* '49, when climate was discovered after the gold was gone, or going. That's why we think our founding fathers here were very wise in choosing this Golden Heart for their " last big camp."

This is always the cycle of the gold camp: first the lone prospector with his dogs in winter or his crudely homemade boat in summer; then the gold rush, when he strikes it rich and the good word spreads; next come the groups of miners who work the richest gravels only, with simple pick-and-shovel man-power methods, for, as old Herakleitos wrote long centuries ago, " Those who seek for gold dig up much dirt, and find a little;" and then, when high-grade ground has all been worked over, the great gold boat or dredge will come, built and operated by some wealthy mining company. "Gold Boat" in the miner's parlance does not connote a Roman emperor's barge on Nemi, marble paved, bronze beaked, and silk pavilioned! Far from it. It means instead a large scow with heavy machinery and housing on it, floating in a little pond of water which it opens ahead by digging in, and closes up behind as it edges slowly along a creek bottom—like some prehistoric monster reaching out its long neck of chain-and-buckets, rooting in the earth with its metal snout, and drawing in enormous daily meals of golden gravels. One of the dredges operating near Fairbanks on Chatanika weighs 2,000 tons, can dig down 80 feet, handles daily between 7,000 and 8,000 cubic yards of dirt, and requires only four men to handle it, each shift. The very last speck of nature's precious metal deposit is sucked up, digested, and the refuse gravels are spewed out in unsightly tailing piles along the creek bottoms, to make ideal road metal for our many motors.

About Fairbanks, as about Dawson, there is a network of little streams each with its tributary "pups." This is the placer ground-plan. And here centuries of dripping water, the pull of gravity, with constant cross erosion of drifting winds that scatter and rains that leach and frost and ice that grind and nibble, have patiently been at work. "As there is a constant tendency for all weathered material to move down the slopes," the geologists say, "most residual gold soon becomes eluvial," with concentration of heavy material. In general, a stream will carry coarse gold one or two miles from its source, and the richest pay usually lies either on bed-rock or in the lower ten feet of the gravel resting on bed-rock. That's why " to get down to bed-rock " means business to the placer miner, for that's where the gold will lie, if any.

The geologist, casting his eye over the Fairbanks creeks, sees that one type of placer here occurs in deep channels lying on the bed-rock floor, in what were formerly broad valleys with gentle slopes. But time has changed the faces of the hills, and this ancient topography has been obscured and written over by the valley's filling with talus from adjacent hill walls. A second type, the bench placer, is the result of archaic erosions and deposits, and may have small relation if any to the present valley formation. Water and wind and slipping time have smoothed and massaged the contours and the face of nature until the question which the prospector must always ask and answer, " Whence came the gold, and how? " is indeed a puzzle worthy of real wit.

Except in the rare cases of bonanza gold, exposed and lying right at the grass roots, he must read the ancient story of the hills with all his canny wisdom and then shape his guided guess from what best evidence he finds there. He stakes his claim upon a likely " place," and then he digs a shaft to bed-rock down through the heavy overburden, perhaps thirty feet of it if he is near to the head of an old valley, perhaps nearly three hundred feet if near its mouth. When the depth to bed-rock is less than twenty feet he can mine with open-cut, scraping off the skin-deep tundra if the place is a flat bed, or ground sluicing if there are both grade and water sufficient to wash and carry off the overburden. Around Fairbanks most of the placers lie in flat open valleys, stream gradients are low, and the annual precipitation is so slight there's little flow of water to be had; so hydraulicking as done at Dawson and at Nome is seldom practiced here. In fact, on some creeks, such as Livengood, a season sometimes comes when there is scarcely enough water even to sluice all the gravels that could otherwise be profitably mined. That occasional lack of sluicing water is one of our inner Alaskan problems. As one Livengood friend wrote me, after reading an article I had published in *Scribner's* on "What Does Alaska Want?": "Please tell Mr. Hoover that what Alaska wants is rain in summer, snow in winter—and transportation at *all times!* That's all I'll ever ask of Uncle Sam!"

If the winter snowfall is light, the spring freshets on the creeks may not suffice to wash all the auriferous gravels accumulated by all the hard work of underground deep winter mining; for the deeper gravels have to be worked by drift mining in cold weather, sometimes 200 or 250 feet below the surface. And that's no fun! If the summer rainfall is too light, then the open-cut gold production may be low that year, for the little streams will not furnish sufficient water for the needed sluicing and cold-water thaw.

Except for the practices of thawing frozen gravel, and occasionally of freezing thawed gravel to hold back a flow of water, mining methods in Alaska are very much the same as elsewhere. But here Frost is, in many ways, the miner's best friend, incongruous as that may seem. Deep ground-frost enables him to remove larger blocks of ground without using expensive mine timbers to support his drifts. Frost is a rigid force and holds tight for him his winter minewalls, even although they may be composed merely of loose gravels. All he needs is timber for his hoist-shaft and those tunnels which have tracks for ore-cars; for exposure to the outside air, combined with the jar of constant vibration, will loosen even frost-solid walls.

At and near Fairbanks the alluvium in many places is frozen down to bed-rock, and beautiful, crystalline, gleaming ground-frost can be seen upon the black walls of mine tunnels 200 feet below the surface, the year round. Unless the moss is stripped, in summer the ground will thaw but two feet at most. In all this Yukon basin permanent frozen ground is the rule, due to the heavy overburden of moss which holds the cold but will not admit the sun's heat; so that in drift mining the stratum of gravel which contains the pay, lying down close to bed-rock, must be thawed either by steam or water. In the old days steam thawing was the custom; but with wood costing from ten to twenty dollars a cord, and a cord of wood thawing less than two hundred square feet of bed-rock, steam thawing proved too expensive for any but the very good ground. Recently cold-water thawing has been used with very good results. The ground is stripped and laid open to the sun and to innumerable streams of water, forced down into it through about a thousand half-inch, ten-foot, strong, steel pipes driven in at a time. With a pressure of about 25 pounds per square inch, and the points spaced from 4 to 16 feet apart according to the nature of the ground, a large area can be thawed in one season, and for roughly half the cost of steam. This method, which has been perfected only within the last ten years or so, has proved a great boon to miners on certain medium and low-grade grounds. To-day these bristling forests of thaw pipes, planted like thick-set, grotesque, branchless trees, are to be seen in many places pouring their constant streams down into ground which, loosened thus and thawed, is soon removable and workable.

Modern science has been defined as the understanding and employment of natural forces, to control natural forces; and we Alaskans are always hunting new methods to use our great God-given cold-storage plant to our own advantage and make the cold work for us. We housekeepers do it in countless ways. We let the deep cold of winter make our ice-cream, preserve our meat, keep handy and always on tap our stacks of frozen mince pies for the holidays, and perform a hundred other useful housekeeping jobs for us, in our " land of the Golden Freeze." The miners have a trick or two of their own in putting ground-frost to work. Not only do they utilize it in place of mine timber, but they also employ frost as a tool in sinking shafts down to a gold-bearing river bar or sea-bottom, which could not otherwise be reached. In Germany, at great cost, clever engineers are opening up potash mines to-day by a reversal of the steam-thawing method, ammonia pipes being sunk in quicksands and the ground *frozen* around them, so that a shaft can be dug and brick-walled and rich deposits tapped that are otherwise unworkable.

But there are places in Alaska where miners have for years let nature do this for them, and at no cost at all but just a little time and patience! At Unalakleet, for instance, a shaft was cut in the ice *almost* to the water, but not quite. The very cold outside winter air quickly froze the water lying next this hole, and soon the shaft could be cut a few inches deeper, and again the water next the thin ice-floor

KILLARNEY LAKE NEAR FAIRBANKS IS LACE-
FRINGED IN BIRCH.

"THE GRAYLING ASLEEP IN THE RIVER,"
THE BIG HORN ASLEEP ON THE HILL."
ROBERT SERVICE.

Photograph by Cann. Fairbanks.

"BRISTLING FORESTS OF COLD-WATER-THAW PIPES LOOSEN
THE GOLDEN GRAVELS."

Photograph by Cann. Fairbanks.

"GOLD BOAT," A LARGE SCOW THAT ROOTS OUT PRECIOUS METAL FROM
OLD CREEKS

was frozen thick and solid. This process was repeated until a shaft with solid ice walls was opened from the surface to the sea floor. The same procedure has been used effectively on river bars.

One thing always deeply impresses newcomers to our gold camps, especially if they are lucky enough to strike one of the creeks on the day of a "clean-up," and see with their own eyes the heavy yellow gold catching in riffles like wheat grains. They say: "You are so *careless* about gold! You treat it as though it had no value! You leave it lying around loose, almost. You never seem to think of thieves."

We don't, for several reasons. One is, there just aren't many thieving-minded people in Alaska's heart. The court records show that—I don't need to prove it. The second is that gold in quantities that would make stealing worth while is a mighty heavy metal. It's hard to "get away with." The third is—Alaska is a "long way from nowhere." The Outside can be reached only by certain definite routes and ports, and any suspected person would find it well-nigh impossible to get out of the country. And where would he sell his gold, if he did go "outside"? While gold dust in a "poke" may be *worth* a lot of money, it isn't money. It has to be turned into money before it can be spent. And who does that? The U. S. Mint, and it is only at the Mint that dust finds ready sale—or at banks in gold-producing regions, which sell directly to the Mint. Here it is assayed for its "fineness" or relative content of other metals, for placer gold always contains some other metal such as silver or platinum.

If you have stolen some one's gold and go with it to a bank or mint, you have to *prove* who you are and where you got that gold before you can sell it. And if you swear falsely, there are a score of ways the assayer can and does check up on you before you ever get paid one cent in coin-of-the-realm. If you should take Alaskan gold to Denver, for instance, and swear it came from some Colorado creek, you'd be arrested as a thief inside of five minutes. You see, there are such differences in the appearance, shape, size, color and texture of gold in different auriferous districts, a clever person knows at a glance the distinction.

My husband employed a chemist who had assayed Alaskan gold for years, and Paul Hopkins could not only tell in a moment whether a certain pinch of "dust" came from the Fairbanks district or from Nome or Dawson, but with a little careful scrutiny he could almost invariably tell you from which *one* of our score of creeks it came. Often he could even name the exact claim on that particular creek from which it had been taken—or which "pup." This is because, to an observant mineral-wise eye, all that glitters is not gold. Virgin gold before it's touched by fire, or changed in shape and color and texture by the process of refinement, has grades and types and classifications. Alluvial gold is associated closely with other minerals of great density and hardness, representing the most durable constituents of the rocks whose disintegration has furnished the detritus whence it came; and the supposedly characteristic yellow color of gold is notably affected by small quantities of other metals—such as copper, lead, or silver—occurring with it. "Raw" gold is almost always silver-bearing, and silver generally contains some gold, so that they are truly sister metals; and the complex problems of "parting" and purifying them are of greatest antiquity. Virgin gold, placer gold, water-washed and cleaned gold, before it has known the refiner's furnace may be reddish, whitish, greenish-lemon tinted, as well as all the ordinary shades of "golden" yellow. Also, the native crystallization will be different, the edges will be rough or worn, and the size of grain or nugget will have been determined by the length of its journey from the Mother Hills to the creek where it is found. That's how the knowing assayer is able to say, off-hand, "It's from Tony's claim, on Chatanika."

And so we "gold-crazed Alaskans," living in the land *we* call "God's Pocket," really take small thought about our precious metal of the hills. I think an experience which my husband had will show you how this works out. Long before the railroad came he was making a trip Outside in late fall, over the Richardson Trail. The snow was already deep on the mountain passes; and while he had left Fairbanks in a motor, when the foothills of the range were reached the stage passengers were transferred to sleds, each drawn by one horse which followed the foremost sled and driver in line, up on the summit trail. There was no need of reins, for there was no need of driving. The horses were honest and trained and knew their business.—But let him tell the story.

"Each sled contained one passenger and some mail sacks or express. The slow walk of the horse —and I could see nothing past him, of course—made me sleepy. I was all bundled up and as comfortable as the proverbial bug, in all my wolf robes, and I thought I'd take a nap. Well, the express box I was using as a back-rest, sitting up, was too high for a pillow. So I pushed it down and used it for a foot warmer! I thought at the time it was mighty heavy, for I couldn't lift it. Felt like lead. But finally I got fixed and slept all afternoon, until we got to the roadhouse for the night.

"When the horse stopped, I woke up. It was pitch dark, and just as I was crawling out of the furs, sort of dazed, Beckett the packer came up and ran his hand along the sled. All of a sudden he yelled: ' Good God, Davis—where's the bank's gold? There was a hundred thousand of a mint shipment I put on your sled and fixed for your back-rest, and it's gone! '

" ' O—that! ' I said. ' Don't get all het up over that. It hurt my back and I just shoved it forward. Here it is! '

"Well, he breathed easy then and helped me unwind myself, and after we'd unhooked Old Dobbin for the night I said: ' Say, don't you want me to lend you a hand with that box? It's pretty hefty.'

" ' H—— no, she's all right, here. We never bother to fetch in any little thing like that. What's going to harm her? "

Well, what was? And nothing ever did. But now, we send out gold by plane. Time flies in our High North, but so does gold dust. The old generation of prospectors is a vanishing race, but some type of prospecting for the precious dust is an ever-continuing pursuit, as it has been since time's golden dawn. The search *must* continue, for the business of the nations is done in terms of yellow gold; and though Uncle Sam's credit is of the best, and he has goods galore to barter, to keep his self-respect he must also have some minted money to jingle when he thrusts down his hands into the pockets of those long striped trousers of his!

XV

The Camp of the Spoilers

NOME'S only past lies in its golden sands. When these began to run, Time then began for Nome. The sands are still golden but are running now more slowly, since the jolts of big strikes have ceased to joggle the glass. Nome, too, with all its many associated mining districts on Seward Peninsula, is passing through the dredging and hydraulicking phase which all great gold camps reach, when only big and well-organized companies can handle, at little profit per yard but in enormous yardage, vast quantities of that low-pay ground from which the early comers skimmed the highest values and then departed. Our own Nome contacts were made in 1918 and 1924, when the entire summers were spent going and coming on and about the Seward Peninsula.

This is the one great section of Alaska that is not easy of approach. It lies 6,000 miles from New York, with six hours difference in time. It is almost within sight of Asia, and is the most westerly " white man's town " of all the continent. It is nine days by ocean steamer from Seattle, and in 1918 it took us fifteen days (counting necessary trans-shipping delay at St. Michael) to reach Nome in July from Fairbanks. Now the same trip is made by plane any day in the year, with but one stop en route for re-fuel; and non-stop through flights have been made in four and a half hours. What used to mean a dreaded, entire summer's delay-ful inspection trip for mining engineers, road commission men, geologists, bishops, school superintendents, governors, politicians, and all the scores of commercial people who had to make the Nome trip regularly each season, can now be accomplished in comfort and ease, over the week-end. No section of Alaska has more cause to bless the coming of our airplanes than has far-lying winter-frozen Seward Peninsula.

Nome is the only one of all Alaska's ports which is frozen in winter, however. The others—those splendid, armada-enclosing, sapphire bays of the South Coast or the many busy fishing and mining ports of Southeastern Alaska—are all upon open sea-water of the North Pacific, kept warm and navigable the year round by friendly auspices of Kuro Shiwo, which spends its heat there. But Nome lies well north on Bering Sea, on a roadstead and harborless, so that freight and passengers must be lightered in; and Bering Sea is a shallow, bowl-shaped basin here, underlain by a long out-jutting of the continental shelf. It freezes readily and early in the fall, when northeast gales drive heavy ice floes down through Bering Straits and the sea is soon covered with a mass of broken ice, cutting off communication with the outside world by water-lane until the following summer. The ice may open late in May but sometimes it does not break until the very last of June. I have pictures of several vessels trying in vain to land at Nome on June 25, but caught in the ice still many miles out at sea.

It's here one realizes best just what the Japan Current means in terms of warmth and transportation, at this one of all our ports which lacks its friendly influence. For, as you will see by looking at the map, the long line of the Aleutian Islands, far to the

Photograph by Lomen Brothers, Nome.

EAST CAPE SIBERIA LIES SO NEAR THAT WE CAN REALLY LOOK AT ASIA.

Photograph by Lomen Brothers, Nome.

ARCTIC ICE-PACK LIES BELOW BUT NORTHWEST PASSAGE OF THE AIR
IS OPEN.

"DOUBLE-ENDERS," THE OLD WINTER WAY OVER THE PASSES TO THE COAST.

Photograph by Lomen Brothers, Nome.

ICE STILL LYING OFF NOME ROADSTEAD IN LATE JUNE OF 1918.

south of Seward Peninsula, effectually deflects the
warm waters of that stream, though they are poured
out toward it, and like a fine mesh keeps them from
modifying the temperature of upper Bering Sea, to
any real extent. In the late spring a strong current
sets in which breaks and pushes the immense fields
of ice up swiftly through narrow Bering Straits into
the Arctic, and so sweeps the sea clean for the summer. In October the Arctic ice pack moves down
again and the port of Nome is closed to navigation
for eight or nine months. In the past, because of
the hard winters and because there was not much
work which could be done then, many Nome-ites
left in early October for the States and returned
again in the summer. They had a saying in Nome,
" Even God leaves on the last boat! "   Old-timers
say, " Before we had the planes, there were but two
seasons in Nome—July and hard winter."

But Nome people enjoy their climate and are loyal
to it, just as we of interior Alaska enjoy ours and
are enthusiastic about it. Nome has greatly suffered
from fiction writers, and her people say, " We ought
to let it be known that we really live like any other
people in the United States, strange as it may seem,
and that we are not burrowing into snow-houses and
living off blubber or performing any of the antics
that some gullible people imagine to be our regular
practices."   Though all about is heart of Eskimo
country, Nome is itself a very white man's town;
and I myself have never had more royal good times
than with the hospitable Lindebergs and Lomens
and many other " first families " there. Nome has
the most truly Nordic past of any Alaskan settlement, I believe, for gold was first discovered here in
payable quantities late in 1898, when Jafet Linde-

berg (whom Stefansson has called " the most romantic pioneer and leading mine operator of western
Alaska ") with Erik Lindbloom and John Brynte-
son, uncovered a rich pay-streak on Anvil Creek,
about three miles from the present townsite of Nome.
Lindeberg's father owned copper mines in Norway,
and the young man had lived in Siberia, so he knew
the mining game well.   These three formed the
Pioneer Mining Company, and staked claims on
Anvil and the other creeks.   Thousands of disappointed Klondikers, returning down the Yukon for
the States, stopped off instead at Nome; and at one
time the town held more than 20,000 people and
70 vessels rode at anchor off shore, waiting to unload
impatient passengers and tons of mining outfit and
grub-freight.   A tent city had sprung up, where all
men did was dig and wash and pan and make great
fortunes over night, it seemed.

Meanwhile paystreak gold had been discovered
upon the beach by "Toughnut" Jack Clunin, who
set up crude mining equipment there and was taking
out as much as 50 ounces of fine gold dust a day.
But The Beach was No-Man's-Land, and there was
no law or tradition to govern its staking.   So a great
miners' meeting was held and the decision made
that each man working on the beach should be
entitled to " foot-possession " of as much ground as
he could reach with his shovel, from the edge of the
hole in which he was working.   Tex Rickard's
saloon, the famous " Northern," was in those days a
tent structure with a board floor; and it was here the
miners met and thrashed matters out, for the popular
hangout was " Tex's Place."   The first court in
Nome was held in August, 1899, in a lean-to back of
this well-known resort.

But there was constant trouble, even riot, due to conflicting claims of beach and bench stakers; the military intervened and, yielding to the importunities of certain factions, put hundreds of beach workers under arrest; and officials sent to Nome to establish civil order added instead to the commotion and confusion by conspiring to loot the camp's golden prospects—a scheme which may sound like fiction, to-day, but it took six months, then, to make a trip to Washington and return, and a lot of mischief can happen in six months. But one man slipped through the "legal" cordon and made his way back to the States, and by his energy and courage forced an investigation. In passing down a decision, whereby many Federal officials incriminated in these doings were sent to prison, a Judge of the Circuit Court of Appeals in San Francisco characterized the acts of these "spoilers" as "one of the most villainous and outrageous conspiracies in the history of jurisprudence."

"The Spoilers" gives an unforgetable picture of the early days of Nome, and I recommend it to any who have not already enjoyed those graphic pages of Nome's beginnings. Many of my Nome friends are the real people whose adventures and early lives Rex Beach, who knew them well, put into this amazing tale of those high-wide-and-handsome (as well as crooked-dealing) days; and we ourselves once made a trip north from Nome with Sliscovitch, that stocky Slav who was the roadhouse keeper of Rex Beach's story, "The Thaw at Slisco's."

That was a curious journey, full of many queeriosities, not the least of which was our pup-mobile transportation! Back in the early days a narrow-gauge railroad was built out through the tundras to tap mining fields in the Kougarok district; but it had water competition and did not carry much freight, fuel was high and scarce, and by 1911 the taxes on it were greater than the gross earnings, so it ceased to operate. But the tracks and little bridges were still there and remain, and tracks are better going than tundra. So, when miners operating in that section beyond Nome wish to travel, they hitch their dog teams to a little flange-wheeled toy car not much bigger than a boy's express wagon, hop on board, shout " Mush " to the huskies, and are off. It's splendid going and one bowls along at a fine rate— unless the dogs spy a rabbit in the brush and take off after it, suddenly spilling you! Thick patches of blue forget-me-nots, Alaska's suggestive Territorial flower, make dots upon the richly-colored tundra as we pass, and salmonberry scrub, fireweed of magenta, and purple iris, all blob the hillside.

The dogs get very wise on the pup-mobile trail. As we were rolling along and had just reached the top of a long easy grade, I was amazed when the dogs came to a sudden stop, whirled about, and began climbing into the little open car—right up into our laps, almost. One big husky settled himself comfortably by crawling between my legs, pushing me aside to suit himself and resting his nose upon my heavy boot; and then with a grunt he fell instantly to sleep. Others sat up and looked about, with wide grins and dripping red tongues, as if to say: " Well, boys, here we are. What are we waiting for? "

Sliscovitch laughed aloud at my startled face, got out and gave the car a little push, then jumped back on again as we rolled off with gathering swiftness down the curly, hair-pin, tundra-heaved, flimsy tracks, bounding and bouncing. He yelled: "The dogs know this is where they coast! It's a long grade!" He *had* to yell, for two or three of the team began to yelp and howl, with exquisite pleasure at the ride, apparently, and kept it up the whole way down; while we grabbed leather and held on for dear life, as we tobogganed around curves and shot out over narrow teetering bridges built over gulches. It was a wild ride, if ever there was one. As the car slowed gradually, rocked, and finally came to a standstill at the bottom, the dogs without a word of command untangled themselves from our feet, straightened into their harness after a snap or snarl or two of adjustment, lined up in the tugs, got into the collar, and we were off again. We had twenty-five miles of this dog-auto ride, each way, and I think it was the most exotic, unreal travel I ever indulged in. I felt like a comic-strip performer!

When we came to Slisco's creek he unhooked the dogs, tied up their dangling traces, tipped the car off the track, and we started off across country for his claim—the dogs following, after he had put little pack-sacks of provisions on the backs of some of the smallest.

"Why do the littlest dogs get the packs?" I asked. "Can't the big ones carry them better?" He grinned and said, "Wait. You'll see."

Soon we came to a very swift stream which poured down from a hill. This we must cross, and I was just preparing to wade in when I was picked up by the middle, thrown on Slisco's shoulder like a sack of flour, and off we started. He handled the hundred and seventy-five pounds of me as though I were a baby. As he set me down on the opposite bank, I protested.

"You shouldn't have done that. I'm tall, I have high boots, I can wade. It's kind of you, but please let me cross the next, myself."

He grinned again, a row of clean white teeth like a hound's, and pointed a long finger at the stream. The dogs were coming through, and while the little ones with packs were making it quite easily, the bigger dogs were struggling to keep foothold and were being pushed downstream so fast they could hardly make it through. "Look!" he said. "You ask why little dogs take packs. You see now? Little dogs *need* packs to hold their feet down in the fast water. I am a little dog. You are my pack. You make a good weight on this little doggie's back and hold his feet down so the water does not push him."

It was so funny, looking at that burly frame, that we all three burst into delighted laughter, and, in spite of protests, I continued to be "packed" until we reached the little cabin at the gulch top.

Nome is a comfortable and hospitable town of many frame houses, law-abiding and cosy after its rough, tent-city, hard youth of graft and vice and robbery. Electric lights, a theatre, a good water supply from Moonlight Springs, help make for good living here the year round; and any one who eats at Mrs. Neibling's place wants to return. Nome friends who were great friends of Amundsen (as well as Stefansson) wrote an amusing account of the return of the *Norge's* crew to Nome, after the great trans-polar flight. It seems that on the voyage from Spitzbergen to Alaska, Amundsen kept telling Ellsworth about the wonderful Spanish omelets to be had in Nome, but Ellsworth said he'd never seen an omelet that compared with good old ham and eggs!

When they finally arrived in Nome, after the forced landing at Teller, they found Mrs. Neibling's café closed for the winter; but after much dickering on Amundsen's part, Mrs. Neibling was persuaded to reopen it. The four friends appeared for breakfast, Amundsen, Wisting, and Omdahl ordering Spanish omelet, while Ellsworth stuck to his favorite ham and eggs—until Amundsen placed an omelet directly under his nose and the flavor so fascinated him that " ever after he has ordered two Spanish omelets each day. He also falls heavily for reindeer steaks! "

On one trip north from Nome we touched the Arctic ice pack, a sight most memorable. It moves several miles an hour, with tide and wind, and is an awful force to find bearing down on one—a moving field of ice, miles wide, crashing and crunching against the loose floes as wind and current push it irresistibly down out of The North—crumbling in towering cracks as pressure ridges form and break or rear in sixty-foot walls above the waterline, to make our schooner seem the fragile toy-like plaything of a child. The off-shore lane of " thaw water " (formed by the warmer land streams and the shallow beach) seems precariously narrow between the margin and the ice, and may close any moment in those late summer days, even for our little boat of less than four-foot draft and centerboard. The barrier-ice is riding down to crush through past the tiny Diomedes and close the Straits and Nome and Bering Sea once more to all passage except by fairways of the air. The loose float ice shifts and moves, but any moment may congeal and hold. The great pack has all the force of a glacier, but instead of moving two or three feet a day, it is moving two or three miles an hour. Look at a piece of ice floating in a goblet and you will get a notion of how great that ice mass is below the sea, if sixty feet of it project above! It carries frightful weight of ballast in the hold. The ice blink from the great polar fields reflects against the low sky, and it's time to be starting home again, to the safety of the Great River and our Inner Lands.

But here at Cape Prince of Wales is the westernmost thrust of America (nearly four hundred miles further west than Honolulu), and from its great headland one may climb and look with a strong glass over into Asia, just across. These Straits are almost never wholly free from ice, and when in spring and fall the ice pack pushes through this narrow hole in the continental wall, the din of its crash can be heard for miles.

And yet, from earliest times, the Eskimo inhabitants of the Diomedes have been the middle men between Asia and America. Across these stepping stones of humped-up granite, piloting their tiny boats, perhaps came long ago the very first human beings ever to set foot on American soil. Who knows?

Nome answers—Nome by this Asia-facing sea, warden of the northern marches. Nome looks across to this inscrutable Asia, and the very name of Nome is answer to the query, "Whence came the first American?"

"Ka-no-me," said the Eskimos, when white men asked what place this was: "I do not know."

And so the place was called: Ka-no-me, Nome, "I do not know."

XVI

Muk-pi and Her People

SIR HUBERT WILKINS, who with our own truly heroic "Fairbanks boy," Ben Eielson, made that great flight over uncharted polar seas, once said to a group who are his friends here: "Most of you have been to college and derived some idea of polar conditions. I, too, studied these conditions in school, but in late years I have found that most of the facts about them which I learned in school were wrong, not because the teachers intentionally told us anything that was wrong, but because *they* had been misinformed."

Now I am inclined to believe that most of us approach the Far Northland as did Sir Hubert, with a great many pieces of misconception and misinformation in our mental luggage. I know that I did. For one thing, I was taught that "Alaska is the land of the Eskimo," only to find out when I got here that only one quarter of Alaska is Eskimo inhabited, and that only one quarter of its people are Eskimos, another quarter being Indians, and fully one half of Alaska's population being white colonists, even as I myself.

But Nome lies in the center of that quarter of Alaska which really is Eskimo Land, and I was fortunate in having a very dear Eskimo friend, even before I first visited Nome, ready and eager to show her people to me. This little woman, scarcely more than a girl in years, had been for five seasons on one of the famous exploring expeditions into the still further North, and, although born and brought up near Nome, was considered by her own people to be most widely travelled, sophisticated, and learned in the curious ways of the curious white man. Muk-pi, you see, had had " advantages! "

To me, Muk-pi was like a bit of old China. Though a full-blooded Eskimo, she might well have posed as an oriental girl any place in the States. She looked and was a Madame Butterfly, a child-woman of really singular charm. Muk-pi was dainty—even fragile in appearance—and yet I knew that she had mushed the longest darkest Arctic trails practically alone, and that her firm little body was tempered as a strong steel spring. To any one who had been taught to think, as I had, that Eskimos are " a filthy and benighted people, living on the fringes of desolation," this very dear friendship which I came to share with Muk-pi was a revelation. She had the finest sense of courtesy, a wisdom that was deep and old and penetrating—the wisdom of a life lived close to great Earth Mother, who had been her teacher. With all her childlike sweetness, she held the philosophic wisdom of the Orient in those dark Mongol eyes, and blended with it was the practicality of all genuine North-dwelling people. When with her I was but a humble learner, for there was nothing in the lore I had which seemed worth telling in exchange for little Muk-pi's rich good sense, the fruit of all The North had taught her cheerful, hospitable, and family-loving folk, in all their years of perfect adaptation to its rigorous ways.

And I was humbly glad, too, that Muk-pi and her brothers, Tuk-tuk and Chick-em (and her brothers' wives whom I came, too, to know) were tolerant of me. The brothers were great seal and walrus hunters and skilled ivory workers, and they, too, had been on many trips with whalers and explorers; and in the hard school of travel and experience they had learned a tolerant amusement for our peculiar, unreasonable, and ofttimes silly-seeming white-man ways. They were too cosmopolitan and humanist to believe that what is different is necessarily inferior, or to distrust the strange in us, as we so childishly are apt to do in them. This Eskimo family which I came to know so well were aristocrats among their own people, unusually keen and, too, perhaps unusually kind, because I had truly been their sister's friend. I write of them—and must—in friendly prejudice, for I can write no other way of what I saw and know. All Eskimos are not, perhaps, like Muk-pi, but of her many people whom I met, she was the one I knew most intimately.

Muk-pi was a pure type of Eskimo, a girl of perhaps twenty when I first knew her, and similar to a high-bred Mongol girl in feature and copper hint of color, with the same dark oblique eyes, the same black stiffish hair, high cheek bones, patrician smallness of well-shaped hands and feet, gentle manner, subtle poise and delicate humor. I have no friend in all the world to whom the good word "lady" could be more justly given. I learned from knowing her that Eskimos are human beings, not mere quaint curiosities. When with her I was often paraphrasing, in my mind, hurt Shylock's tragic cry of a misunderstood and often a misvalued race: "Hath not an Eskimo eyes? Hath not an Eskimo hands, organs, dimensions, senses, affections, passions? Fed with the same food, hurt with the same weapons? Subject to the same diseases, healed by the same means, warmed and cooled by the same winter and summer?"

My little Muk-pi—strong, gay, full of bubbling giggles of rich fun, so happy in the warm home life of her own people—but "subject to the same diseases!" Will Shakespeare truly put his finger there upon the root of my dear little friend's deep tragedy.

Nome may seem to you an outpost of civilization, but to the Eskimo it is a great city; and many of them, such as my Muk-pi's family, live in its suburbs on the Sandspit. These "city Eskimos" seem very urban to their country cousins who come to see them each summer: King Islanders, Eskimos from St. Lawrence Island and the Diomedes, families from Bering Straits and the Shismaref and Kotzebue country, with kindred Chuck-chee Siberian natives as well, all come in their skin-boats to Nome to trade, to visit, to sell their furs and lovely fossil ivory, to make merry in their own care-free, happy, summer-holiday fashion. For a people who live through the long winter months so close to imminent death, whose days are so compact of hardship, who know so well the tooth of hunger and the bite of winter cold, whose near neighbor is the paleocrystic sea, whose very name for winter (Uk-shuk) is a verbal shiver—to possess such amazing humor and sweetness and amity as I witnessed those long days I spent among Muk-pi's kinsfolk, was beyond my comprehension. Kind, courteous, and unbelievably hospitable, a highly intelligent although in many ways an undeveloped race, I found them much more pleasant, quick, adaptive, eager, than many of our pure-blood Interior Alaskan Indians with whom I've come in contact.

I have travelled about a good deal upon four of

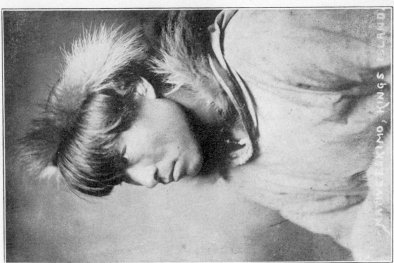

NATIVE ESKIMO, KINGS ISLAND.

Photograph by Lomen Brothers, Nome.

THIS ESKIMO FROM KING ISLAND IN BERING
SEA IS A SUPERIOR TYPE.

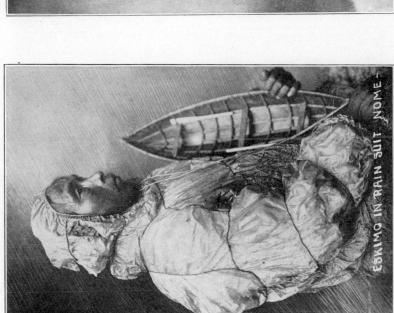

ESKIMO IN RAIN SUIT, NOME.

Photograph by Lomen Brothers, Nome.

THE ESKIMO RAINCOAT IS MADE OF LIGHT BUT
STRONG SEA-ANIMAL INTESTINES.

EAST CAPE ESKIMO ARRIVING IN NOME, ALASKA

Photograph by Lomen Brothers, Nome.

THE ESKIMO SKIN UMIAK HOLDS UNBELIEVABLE FREIGHT.

Photograph by Lomen Brothers, Nome.

WE SAW AN UMIAK UNLOAD ITS HUMAN TONNAGE ON NOME BEACH.

our major continents, and I have never seen a people
more perfectly related to the earth on which they
live, in their social organization and in their technique of comfort, than are the Eskimos. We make
a great mistake if we are sorry for the Eskimos, and
we make an even greater mistake if we try to change
their ways too much toward our ways, for they have
acquired social and domestic and economic habits
marvelously well suited to their environment. I am
speaking from my own experience among them, and
some of my very best Alaskan friends violently dis-
agree with my feeling about the Eskimos. Many
think that *all* their ways are bad and should be
mended. I feel that many of their ways are very
good, and should not be disturbed. If we can give
them of the best of our civilization without destroying what is best in theirs, then only, I believe, will
be a happy outcome for this contact of cultures.

We white colonists in Interior Alaska are not to
be pitied, for we are here because we love it here.
And neither are the Eskimos to be pitied because
they live on Bering Sea and Arctic Slope. As
Stefansson again and again reminds us, *the North is
not terrible to people who LIVE in the North*. And
these Mongoloid Eskimo people, who long ago
moved North out of the great central Asian breeding place of races to take up new land, not only live
here to-day but have occupied this country gradually,
have reshaped their hands and minds to its conditions, have chosen it, prefer it. In every contest
(and there have been many in the past) between the
Eskimos and the Indians living south of them, the
Eskimos have been both the aggressors and the
victors. If they had wished to move south, if they
had preferred the sheltered inner valleys, there was

nothing to prevent their going. The Indians are and have been much more afraid of the Eskimos than the Eskimos have been of the Indians. The very word "Eskimo" is proof of this: "Those who eat raw flesh," a name given to the Innuit by southern Indian tribes who feared their fighting qualities. Do not for a moment think that Muk-pi and her people live on the northern shore through anything but choice and preference, or that they have been crowded out from below by a more powerful folk into an undesirable or unwanted place which they now inhabit. Stefansson, who's very blunt and practical about such matters, shows up the silliness of this notion that north-dwelling peoples only live north because they have to, when he says: "Do the British inhabit England because crowded by the French? Are the inhabitants of the northern U. S. A. inferior and crowded north by the southerners?" It's a thought worth digesting!

I have never been able to decide in my own mind whether Muk-pi and her people are so happy in their simple primitive ways of life because they are philosophers at heart, or whether, being philosophers, they have evolved such perfect tools to meet their chosen environment. They are like supercheerful Yankees in some things, for they are great contrivers. They love tinkering and fixing, they are great natural mechanics, they like to do "neat jobs," they are "faculized" (as Nantucketers call it), and all for much the same reason as the typical old-time Yankee is all these things: because they have few resources at their command, and therefore make the most of those they have. And though, like the true Yankee—Nantucket and New Bedford and Salem men of old—they respect the northern sea, they do

not fear it, but use it and make an honest living from
its waters, reaping the harvest of the moving
meadows of the untilled sea with skill and patience.

But Chick-em is an ivory hunter, too. Over that
ancient bridge to Asia, in prehistoric days, came
hairy mammoth with great curving tusks, and they
ranged everywhere over what is to-day Alaska, the
most abundant animal in Pleistocene times. The
bison followed, and then horse and caribou in lesser
numbers, so the archaic searchers say, and other
mammals of that age and time. But the great
Elephas primogenius, the woolly or northern mammoth, left his remains all over this then forested
north country, where large fossil trees of that day
still remain but where now are barren tundras with
frozen subsoil. Osborn says one can imagine "moose
and reindeer in these forests, horses and bison grazing on the uplands, elephants and rare mastodon
browsing on forest borders," in days when forests
stretched clear up to the shores of the Arctic and
the elevated western shelf now submerged was "an
enormous level plain covering most of the present
area of Bering Sea; and the diminished body of
water, in connection with the prevalence of northwest trade winds, would have given to this region a
very dry climate." Mammoth have been found here
recently, in places such as Elephant Point, where a
sealing of soft mud and a later complete freezing
have perfectly preserved both skeleton and hair from
any bacterial decay; and dogs and men millennia
later—even the last Tsar of the Russias, at a great
imperial banquet—have actually eaten the strange
flesh of prehistoric beasts, dug up in Siberia.

Mastodon ranged into Alaska in the interglacial
stages, when the climate was much milder than now,

and this southern species could therefore spread; and rare and beautiful, dark-colored, mastodon ivory, as well as the more common mammoth tusks, are hunter's trove for Chick-em and his ivory-worker brother. Fossil ivory has been long prized for its beauty of color and texture, both by the Chinese and the Russians. We have a record that in 1771 Liakhoff obtained exclusive rights from the Empress Catherine " to dig for fossil ivory in The North," and ivory of mammoth, mastodon and walrus has been to these Eskimo people possessing few metals a substance useful, necessary, and long sought. The walrus hunts yield tough strong hides of leather for all heavy purposes, as boats, but the tusks serve both as wood and metal to this resourceful, Yankee-contriving people of my Muk-pi.

Old ivory has for ages been precious for its lovely soft color; and tourists in Alaska to-day pay high prices for long strings of exquisite old ivory beads. But I warn you, before buying, to consult one who knows, just as you would in buying rare furs or precious stones. The soft velvety colors of truly prehistoric mastodon are so prized that sharpsters have discovered artificial means of coloring new walrus ivory (by a short boiling in seal oil or, so I'm told, even in coffee!) so that it takes on a temporary coloring similar in appearance to that acquired by centuries of genuine soil burial, though a skilled eye can quickly tell the difference.

The whale is another Arctic Sea mammal, but with the fast-increasing technique in their slaughter, a time may soon come when Arctic and Antarctic whales will be practically extinct. To-day this unctuous sea-harvest is not only being reaped with aid of the explosive harpoon invented by the Norwegian

Svend Foyn (a cannon-like gun mounted on a pivot
at the bow of a small staunch iron steamer), but this
gigantic game is being pursued into its last far polar
retreat by sea-plane-equipped whaling boats, with
Pilots Riisar-Larsen and Leutgowe Hohn, seasoned
polar flyers of the lost Roald Amundsen—experiments off Alaska having shown that whale gam can
be spotted from the air, resulting in a tremendous
kill.

Perhaps you wonder of what use are whales, these
days of collarless and corsetless women who wish no
whalebone stiffening, and these electric-lighted days
needing no whale-oil lamp. I'll tell you a secret. I
know a man who owns and operates a fleet of whaling vessels in Alaskan waters to-day, a fleet which
rides up to the North each March following the
whales arriving. In May the opening of the ice
barrier permits them to resume their northland
journey. Again in the fall they return.

I asked this friend: " Please tell me what the
whales are used for, now that whalebone and sper-
micetti both have so many substitutes and so few
uses. I'm interested, for I have Nantucket kinsmen,
you know. Where do you sell your product? "

He answered in two words, " It Floats! "

For a moment I was puzzled—and then I saw the
point! Since then I've learned that whale oil sells
in the United States for fifty cents a gallon, and is
used to-day mainly in the making of fine soaps.
Soap was old Father Duncan's first missionary Alaskan product, at Metlakatla; and soap is evidently
to be the end product of that once great whaling
industry which has continued for a thousand years—
for there were Norwegian whalers at least that long
ago, as we know from King Alfred's account of

Ohthere's voyage to the White Sea. But Muk-pi's people will not believe the day of whales is passing, and during the whaling season the Eskimos still make their camps out on the ice floes bordering the Arctic Ocean and keep a constant lookout for whales. Then, as soon as ever a leviathan is sighted, a boat puts out in swift pursuit of prey which for so long has meant Goliath source of food and light to the children of the North.

The igloo, the parka, the mukluk, the kyak, the umiak, and a score of other typical Eskimo inventions are the " cutest tricks " imaginable for the purpose to which they are designed and perfectly adapted. White men living in the far North never do more than adopt and adapt the Eskimos' own tools and ways for meeting the exigencies of the North. The failures among northern explorers are those who have refused to listen to their Eskimo friends; the outstanding successes in Arctic exploration and adaptation are those men who have listened wisely.

Take the umiak or long skin-boat, of which I have seen hundreds at Nome and north of Nome—the Eskimo freight boat or "woman boat" thirty feet long, with a frame made of driftwood lashed with leather, covered with skins, carefully stretched and double stitched to water tightness by the expert and incomparable Eskimo workers. It will hold thirty people or a ton of bulky freight, can be carried by any two stout men on portage, can bump into rough ice without smashing (as a whale boat of similar size, but four times as heavy, would surely do), or it can be put on a sled and drawn overland by five or six husky dogs. If it "busts" (though usually even a stiff crack against sharp ice or rock will only make it bounce back like a rubber ball) a new rib can be quickly set, or a patch can be laid on with a heavy bone needle and sinew thread. And what more do you want, for emergency service?

I remember well seeing an umiak unload at the Sandspit near Nome, and being reminded of a conjurer's hat. After at least three full families of Eskimos had piled out (and two by two like Noah's ark, for women and children were carried ashore through the surf, like sacks) I thought it surely must be empty. But then, from somewhere, there scrambled out at least twenty Eskimo dogs, and *then* came the freight of household goods—skins and furs and cooking utensils and gifts for all the Nome aunts and cousins—and fish!

"Muk-pi," I said, "please find out where they came from with all that stuff. It can't have been far, loaded so."

"I no ask, I see him," she replied, in her quiet way. "You see, man parka? You see, woman parka? He Chuck-chee man, Chuck-chee woman."

Chuck-chee! I knew *they* lived in Asia, across the Straits—East Cape—Siberia—Russia—stalwart swarthy Chuck-chees! When I hear certain skeptical, undaring, stay-at-home scientists say, "The earliest Americans could not have likely come from Asia by that perilous northern route, but much more likely by the southern islands," I merely unpolitely sniff! Haven't I *seen* them come, with my own eyes, just yesterday?

When Muk-pi's people wish, they improvise a sail of skin and rig it in the umiak; or when they travel coastwise by a sandy beach, they hitch their dogs and let them out for exercise by rigging up a tow line to the boat, like a canal team's harness, and bowl along in swift style, the happy dogs (as I have seen them at Port Clarence) yelping and scurrying along the shore in joy at stretching of their legs, the happy crew singing and laughing and making summer holiday outing.

The kyak is the Eskimo sport-model roadster, or " personal car," as the umiak is their family car. It is a tricky light canoe of hides, decked over, and into it a man just fits, through a hole in the top. The Eskimo walrus and seal hunter can do unbelievable stunts in this little boat, even to turning completely over in the water and coming right side up again— smiling and all dry below decks.

Mukluks are Eskimo boots, made with durable oogruk or bearded-seal-hide soles and water-shedding reindeer legs for tops, all brightly decorated with intricately matched brown-gray and white checkerboard-pattern collars at the top and bright red strips of root-dyed walrus stitched above the black turned-up sole. Muk-pi made me a pair and gave me several others of various types and kinds; for the design of the mukluk has social significance, and no perfect Eskimo lady would be seen wearing a *striped* mukluk, just as no Seward Peninsula Eskimo man would be caught wearing a scalloped or apron-shaped parka, with its two wide dips, fore and aft. Men's parkas here must have a straight edge. These are very serious matters, and to offend such ancient customs would brand you as ignorant, or revolutionary and radical.—Watching Muk-pi and her sisters-in-law, O-ti-ouk and Maw-graw-gee, at work upon my lovely mukluks, I realized what matchless needle-workers these Eskimo women are, their stitching so perfect, their seams absolutely waterproof without any greasing. Muk-pi, when the

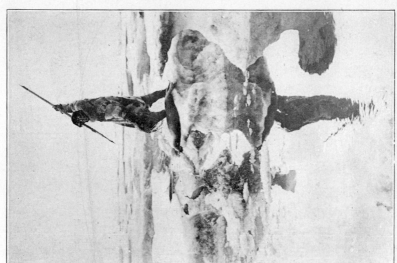

KINGS ISLAND NATIVE

Photograph by Lomen Brothers, Nome.

MUK-PI'S BROTHERS WERE OF THE STURDY HUNTER ESKIMO STOCK.

Photograph by Lomen Brothers, Nome.

THE ESKIMO SEAL HUNTER REAPS HIS HARVEST FROM THE SEA.

THE DECKED KYAK IN WHICH THE ESKIMO HUNTER CAN DO WON-
DROUS WATER TRICKS

Photograph by Lomen Brothers, Nome.

SIBERIAN ESKIMOS AT THEIR SHORE SUMMER-COTTAGE MADE OF SKINS.

mukluks were finished, blew them up like a balloon
and tested them for air leaks like a tire, against her
face as well as over a flame. There was no flicker,
for the job was featly done. I once heard Stefansson
say, "There are few man-made articles more nearly
perfect as to comfort and durability than the foot-
gear of the Eskimo." Just like a man, for the mukluks are woman made! Hay, dried from sweet-
smelling seashore grass, is crushed into a little bed
or mat and wadded all along the sole, you wear a
double pair of woolen socks, and then you can mush
thirty or forty miles a day in them—if you are a *real*
musher—and never tire or get a blister.

The Eskimo parka is the perfect winter garment,
and is an especial boon to aviators. It is a one-piece
knee-length coat of fur (reindeer, "sik-sik-puk," or
the soft under fur of muskrat) slipping on over the
head like a sweater, with no fastening at all, and no
opening but the face hole of the attached hood,
which may either be worn over the head or thrown
back. This hood is faced with wolverine, for the
Eskimo has found that, due to some peculiarity of
the hair shape or oil distribution, wolverine is the
only fur that does not hold frost from the breath;
and to have a frosty fur next the face would not be
pleasant in extreme temperatures. The parka hood
has also a wide fringe or ruff of wolf fur, coarse and
long. In windy weather this projecting ruff is
whipped across the face constantly, and sets up a
stimulating circulation, keeping one's face from
frosting. Being of one piece and fitting snugly
about the head and shoulders, no cold enters and no
warm body air is lost, but all is conserved inside.
So warm is a well-made parka that, when exercis-
ing, it can only be worn in comfort during extreme

temperatures.   Parka is but one of many non-patented gifts of the little brown Eskimo to all who live and work here in the North.

I never saw a people more devoted to their families than are Muk-pi's people. Though many children are not the rule, the parents are slavishly fond of those they have; and while the round chubby youngsters, who always smile, never seemed to me to be punished, they are put through an early rigid training to fit them for their future existence as good clansmen and family providers—both boys and girls. Because their diet is of necessity so nearly all a meat diet, babies are often nursed by their mothers until they are four or five years old, or until their teeth are strong enough to chew meat.   Teeth are terribly important to the Eskimo.   Fuel is scarce, and half-raw meat must be eaten (and is preferred—so they're in no fear of scurvy!) ; and Tuk-tuk the ivory worker told me that a man of his people must be very careful when choosing a wife, to pick one with good teeth!   For mukluk soles must be chewed into shape, and if the wife and mother has poor teeth, then the family cannot have proper mukluks, and a leaky mukluk may well mean a frozen foot, a gangrened limb, and death.

Muk-pi loved song, her people all love song, and use music as well as enjoy it.   It is a fruit of life with them, a flowering of experience.   They sing of what they know, of hunt and chase, of beasts and fish, of tribal lore and custom.   They sing when sad, and then (as Muk-pi told me when I found her first, near starved, deserted, in a stranger's land) "make song, no hon-gree, no catch him big pain—here!" They sing when glad, too, and make a happy music to all sport and family gathering.   And they even mix music with jury duty! For some groups of more eastern Eskimo have a quaint, old, and now passing custom, the nith song, by which controversies used to be settled, before we brought our white man's courts to Nordland. They knew no lawsuits in the old days, but parties to a dispute came before a gathering of all the people in the community house and here sang *at* each other, before the council of their peers. They " sang their man down " until the laughter of his own people proclaimed one man the victor. White men discouraged this charming custom. They didn't think it " serious enough " and it " wasn't the civilized way to do things." Had they forgotten troubadour and minnesinger, " The Hall of Song," " Tannhaüser und der Sangerkrieg auf Wartburg? "

But music still envelops all the life of Muk-pi's people. They live by and they live to music. Is that why they are such a happy people, because they live with laughter and with song? Or have they that God-given gift because they so deliberately choose to live upon what seems to us least lovely of these continental shores, and make themselves so usefully content there?

Half of each day, when I was visiting Nome, I always spent with Muk-pi and half with my white friends. My white friends gave me of their best, in royal hospitalities; but Muk-pi and her people gave me more. She gave me of her very self; and from my little Eskimo Butterfly I learned, upon the wind-blown barren Sandspit, that courtesy and courage are close kin and may be found under a wolfskin parka hood as well as under the white helmet of magnanimous Navarre.

XVII

The Deer That Went to School

TO-DAY, because one can fly to Nome so easily
from Fairbanks in a few hours, few use the
old-time Yukon waterway of long ago, taking
monotonous weeks in transit. There are no fine,
modern, tourist-equipped vessels on the Lower Yukon,
as on the upper river; and in keeping with Alaska's
paradoxical ways, as the Great River grows wider
and wider in its perpetual rolling to the sea, the
boats you take to travel on it get smaller and smaller
as you near the deltic mouth and the once busy port
of St. Michael.

Here, where the now old weary river flows
through wide mouths its " somewhere safe to sea," is
to be found a very different land from the tremendous majesty of the Upper Yukon. There is very
little timber on the coastal areas and none at all over
the major portion of Seward Peninsula; indeed, the
old Russian round tower at St. Michael is built of
timber brought from Asia, men say who have ex-
amined it closely, though it is well known that
material for the Russian Fur Company building was
brought from Sitka in 1833. There is practically no
timber over the belt immediately back of the coast,
and only very scattering stands across the neighbor-
ing inland areas back as far as the Endicott and
Alaska Ranges. The coast lands are hummocky
moist ground called tundra or niggerheads—dense,

matted and profuse growths, but unsuitable for agriculture. On small areas of sandy soil along the
beach the grasses are three to four feet high, and in
many places the typical tundra growth of mixed
sedges, grasses and lichens form a sponge mat ten to
twelve inches deep, making any long mush across
them a leg-weary toil. Thickets of scrub willow
along the stream course and scattered stands of alder
or birch along the larger river valleys or upper roll
of slopes, mix with a growth of ground birch, ground
willow, huckleberry, salmonberry, cranberry, crow-
berry and " Alaska tea." Those white spots flying
overhead are Arctic swans seeking a north place for
the summer season, where the sun never sets. Those
darker wedges are migrating ducks and geese. Except for their far lonely cries the land lies silent,
waiting for some far-seeing mortal to sense the quick
life dormant in these sedgy tundras and turn this
corner of the Great Country to usefulness and purpose. Nor do we have to wait long for an answer—
it has already come. The magic of an idea, born
out of human compassion, is even now transmuting
tundra into meat.

There is one animal and one alone, known to man
since man himself has first been known, that thrives
on land like this—an animal long domesticated, a
native to the North, " the most widely distributed
mammal in the world," whose range has been a territory far exceeding in size all of Europe. The reindeer is the answer to that question of how the peculiar and abundant vegetation of this quarter of
the High North can be converted into food for
men, instead of food for wolves and foxes; for reindeer and reindeer alone of all domesticated animals
can best convert into the most delicious meat the bil-

lions of tons of edible vegetation which yearly in the past have gone to waste on the swelling slopes of these northern prairies. " Reindeer moss "—that gray, gelatinous, slightly pungent and acrid lichen, shaped like branching coral and the most common form of vegetation in this section of the North— cannot be eaten raw by man, but it can be eaten in the most palatable wise imaginable, after it has been built solidly into reindeer meat. And Alaska has in the Lower Yukon-Bering Sea section grazing land sufficient to support three to four *million* reindeer. Already there are nearly a million reindeer being herded by Eskimos and whites in this section, and already the net profits from this youngest of Alaska's great industries have reached a sum that more than pays back Uncle Sam's sometimes begrudged pur- chase price for the whole Territory. If the reindeer industry increases in the same ratio as it has been doing, in much less than twenty years the *annual surplus* of the reindeer crop will be yielding a meat production each year worth more than the annual precious-metal yield of the Territory, and second only to the great Alaska fisheries as a permanent income-producing activity.

Wherever wild caribou thrive, why should not the reindeer, man protected, thrive even more lustily? For reindeer are merely caribou that have for long ages gone to school with man and have been greatly changed in disposition and tractability by these cen- turies of domestication—but no more changed in essential physique than wild horses or wild cattle have been changed. And the climate and vegetation of large sections of Alaska are closely similar to those of regions occupied by long-skilled reindeer breeders in the Old World.

Who thought of this, and when? Dr. Sheldon Jackson, U. S. General Agent of Education in Alaska, in 1890 had been granted transportation on the Revenue Cutter *Bear* on its annual cruise into Bering Sea and the Arctic Ocean, in order that he might gain basic information about the possibility of establishing schools among the Eskimos. The *Bear* visited all the important native villages on both the Alaskan and Siberian shores. The Alaska Eskimos were leading a precarious, hunters', hand-to-mouth existence due, as he soon found, to the very patent fact that the native food supply of sea game was fast diminishing, and to the fact that wild caribou no longer ranged this region but were drifting farther inland through central Alaska and the Yukon territory. With the coming of white men and white men's traps and guns, the fur-bearing animals were growing more and more scarce. Yearly, fleets of steam whalers were driving the bowhead farther and farther into the Arctic, and gasoline schooners were decimating the herds of walrus and seal which the Eskimos through centuries of adaptation had learned to depend on for their food and clothing, sewing materials, boats and tools. Left alone, all would have been well, but we had not left them alone; we whites were yearly ravishing their larder and leaving only fast-emptying food shelves for Muk-pi's people. Not only were the Alaska Eskimos in danger of losing their food supply but (and this is equally important in any Arctic climate) their clothing as well. The Alaskan Eskimo was typically a sea hunter—seals, whalebone and ivory tusks had long been his articles of barter with Siberian cousins across the Straits, and in return he brought back reindeer skins from their herds. Dr.

Jackson saw that unless something was done, and done soon, Uncle Sam might have to feed the whole Eskimo population of Alaska—or let them starve to death. This was unthinkable. And yet, as hunting resources were the Eskimo's entire dependence for his claim on life, and hunting resources were rapidly diminishing, the natural consequence would be starvation.

But—across Bering Straits in Siberia and only a few miles distant from Alaska, with climate and country precisely similar, Sheldon Jackson found thousands of Chuck-chees waxing fat on countless herds of reindeer. Why then hadn't the Alaskan Eskimos taken up reindeer herding? The answer to that question runs very far back into pre-history and paleo-asiatic folk ways, but the sum of it is this: While the domestication of reindeer is undoubtedly far older in Asia than in the Europe of northern Norway, Sweden, Finland and Russia, and the reindeer culture of the paleo-asiatic Siberian tribes is very ancient, still reindeer-nomadism as a way of life was taken up by these Asiatic peoples *after* the migration of Alaskan Eskimos to this continent. When they came, reindeer were being hunted and not yet tamed in the old home in Asia, and so the Eskimo continued as a hunter and had never learned to be a herder. Among our own early ancestors reindeer *hunting* was an important occupation, as we know from wonderfully lifelike drawings of pre-historic reindeer made in such caves as those of Kesserloch in Switzerland. Indeed the very dawn of human history has become known as the Reindeer Age, because they flourished so then, and must have been the most numerous large animal then in Europe. But these early European hunters had not yet learned

reindeer nomadism, although cave-dwelling men
have left for us those many skilful etchings of their
favorite *game* creature, done upon cave walls with
a sharp-point flint.

That is the reason why Muk-pi's people did not
bring reindeer herds with them when they came, so
long ago; nor did they need domestic reindeer while
the wild caribou herds were plentiful on Bering
coast, or while they could pursue their ancient hunter
way unhampered on the sea, with undiminished
success. And after the sea food-supply began to go,
Siberian cousins then would neither sell nor lend
their own *live* reindeer, but only trade their hides.
Tradition and a taboo had grown up, absolutely forbidding the sale of reindeer for breeding—a tradition very similar in quality to that of Arabs regarding their pure-bred mares. Nor did the Alaskan
Eskimos know anything at all about herding, and it
is not at all likely that, unaided, they would ever
have considered it, nor, even if they had, would they
have been successful at it. Successful herding is a
trade long to learn, and both the cultural form of
reindeer nomadism and the handy ski for snow-tool
are among those North Asiatic cultural elements
which evolved too late to reach America, and stopped
with the Chuck-chee before reaching the narrow
Straits. The coast Chuck-chee are not herders but
fishermen, and while the inland Chuck-chee breed
large herds of reindeer (often as many as a thousand
to a herd) and live on reindeer flesh and milk and
are generally prosperous, the fishing Chuck-chee of
the Siberian coast villages with whom the Alaskan
Eskimo come most in contact, are very poor, and beg
hides from their richer cousins to make their tents
and clothes.

Although there were approximately three million reindeer among the northern peoples of Asia, Siberian Chuck-chee were most unwilling to part with any live deer—partly on account of superstition, and partly for fear of losing trade. They not only did a good business in skins with Alaskan Eskimos, but among themselves the size of herd was a symbol of wealth, culture, position, and family pride. What houses and lands, motors and jewels are to us, even such are flocks and herds to the pastoral liver. To sell, they felt, would be like selling birthright for a mess of pottage. And the Chuck-chee were a fierce and independent race, who had resisted all attempts of Russia to conquer them.

Both Sheldon Jackson and Captain Healy of the *Bear* were greatly impressed with the thought that it would be a wise national policy to introduce domestic reindeer from Siberia into Alaska, as a source of supply for food and clothing to Alaskan Eskimos. So obsessed was Dr. Jackson with the dual idea of the Eskimos' plight and the feasibility of transplanting reindeer culture from Asia that, after two attempts to get money from Congress had failed, an appeal was made to the people directly through the press of eastern cities, and $2,136 was contributed by benevolent individuals. Sixteen deer were purchased with this in 1891 and a hundred and seventy-one in 1892. In 1893 Congress now realized the importance of the movement and made the first appropriation of $6,000 for the work of continuing the reindeer industry in Alaska. During nine seasons the good old *Bear* carried the agents of the Bureau of Education back and forth between Siberia and Alaska and transported Siberian reindeer to Alaska —1,280 animals in all being imported. From this

small beginning has grown the present Alaskan herd
of nearly 1,000,000 animals.

All this was not done without adventure, work and
risk in the early stages, as well as the skepticism and
cruel wit which always attach to a new venture.   In
1901 Lieutenant E. P. Bertholf, U. S. Coast Guard,
was sent to Russia, provided with proper credentials
by the State Department, to arrange through imperial official channels for the purchase of reindeer;
for Dr. Jackson and Captain Healy had both of them
learned the deep-rooted feeling of the Chuck-chee
against the sale of their animals.   Armed with the
necessary permits by governmental authority at St.
Petersburg and Moscow, he travelled across Siberia
by rail and sledge to Ola, on the Okhotsk Sea, where
about four hundred reindeer of a superior breed
were bought with trade goods from the Tungus, a
northern wide-spread Asiatic people of Mongol-
Tartar family.   These animals were taken to Vladi-
vostok where a small steamer was chartered and this
shipment of deer transported, with 2,500 bags of
reindeer moss for food during the voyage, to Teller,
on Port Clarence, which was Alaska's first reindeer
station.

At first, Siberian natives were hired to come over
with the herds and teach the Eskimos the care of
deer, with herding, breaking deer to sled, lasso
throwing, corralling, and all the other tricks of
herdsman art.   But they proved poor teachers—in
fact, unwilling instructors and quite greedy of im-
parting very much of what they knew.   They seemed
jealous of their craft and wished not so much to
teach as to conserve their present good jobs—which
was but human nature, perhaps!   Accordingly, in
1898 Uncle Sam invited a few intelligent and ef-

ficient Lapps (a people who had reduced reindeer raising to a science in the north of Europe) to come over at his expense, bring with them some of their own sled deer, and help him train his Eskimos to be good herdsmen. We know that the Lapps have been breeding reindeer in Norway through long centuries, for Ohthere the Norwegian (who said that he " dwelt furthest north of all the Northmen," made the first voyage around North Cape, and discovered the White Sea) in the ninth century speaks of a herd of six hundred head and told our own Saxon King Alfred all about reindeer herding, in a manuscript still preserved in the British Museum.

Under this white-man expert tutelage the Eskimos, like the Mongoloid quick-wits they are, proved excellent imitators and soon became proficient. An ingenious system of four years' apprenticeship was inaugurated, an apprentice receiving six, eight and ten breeding deer at the close of his first, second and third years, respectively, and ten more at the close of his course of training. He then becomes a herder on his own, in entire charge of his own herd, and hires apprentices to serve under him on the same terms, thus creating an endless chain of trained producers. This is the excellently devised system which in one generation has elevated a large portion of the Eskimo population from a hunting to a herding culture, based no longer on a gamble with the winter sea but on the sure increase of herds which now run from less than 400 up to 12,000 head—great herds of meat creators on a thousand tundras, located, visited, and inspected to-day by men in airplanes, conquering space.

Our own good friend Jafet Lindeberg, " The Father of Nome," came to Alaska in 1898 as one of these foremen brought by Uncle Sam from Norway with the reindeer. But Lindeberg did not have to wait for herds to make *his* fortune, for he was, you will remember, the lucky discoverer of Nome's gold fields. It was Jafet Lindeberg, at Unalakleet on Norton Sound, who gave me my own very first sight of a great reindeer herd. Surely no man's eventful life has been more bound up with the development of this Northwest Province. The herd we saw there Lindeberg owned jointly with the well-known Lomen family of Nome, and the Lomen Reindeer Corporation is to-day the greatest single producer of reindeer meat in Alaska. This company ships reindeer meat to the States, where it is served as a great delicacy on dining cars of most of the finest railroads, and in many of the better-class eastern hotels and most exclusive clubs. The States Restaurant in San Francisco is the largest user of reindeer meat in America, I am told. They order it by the carload and now serve almost as much of it as they do beef! Indeed, it has become so swiftly popular that I believe it's scarcely necessary to describe its taste, which lies somewhere between beef and mutton, with just the faintest suggestion of duck. Only the dressed meat of young steers is shipped out of Alaska, and this has no gamy flavor, only a little spicy tang like well-fed duck. While the best cuts for household use are round, loin, ribs and shoulder, there is practically no part of the animal inedible; and chemical and biological analyses of reindeer meat, made by the Department of Agriculture, show that reindeer, about halfway in size between beef and mutton, has good texture and very little difference in proximate composition as compared with other meats. The distinctive differences in quality are that it is high in protein, low in fat, and of relatively low moisture,—that is, high nutritive value in proportion to weight,—a valuable factor when, as from Alaska, it must be shipped long distances.

The word " reindeer " has long been associated in our minds with Santa Claus, and this association need no longer be considered a childish fancy; for the reindeer did come first to Alaska as a left-handed gift of Uncle Sam himself, and to a people whom he, in his solemn treaty with Russia three quarters of a century ago, had undertaken to protect and not abridge in their natural rights. But reindeer have proved to be so well adapted to this peculiar environment that they have developed with leaps and bounds. To-day Dasher and Dancer, Prancer and Vixen, and all the rest of Santa Claus' antlered ponies, are clattering loudly with their far-from-tiny hoofs of infant industry upon the very roof of Uncle Sam's attic.

This vast, fallow-lying land of the Lower Yukon, Kuskokwim and the Northwest Province contains millions of acres of good reindeer grazing. As a great portion of this land is not used for anything else at the present time, it would seem that the reindeer industry is the fitting business to encourage here. In the spring and summer the deer feed on grasses, willow leaves, buds, mushrooms and marine algæ; in the winter on the lichens which have been slowly growing since last season. Each animal needs for range the same acreage as do western cattle—that is, about two and a half acres per head per month. Only the white owners (who secured the nucleus of their herds from the Lapp herders, who in turn secured their herds on shares for their work) are at present shipping meat to outside markets, and about

ESKIMOS SOMETIMES CUT OFF ONE HORN OF THEIR DRIVING DEER.

A RACING REINDEER FOUR-IN-HAND IS REAL WINTER SPORT.

SINROCK MARY, QUEEN OF ESKIMO-

Photograph by Lomen Brothers, Nome.

SINROCK MARY OWNED SO MANY DEER THAT
SHE WAS CALLED A QUEEN.

Photograph by Lomen Brothers, Nome.

REINDEER ON SUMMER PASTURE HAVE DARK
COATS AND VELVET HORNS.

two-thirds of the herd are still owned by native Eskimos. Here in a region not as yet proven favorable to the pasturage of cattle and sheep, a great domestic-animal industry is being built up, reindeer furnishing food and clothing and labor and spending money to the people of one section of the far North, and an increased meat supply to all of Uncle Sam's children below stairs.

The herds double every three years, allowing for an annual kill of ten per cent., and more than 250,000 animals have already been butchered for food and clothing. The average fawn crop runs about sixty per cent., and the average life of the reindeer is about fifteen years. Approximately five thousand people of Alaska, native and white, are now engaged in this industry. The government itself owns from five to ten thousand reindeer in Alaska, several of the missions own small herds, and the big Lomen Corporation, who are the main shippers commercially, own or control about 200,000 head. Nearly 2,000,000 pounds of reindeer meat were brought into the United States in 1928. While the ultimate object of reindeer breeding will doubtless be the largest possible meat production, and the industry has grown far beyond the original conception in that a new meat supply has been tapped for *all* United States citizens, and the nation's possible grazing areas have been vastly enlarged, the original idea of new and better livelihood for Eskimos and a means of their development into useful, producing, self-supporting citizens has never been lost to sight and is even now being accomplished.

The reindeer is the best solution for the high cost of living in this section of the High North. Interior Alaska has its huge wild caribou herds, which are nothing more nor less than feral reindeer; and any hunter during the great caribou runs or migrations, when they sweep in countless tens of thousands past our villages, can kill his winter's meat. But these wild caribou range over from western Yukon Territory, from just south of the Tánana to a little west of Fairbanks and then north to the mountains. We know from long experience the usefulness of caribou, least shy of all deer and a very practical animal, furnishing food and clothing to thousands of northern Indians. This native caribou is an animal closely related to the original progenitor of the reindeer, but is to-day larger and more slenderly built, less blocky and with longer legs than the domestic reindeer which remained an exclusive cultural property of the Old World before this Alaska importation. Valuable experiments are under way, crossing reindeer with wild caribou, resulting in a larger beef animal.

But above all else, the reindeer is a civilizer. Before Sheldon Jackson conceived his wild dream, the culture of the Alaskan Eskimos was in a state of disintegration due to changing conditions. The sure way of life which their ancestors for centuries had followed and had learned so well, was being lost through circumstances which they could not control. The Eskimo is much like an uneducated European peasant, possessing a large amount of native wit and an intelligence that lies fallow but is readily tapped. Sheldon Jackson did the tapping when he brought the reindeer, for Eskimos delight in this new craft which makes them independent financially. Through this industry the Eskimos have now taken the first step up on the grade of civilization, a step our ancestors took long ago; that is, hunters are now becoming herders. We must be patient and not expect too much, too soon, for it's a slow process, and new and steady qualities need to be developed. But Muk-pi's people are quick learners, and Eskimo and reindeer have been developing in a similar environment through brooding long dark ages, and they possess the same affinity for space and mystery.

Nomadic hunters, primitive men, are to-day taking this step up into the pastoral stage—with herds to assure support for themselves, with opportunity to acquire real wealth, with vocational training adapted to community needs, with independence and responsible citizenship just ahead around the next corner. The " pasture deer " of the Old World for centuries went to school to men. Having proved good scholars, they have now become teachers— teachers and civilizers of men.

XVIII

Copper Gate and Iron Musketeers

THE Richardson Trail from inland Fairbanks to the Pacific Coast is Alaska's longest and most ambitious piece of roadwork. It is unique in many ways, one being that in all the three hundred and seventeen miles from the outskirts of Fairbanks to the town of Chitina there is not one single crossroad. No wonder our Alaska motorists love The Trail!

But our affection goes far deeper than mere present-day motor pleasure, for those who have lived long in Interior Alaska see in the Richardson Trail an index to the whole past development of the great and fertile hinterland province, quite as surely as they see our future here linked with the new railroad. First treked out and cleared in 1905 by the War Department as a crude trail, in 1907 it had become passable for dog teams in the winter and sourdough prospectors with pack animals in summer. By 1910 there was heavy traffic over it, both summer and winter, for it made an overland "all-American" short-cut from tide-water—avoiding the great time-consuming loop from Skagway to Dawson, down the Yukon and up the Tánana—some 300 direct miles as against nearly 1,500 of detour. Light horse-drawn wagons were used on it in summer and double-ender bob-sleds driven by "the trail hounds" in winter; and, once the river closed in October, the

trail was then the only route to the Interior until
July, and our one fine-drawn link of transportation
between The Last Frontier and all the outer world.
No wonder we sentimentalized The Trail, and this
condition remained until the completion of The
Alaska Railroad in 1923. In 1913 an automobile
(a Ford, of course!) was driven by that gay-hearted
pioneer, Bobby Sheldon, on the first through motor
trip from the Interior to the Coast. Yet when he
first suggested it, other old-timers thought that Bobby
should either be given the lunacy test or shipped out
at once to Morningside Asylum! Although Sheldon's trip proved that The Trail *could* become a
motor way, because of the War very little was done
to improve it during the following years; and much
of the mileage previously established fell into
grievous disrepair, due to lack of appropriations.

But in 1920 the present Alaska Road Commission
came into being, and too high praise cannot be meted
to the work of this efficient, practical and visioned
organization, as all who know Alaska will, I think,
agree. Those of you who live in sections of the
States where good roads have come into being during
the last decade, after a long period of hub-deep mud,
will know in your own hearts that a road is more
than a fact of transportation. It is a symbol. It
means touch, that closest of all our senses—to be in
touch with kindred life, with other communities of
citizens, with one's own kind. You can imagine,
then, how much more a real road meant to us who
inhabited "the pastures of the wilderness." After
days of mushing across miles of glutinous gelatinous
sponge, to come upon even a wagon track! The very
sight of it turns your heart tumbling inside of you,
and something catches in your throat. A road!—

Dear Uncle Sam, we pray you for our Alaska roads, for they are the very life-blood arteries of our colony, through which our continued well-being flows.

Since 1920 the pioneer period of the Richardson Trail has ended and its larger purpose has gradually been achieved. Now it is justly called "the best dirt road in America." It is drained and graded and gravelled throughout, dangerous curves have been widened, and the larger streams are bridged, so that it may now be travelled by good cars and at comfortable speeds (the entire distance can be driven in one summer day), affording colonists and tourists alike a way of unexampled beauty from the Golden Heart out to the Copper Gateway of Alaska. Many tourists (12,000 came our way last summer) patronize the regular summer motor-bus service between Fairbanks and the coast. A score of prominent travel organizations in the States arrange conducted parties each summer by this route, making what is known as the Golden Belt Tour in over The Trail to Fairbanks and out through different but equally interesting country by the Alaska Railroad. Only last season a new extension from Fairbanks north to Circle City was opened, making now a continuous motor route from the Pacific at Valdez to the Yukon River, 531 miles. New colonists often bring their own cars, and fetch in trailers their camping outfits and lighter possessions. The Trail has afforded to many an unequalled chance to drive in comfort and in leisure through some of the most lovely mountain scenery that I know in all the world, for the way crosses four ranges, although the greatest elevation of The Trail itself never exceeds 3,310 feet. Constructed as it is in such a remote land, through such sparsely settled country (for there is not a real town in all its

MT. MCKINLEY 20,360 FEET HIGH ALASKA.

DENALI'S SOUTH SIDE AS IT WAS PAINTED BY SIDNEY LAURENCE.

MT. MCKINLEY, ALASKA. 20300 FT.

Photograph by Cann. Fairbanks.

MOUNT MCKINLEY OR DENALI FROM ITS NORTHERN KANTISHNA SIDE.

Photograph by Lomen Brothers, Nome.

CORDOVA HARBOR IS BUT ONE OF MANY SAPPHIRE BAYS ON ALASKA'S
COAST.

THE RICHARDSON TRAIL CROSSES FOUR RANGES TO REACH ALASKA'S
HEART.

length), it represents the utmost in engineering patience and skill; and yet the total cost of building this road and maintaining it for twenty-four years has been less than $12,000 per mile.

The Trail passes through the heart of big-game country, and sportsmen have little trouble in securing a limit bag within a few miles of the highway. It's no uncommon thing for automobiles to be held up while huge herds of caribou, on their annual migration, sweep across from hill to hill in thousands like the half-wild cattle of early western days. The way skirts many lovely lakes rich in fish—popular boating and swimming places for Fairbanks week-enders. If you are interested in shooting, either with camera or with gun, engage a guide such as John Hajducovitch to take you into the Upper Tánana country and there you'll find (as W. N. Beach, of the Camp Fire Club, and his sportsmen friends have found) a veritable treasure house.

After one leaves the town of Fairbanks and the pleasant farmlands stretching out near by, the road slides away for miles and miles—not like a ribbon of dental cream, as are so many eastern roads, stiff and unyielding and alien, but built here out of bones of the soil's self, springy but firm. Through the cool green tunnel of the trees, past moose pastures flooded with flowers and hilltop lakes of bluebells soft as the lip of heaven and wind blown into froth of Queen Anne's lace, gradually we climb by easy stages on and up into the shadow of the peaks, so massive, so impassive, ineluctable. Alaska is "long" on highest mountains. Within her borders are no less than eight peaks loftier than Mt. Whitney, the greatest in the States: Mt. Hayes is fourteen thousand, and Sanford and Blackburn (nearly half a mile higher) may be seen from many points along The Trail, as may also the sugar loaf of Mt. Wrangell. The frequent log roadhouses along the way offer not only the friendliest of shelter but food that tastes ambrosial, after these miles of open air and land. One surely should experience The Trail, to see what "The Interior" really means.

At Willow Creek The Trail forks, and one may go on all the way by road to tide-water at Valdez (an alternate route which makes the Richardson Trail 410 miles from Fairbanks) or direct to Chitina on the Copper River Railroad and thence by train to Cordova. It's hard to say which way is finer, for the rugged grandeurs of the Copper Valley are unsurpassed, and yet the Keystone Canyon into Valdez is also ethereally lovely in its drape of spray-blown waterfalls. Lieutenant Allen spent weeks of "discomfort that beggars description," cold and half starved, to make the first white trek up the river from the coast to Chitina, in the early spring of '85 —a distance of 131 miles which we cover to-day in a few hours of Pullman luxury and dining-car service.

This railroad was built to tap the rich copper lodes of the Kennecott, and the discovery of these lodes was itself dramatic enough, in all conscience. Katherine Wilson of Cordova tells how, one day some thirty years ago:

In the late afternoon Tarantula Jack and his partner halted their pack-horses. It had been a long day's tramp, and the foothills of the Wrangell Range offered nothing of shelter or food for man or beast. Naked and glacier-scarred, the mountains rose at their approach in lowering unwelcome and retreated darkly into their high-up ice caves. It was while the prospectors were loosening the pack-straps to get at the shrunken food-bag for the animals, that the eye of Tarantula Jack was caught by a patch of green apparently overgrowing a slide well up the face of the mountain. " Looks like that might be grass up there," he observed to his companion. And as he staked out the hungry horses and gave them as much as he dared of the feed, he kept glancing now and then at that vivid patch of color so promising of fresh forage.

When the flapjacks and coffee had been disposed of and pipes lighted up, Tarantula rose to his feet. " Think I'll take a turn up the mountain and prospect that vegetation," he announced. He was gone some time. He returned two steps at a jump.

" Grass? " his partner ventured.

Tarantula Jack spat explosively. " Grass nothing! " he fumed, in disgust. " That there green is malachite and chalcocite—copper ore, or I never saw Arizona—and a whole blamed mountain of it ! "

And so was discovered the Bonanza mine.

The partners staked out claims—a dozen or so. They located in their own names, Jack Smith and Clarence Warner, and, to cover as much ground as possible, in those of a trail party with whom they had travelled inland as far as the Chitina.

Months later at Valdez they notified the others of their find. The latter were but mildly interested, a copper property not being like a placer, a poor man's mine. However, a dozen of the " sourdoughs " recorded their claims. But when, the following year, they were offered what to them was the fabulous price of twenty-five thousand dollars apiece, seven of them—and with alacrity !— sold their interests to a " green young college feller " from New York.

That young " college feller " was Steve Birch, the empire builder. That " patch of green " became one of the world's greatest copper mines, the Kennecott, which was primarily responsible for the melodramatic building of the Copper River and Northwestern Railroad, put the now prosperous "Red Metal Metropolis" of Cordova on the map, and made possible the establishment of one of the main steamship lines now plying between Seattle and Alaskan ports. Great fortunes often breed great jealousies, but Stephen Birch is still "Steve" to many old-time Alaskans who knew that young mining engineer when he first came here directly from Columbia University, back in the days of '98, and followed Lieutenant Abercrombie on a scouting trip to reconnoitre a military road (our present Trail) inland from Valdez. On the way back he picked up news of Tarantula Jack's discovery, took an option on the Bonanza at Kennecott and has been with it ever since, rounding out one of the most striking episodes in the history of the Territory. During the late War *one shipment* of copper ore from this property proved to be worth more than the whole sum Uncle Sam once paid for the whole Territory of Alaska. The Copper River section supplies the highest grade of copper ore being mined anywhere in the world to-day, and a constant stream of the red metal flows through the port of Cordova, aggregating nearly a million dollars every month.

But before there could be this great copper production there had to be a hundred and ninety miles of railroad; and few believed that possible, up the canyons and past the great glaciers of raging Copper River. There was in those days, however, a certain intrepid Irishman abiding in the land, Michael J. Heney. He had been the contracting constructor of our White Pass and Yukon Railroad from Skagway over to White Horse, the only railroad then penetrating into the North from the Coast; and, having

already built one " impossible " road, he saw no reason why he could not build another! The word " impossible " was always a red rag to " M. J.," at which
he first snorted, then charged; and the road is a picture of the man, stopped by nothing in heaven or on
earth.   Surely no one but " a wild Irishman " could
have conceived it, surely no one but " a black Irishman " could have built it.   For three miles along the
river's edge there lies Child's Glacier, raising its
frigid bulk three hundred feet high in a solid wall,
with the torrential river swirling and undercutting
at its base.   The glacier moves three and a half feet
a day, and every few moments giant bergs break off,
some weighing thousands of tons, and splash mightily
into the water.   Just across is Miles Glacier.   The
dual sight is tremendous, and when President Harding was here, Cordova people who brought him out
to see it could hardly get him to go back!   No one
of his party had ever looked on such a thing—and
no wonder, for there is nothing like it elsewhere.

A fine sight—but not for a prospective railroad
builder who must rear a bridge across the river between these glaciers, and slap its twin steel threads
against their very faces.   Working day and night all
winter, with hundreds of men, " M. J." reared the
false-work for his bridge *upon the river ice*.   But an
unprecedented early spring came, the ice began to
thaw and shift, and the bridge was not yet completed.
If the river ice moved before the last span was in,
the whole huge structure and a year's full work were
irretrievably lost, and surely no one then would back
another such venture.   The ice went out—less than
one hour *after* the last bolt had been placed in the
connecting span of the mighty steel bridge, now rising secure and high above those glacier-strewn

waters. "The Iron Trail" tells the romance of that building, first daringly plotted by three iron musketeers of Alaska—Heney the contractor, Macpherson the engineer, and Dalton the famous old Alaska sourdough; the first train over it in 1911 brought out the most valuable consignment of copper ore ever moved in the history of the world.

Alaska has several railroad towns that either grew up directly because of a railroad built out from them, or have derived their chief support from a railroad. And Cordova, like Skagway, is the place where Iron Trail and Pacific waters meet—in a harbor here more beautiful, I think, than even justly-famed San Francisco Bay, an ample area of good anchorage and probably the finest naval harbor in Alaska. Cordova is a modern, clean-built city of to-day, not only tide-water outlet for the richest copper mines but also gateway to the Bering River coal and oil fields and the Interior placer and quartz mines. It is the home of salmon and clam industries and the epicure's Cordova crab, a deep-water crustacean which cannot be equalled anywhere. Lying on the east side of Orca Inlet at the entrance to Prince William Sound, it is laid out with a view to the future, with well-graded wide streets, substantially built houses, a good water system, electric light and power, attractive homes, excellent schools and churches, "the finest docks in Alaska," cable connection with Seattle, telegraph connection with the Interior, and a powerful wireless station. The site was named by a homesick Spaniard, Caamaño, sailing up this coast in 1792 on that restless search for gold which, like a gadfly, drove his people fruitlessly so far afield, into Florida and California. Here again they found no trace of golden treasure, for they never penetrated behind the ranges but went away discouraged after naming the bay for the most strangely haunting of Spanish cities. Cordova is but one of many high-sounding names of old Spain that have been left upon this coast—but of Spaniards themselves, no colony or trace remains. The land was waiting for the touch of another master.

Prince William Sound is perfectly landlocked and surrounded by high mountains. Like most of the South Coast harbors, it is an unspeakably beautiful mountain-fast bay. The entire southern coast of Alaska is very irregular and precipitous, with only slight stretches of beach varying the rugged contours of the piled-up mountainy wall that seems to forbid all entrance to the inner lands. Here are the islands so sought by fox farmers, here are the greatest bears in all the world. Fishery experts tell that the waters of Prince William Sound contain 250 varieties of edible sea foods. The near-sea valleys are full of ferns, anemones, forget-me-nots and buttercups, for the climate here is but the climate of Scotland. A zero day in Cordova is so unusual that the local papers will headline it; whereas in the mild January of 1926, grass crops and strawberries were growing at Seward, mosquitoes and alders and cattails were reported coming out at Cordova, and fox farmers along the coast were complaining about the " heat!" Mild and moist conditions are usual here, Latouche one year recording no less than 249½ inches of rainfall! For the high peaks, rising literally from the tide line, form a great barrier which not only opens few natural doors to the Interior but catches upon its jagged summits all wandering rain clouds from the warm sea and casts them back once more in water that hurries down the slopes in swift rich salmon streams. Year in and year out this monstrous game of catch as can continues, and few indeed are the stray puffs and whiffs of moisture that slip through the fingers of these big-league mountains. And so many are the islands, bays and headlands of this ragged coast that they draw out Alaska's five thousand true miles of continental shore line to more than five times that length, if all their irregularities are measured.

Valdez is another warm rich Spanish name, and the town of Valdez is one of the old gold-camps of Alaskan story. It, too, lies at the feet of great mountains and is reached from Cordova by slipping along the coast back of that Hinchinbrook Island where Lieutenant Allen was landed, at Point Eteches, to begin his once adventurous escapade into the Interior. Across the sound are white-capped mountains, thick in green vegetation from the snow line to the water's edge. You pass Fort Liscombe, steep granite slopes which are the haunt of mountain sheep and goats, fine trout streams, and many mines and prospects, for this whole region is one where both gold and copper ore are widely distributed. "Red" Ellis put Valdez on the map as a mining town, for, after locating a good gold prospect near by, he talked the inhabitants of the town into raising $10,000 on shares for a plant, and the mine paid eighty per cent. a month—a good community investment! Valdez to-day impresses visitors not only by its small but well-laid-out golf links, open to the use of all, but by its beautiful gardens in the courthouse yard, where flowers are free for the picking, and the municipal strawberry beds where the stranger within her gates is invited to go and pick and eat to his heart's content. For Valdez, like Skagway, has turned its early

wildness into present beauty. It was one of the
bustling busy towns of olden days, a place of gusty
miner's meetings like Nome, in 1910 when Cliff
Mine was at its best; and Valdez was outfitting point
to Fairbanks, Copper Center and other Interior
camps before Cordova got the railroad built. Fourteen miles back of town is lovely Keystone Canyon,
with the road to Yukon valley stretching away to
the north, one fork of to-day's good trunk line over
the mountains.

West and south, on Resurrection Bay that runs an
arm back into Kenai Peninsula, lies Seward where
Uncle Sam's own railroad reaches down to sea. How
those early Russians sprinkled our Alaska map with
holy names! Each new discovery of theirs was, for
good luck, most apt to bear the name of that particular saint or feast day. Many of the old Indian,
Spanish and Russian place names have since been
translated into English, and only research or tradition reveals the older and often softer-sounding form
of word. But any collection of syllables like the
Spanish Revillagigedo—the island named for that
up-and-doing Don Juan Vincente de Guemes
Pacheco de Pedilla, Count of Revilla Gigedo and
viceroy of Mexico—has proved almost too much for
Saxon mouths to master! So this present-day busy
city of Seward, named of course for Lincoln's forward-looking Secretary, is built near the site which
Baranof, "the Iron Governor," selected in 1792 as
the proper spot for a shipyard and called Voskresen-
skaia—which means Resurrection, and also Sunday.
Here was launched in 1794, the *Phoenix,* the first
vessel ever to be built in the territory now Alaska.

Seward, a couple of thousand miles nearer the Far
East than Bremerton or Mare Island, tapping with

its railroad both the Matanuska and Nenána coal
fields as a coaling station, outfitting point for the big
game district of Kenai peninsula, transfer point to
" The Westward " and the Valley of Ten Thousand
Smokes, was founded about the same time as Fairbanks by just one white man named William Lowell,
said to have been descended from the famous Massachusetts clan of that name. His homestead, containing about a hundred and sixty acres, was bought
up and laid out as a townsite by the Ballaine brothers, who were then interested in the ambitious plan
for a railroad from Resurrection Bay to a point on
the Yukon River. While the Alaska Central Railroad Company has passed into the things that were,
its projectors builded better than they knew; for the
Government Railroad, now in operation, absorbed
the seventy-odd miles already built across the peninsula and stamped the name of Seward indelibly upon
Alaska's map—where no man's name has surely a
better right to be!

One passes through a protected channel into Resurrection Bay, fifteen miles wide, a long straight
passage like that of Seattle's harbor, and large
enough " to float all the fleets of the world." Ice-
free and always open, Seward is near great fishing
banks and great coal fields, is a cable terminus, and
all of surrounding Kenai Peninsula is highly mineralized territory. From Nuka Bay to Willow Creek,
mines or prospects are to be found every few miles.
There is a fine stand of timber here, and logging in
the woods is carried on year round. A delightful
roadway connects the city with Kenai Lake, and this
is the heart of moose, sheep, bear and goat country
for the sportsman, and Alaska guides, as Arthur
Thompson says, will " do all but tie the animals! "

Paradise Lake is a hatchery where any one who asks questions may learn the fascinating romance of the salmon cycle.   Backed by great hills which break only at that notch through which the railroad drops from far-off Fairbanks, Seward on its quiet bay, built up on rising ground of slate that drains and cleans ideally, stands a secure metropolis of the North to justify its historic name.

The builders of the Alaska Central Railroad planned to tap the Matanuska coal measures two hundred miles inland, and then push on to the Yukon drainage; for although only one fifth of Alaska has been geologically surveyed to date, its known coal fields include twelve thousand square miles, and skilful geologists compute Alaska's ultimate coal resources at a hundred and fifty *billion* tons—far beyond the original supply of Pennsylvania, the largest coal producer of the States.   The Matanuska field lying back of Seward and Anchorage is rich in high-grade bituminous and anthracite coal, equal in quality to that supplied by Montana and Utah mines, while the Nenána field that lies along the line of the present Alaska Railroad is one of the largest and most promising of " lignite " fields, really an excellent slightly sub-bituminous coal.   In fact, at one point on Healy River near the railroad line there are four beds exposed, one above the other, separated by narrow layers of shale and sandstone, totalling a hundred and thirteen feet of coal.   Some of the coal beds in the Nenána River region are forty-five feet thick.   These known coal deposits of the Matanuska and Nenána valleys were largely responsible for the construction of the Government Railroad and for the existence of Anchorage, Nenána and a number of other smaller communities along the right of way, for here were more wide pastures for the Iron Horse to feed upon. The Government Railroad also tapped the Willow Creek lode gold camps of the lower Susitna and the extensive placers and agricultural development already well under way in the Fairbanks district. The Matanuska Valley, too, has its fertile farms; so that Uncle Sam's railroad, built as it is upon the known facts of coal, gold and agriculture, has a mighty firm foundation.

From Seward to Anchorage most of the route is along the old Alaska Central right-of-way, now taken over and re-graded by the Government—past Kenai Lake, across the ridge of mountains which march in 6,000 to 8,000-foot peaks down the spine of the peninsula, past larger glaciers than many you go miles to see in Switzerland, by waterfalls and swift tumbling streams, to drop steeply down to Turnagain Arm on Cook Inlet and around to the railroad-built and modern town of Anchorage, on Knik Arm. Except for the Bay of Fundy, I am told, Cook Inlet has the highest tides in the world, the extremes being sixty feet and the incoming water rising to a bore eight to ten feet high. Sometimes the tide meets itself going out, and the waters are then as thrilling a scene to watch as you can imagine. Cook, the great navigator, went up this large indentation from the Gulf of Alaska, thinking he had at last found a northwest passage. However, when he saw that the tides were running so high, he concluded that this was not the channel and, in disgust and disappointment, he named the bay Turn Again Arm.

Anchorage is much more than a railroad town, however, for it is one of Alaska's real cultural centers, a little city of 2,500 souls, now building a $50,-000 high school. I shall never forget my own first visit there, the woman's club I attended, the splendid papers read and book reviews given—and the marvelous refreshments! For Alaska's women are famous cooks, wherever you go. I sometimes think that this is true because most Alaska husbands are themselves good cooks, having mushed and siwashed and camped so much "on their own." Wise in the ways of cookery themselves, this knowledge makes them intelligent cook critics, and therefore sets a high culinary standard! But Anchorage is also an art center. Here Sidney Laurence lives, whose celebrated pictures hang in the most discriminating galleries of America and Europe. For years he has made a study of Mt. McKinley from this southern side; and he has painted the majesty and mystery of that great mountain, in all its moods, with the care and shading of true lover as well as of consummate craftsman. His wife is also an artist, making her study one of Alaskan life, its sled dogs in special, in all their types and poses. Seward has the Dutch artist Jan Van Emple, who ran away and came to the New World as a cabin boy, is now a member of the Whitney Studio Club in New York, and has taken part in a number of eastern exhibits. He has done a very unusual reredos for St. Peter's Episcopal Church in Seward. The upper portion of the painting shows the familiar figure of the Christ, with angels kneeling at His feet; but the background of the Resurrection scene is formed by the mountains and waters of Resurrection Bay itself, and in the foreground stand Alaskan natives, miners, and settlers grouped about the open tomb. The prospector stands in his rough shirt and suspenders, rugged, true to life, his shallow round pan dropped from his hand and rolled against the open sepulchre, while the little Indian mother standing near is unable to lift her head to heaven with the rest because her baby weighs so heavily upon her back. The whole conception forms a work of great piety and unusual beauty. Cordova is the home of Ziegler, who has done such charming sketches in ink, as well as canvasses of great vigor and power; and Rockwell Kent himself had an "Alaskan period," when he spent a winter here and first caught that glory of a beetling, severe, rock coast which later was to send him with his lively master's sketch book to far-off Patagonia and to Labrador.

A far cry back from Rockwell Kent to railroads! But the first time I came to Anchorage it was in late winter, and to embark upon an adventure from which the kindly Anchorage women tried their hardest to dissuade me. Steel had then been laid from Anchorage north, and from Nenána south, but there was a gap in the midst of the mountains that had merely been surveyed, for which there was as yet no building appropriation. We planned to go to end-of-steel, secure our own dog teams there, and mush over The Pass to end-of-steel on the Interior side. It was about the worst time of year to attempt it, we knew, but we were determined to see the country lying under Mt. McKinley and cross Broad Pass before the railroad "messed it up," as I expressed it. We saw it with a vengeance, for a great blizzard came just as we reached The Pass and we were caught crawling along like flies upon that mountain slope—frail human things, with slippery hope below. Three times in one short day snow-slides swept down on us with that preliminary hiss, that unforgetable and culminating roar of blind, brute, primal gods forbidding entrance to their long-fast mountain home. How we escaped from that crisp clip of Destiny's long shears was something of a miracle. Never have I known that sound so close, and never have I felt so keenly the presence of those irresistible forces whose puppets we seem to be. To step from the facile self-contained pride of newly-building Coast cities into the winter heart of that immensity and cold white silence, gave me a sense of curious impotence I never can wipe out in memory. Here man was still the idle sport of monstrous, shambling, elemental gods who dwell in unremitting habitation within the heaven-topping peaks.

It took us nearly two full weeks to go those hundred miles across The Pass, in snows that were—in places on the southern side—from thirty to forty feet deep. At times we walked upon the tops of trees, at times slid down into the funnels of less close-packed snows around the buried conifers. At times we waited for the storm to pass, at other times we tried to push along, for there was nothing left to eat but dog-rice. Our friends in Fairbanks knew that we had started over, and when we did not come and word was brought of winter storms of long duration and of great intensity raging within the passes, they gave us up for lost. We had the strange experience of reading later in our Fairbanks paper, "W. F.'s" comment on our crazy foolhardiness, the statement that we were undoubtedly lost, and what amounted to an obituary notice—with a few shreds of hope still grudgingly held out to any grieving friends of the deceased!

But not so many years after that deeply bitten-in experience I was again crossing Broad Pass—but this time in a Pullman observation coach. The train rolled smoothly out over a riven gulch between steep-sided slopes, and as I looked far down I recognized from this now conquered height that very chasm of our three-fold avalanche, where we had struggled for three days imprisoned in the mountains' heart, walled with impenetrable snows, against archaic night. This was the conquest men had dreamed, this was the bourne of all those lonely trails. The 470 miles of the Alaska Railroad had been built—to tap large mining districts and open them to ocean transportation?—Yes, but much, much more than that. This was *our* railroad, built not so much from steel and wood but from the hope and the experience and the very soul-stuff of men, grappling here with gray old gods of chaos. Again mere Man had answered the insuperable challenge, with his dream-spun steel.

At yet another time it was my rare good fortune to be the first white woman (so they told me) mushing over to the foot of Mt. McKinley and back from the present site of the railroad, through the then untracked, unblazed high-lying passes of the inner mountains, the home of many thousand big-horned mountain sheep. I myself counted more than a thousand here, in the first three days of this journey, and it too was an adventure long remembered. But today they are building a fine tourist's motor road along those gulches which we ventured, over those passes into the Kantishna country, down to Muldrow Glacier, Wonder Lake, and the foot of tremendous Denali, "the Most High," so that in time all the world may come to see. Forty miles of road, to Sable Pass, already have been built; forty-nine more are to be constructed within the next two years, and a tourist hotel will be erected at the foot of Copper Mountain in time for the tourist season of 1932, whence future thousands will look up at great Denali

—the highest mountain in the world *above its sur-*
rounding base. This park highway, already open
to the traveller, will prove to be, I have no doubt,
one of the most scenic routes in North America,
since it crosses four major passes from which a
remarkable panorama of the Alaska Range is constantly in view. I say "constantly" advisedly, for
even that cloud-gathering giant, Mt. McKinley, was
visible from Savage River tourist camp last year
sixty days out of the season's eighty; and this is a
record, I think, for any tremendous peak—far
greater visibility than for far lesser Mt. Ranier, for
instance. And yesterday a honeymoon couple from
New Jersey left Fairbanks in a plane to fly over to
Kantishna and inspect the mountain, before leaving
the heart of Alaska. Ah, well! perhaps I'd like to
see it from the air myself one day and, in fond memory of that pioneering journey, snap fingers down
at Sable Pass, those icy rivers, and the bighorn's
knife-sharp hills, where cloudy shadows wander so
high and free.

For this abode of silence, too, the truly last frontier, is being entered from the Iron Trail and our
slow unblazed way of long ago is fast becoming an
easy way of rolling rubber. This road is a sure way
to better things for many who have given lifetime
to the inner country; and a road will mean that prospects in Kantishna land will become mines, and little
mines will become real mines, all adding of their
wealth to Uncle Sam's great attic ledger.

Do you wonder, then, that Alaskans are a bit sentimental about "our" Railroad, as we once were about
the Trail? It has come to us as the long-promised
child of our brain and body, born of our hope and
wrought out of long years of work and waiting, until

at last the dream came true. We know what it has meant already to the inner lands, in many ways; we know how it links up with all our future promise. And when, as I once did, we sit in galleries of Congress and hear men state there that the building of this railroad was a mistake,—because, begun in 1914, it cost a little more, due to the intervening of World War, than first had been anticipated,—that the people of Alaska are as yet so " few " and the land so "worthless" (just the things once said about New England, about the Middle West, and later about the Far West, before men *knew!*) then I could cry in rage, or weep in very pity for their blindness!

But there are many folk sitting in Congress, wiser than those who spoke so slightingly of America's Last Frontier. Alaska, thank the Fates, still has her friendly Sumners and her Sewards, brave enough and plain-spoken enough to enlighten the people of the States regarding the real worth of their colonial possession. And knowing this, we wait for Time to bring the needed answer, remembering that pessimism about new and as yet unexploited far-off territory is no new thing in Congress; and Time has an ironic way of reversing such under-judgment, a way in which history (for our delight!) abounds.

When Chicago was a cluster of a hundred and fifty wood houses, grouped about Fort Dearborn in 1825, Senator Benton said of the Great West: "The ridge of the Rocky Mountains may be named as the convenient, natural, and everlasting boundary (of the United States). Along this ridge the western limits of the Republic should be drawn and the statue of the fabled god Terminus should be erected on its highest peak, never to be thrown down." But Benton subsequently changed his mind! Later, the controversy about the great "Oregon Tract" (which embraced what now is Oregon, Washington, Idaho and parts of Wyoming and Montana) brought out a "new crop of congenital unbelievers," as our Alaskan Judge Wickersham delights to call them. Senator Dickenson of my own New Jersey said of Oregon, in that period when national legislators knew as little of this section as some do now of Alaska, "Oregon can never be one of the United States. . . . The Union is already too extensive. . . . A young, able-bodied Senator *might* travel from Oregon to Washington and back once a year, but he could do nothing else."

Even such a paragon as Daniel Webster, that "noblest of our notabilities" (from Massachusetts, too, itself once a mis-prized colony), said of all that region which contains, among other things, superb Puget Sound: "What do we want with the vast, worthless area, this region of savages and whirlwinds of dust, of cactus and prairie dogs? To what use could we ever hope to put these great deserts, or those endless mountain ranges, impenetrable, and covered to their base with eternal snow? What can we ever hope to do with the western coast, a coast of three thousand miles, rock-bound, cheerless, and uninviting, *and not a harbor on it?* Mr. President, I will never vote one cent from the Public Treasury to place the Pacific coast one inch nearer to Boston than it is now."

How Daniel Webster's long-departed spirit must regret those ill-digested, hotly-spoken words!

XIX

What Price Great Catherine's Fur Piece?

R USSIANS were the first white men to see and claim Alaska, and the curtain of history rolls up here in riotous Romanof color, upon a stage of Bakst decor like a setting for "Prince Igor." The names of the first comers are to be read in the age-old palimpsest of the land, for you can tell who came first by the names they scratched upon its early maps.

The Pacific coasts of " Russian North America " were explored for years by the navies of half a dozen nations, as were the Atlantic coasts of eastern America. They came for the same cause that brought Columbus sailing from the Port of Palos—the search for a way between Europe and the East. Frobisher, Davis, Hudson, had attempted it from the Atlantic in the sixteenth century, but Russ and Spaniard and such Englishmen as Cook attempted the supposed passage from the Pacific side in the eighteenth century, " grubstaked " as was Columbus himself to find a new short cut to an old market. For a time the Inside Passage from Puget Sound north was thought to be the long-sought " Strait of Anian," and all the windings and twistings of this teasing water maze were patiently explored. But there proved to be no channel through, but only a strange way of beauty for their pains—" divers Ilands in that Sayling and . . . people on Land clothed in Beasts skins."

But it was the essential northern-reaching nearness of Alaska to Asia, a basic simple fact of geography, which first gave rise to persistent tales of a land to the eastward heard by seventeenth- and eighteenth-century Cossack adventurers in Siberia; tales which, retold at the court of Peter the Great as tales of the Cabots had been retold in the port of Bristol, finally resulted in an expedition to verify the strange account.

Vitus Bering was the first, in 1728; and a village a glacier, a haven, an island, a river, a lake, a bay, a strait, and a sea of Alaska, all carry his name to-day in fitting monument to this man who made a final rendezvous with death upon the gray and foggy islands. He had set out in the days of Catherine I of Russia, illiterate but shrewd peasant wife of Peter the Great. Bering's expedition was the first to make landfall of the continent from the Pacific side, but, like Columbus, he sailed at the command of an alien empress. Columbus was from Genoa, though he rode the unknown seas under the royal ægis of Spain; Venetian Cabots had been navigators for England; and Captain Commander Ivan Ivanovich Bering was the son of Jonas Svendsen by his second wife Anne Pedersdatter Bering, and was born in Jutland in 1681. His mother's distinguished Danish family included a number of great men who had held high ministerial and judicial office, and when John Svendsen's son Vitus entered the service of the Russian navy he took the Russianized form of name —Ivanovich, John's son—with his mother's surname. The insertion of the " h " in Bering, as often written, is merely a form of word " made in Germany."

Bering had been selected for the work of exploring the coast of eastern Asia by no less a man than

Peter the Great himself. The first Kamchatka expedition, as it was called, set out from Okhotsk and discovered and named St. Lawrence Island in Bering Sea, sailed up through Bering Strait, rounded East Cape, and proceeded westward along the Siberian coast far enough to establish the fact that the land, which Chuck-chees had reported as lying beyond Siberia, was no part of continental Asia. So Bering Strait was on the world's map fifteen years before the first white man, La Verendrye the French Canadian, laid eyes upon the Rocky Mountains! The results of this first " Kamchatka expedition " merely whetted the curiosity of the Russian Court to learn more and, if possible, to find a trade route through. Accordingly, the second Kamchatka expedition was organized, again under Bering, with Alexi Chirikof as second in command. They sailed in 1740 on the *St. Peter* and the *St. Paul,* and the plan called for the two vessels to proceed together; but they became separated soon after setting out from Avatcha Bay, and thenceforth the two commanders proceeded independently.

On July 16, 1741, Bering sighted and named magnificent Mt. St. Elias, one of the most prominent features of Alaska's south coast and lying about halfway of present-day Seward and Juneau—its 18,000 feet first climbed by the Duke of Abruzzi in 1897. Bering made a landing near Controller Bay, beneath those blue skies, blue hills and blue glaciers, and not far from the spot where to-day the coal and oil of the Bering River district have created the settlement of Katalla. Remaining but a few days in the neighborhood of Prince William Sound, he sailed to the westward along the coast, touching at several points. But Bering and the whole ship's crew fell ill of scurvy, that greatest peril then to even master mariners, and on November fifth his vessel was wrecked upon an island of the Commander group later to be called by his name. Here Bering died, and those of his crew who survived both shipwreck and scurvy constructed another vessel from the wreck and returned to Kamchatka the following fall, bearing rare treasures of sea-otter skins and telling wild travellers' tales of a land where savages went robed in pelts that might enrich the pomp of kings.

Chirikof also sighted the Alaska coast, probably a few hours before Bering. Commander and crew all suffered greatly from scurvy, his home journey was beset with great difficulty because of his inability to make any landings, due to the loss of two boats full of men, sent ashore for fresh water and presumably killed by hostile natives near the site of to-day's Sitka; but he finally reached Avatcha Bay in October, 1741. Flavorsome old Greek Church names scattered all up and down the coast of Alaska still show that the Russians once passed this way. Etolin and Baranof were Russian governors whose memory remains in place names; and if you care to trace the story of many a Rock or Whale, Long, Big, Spruce or Bare upon Alaska's map, you'll find they are but English translations of words the Russians first put there—*Kamenoi, Bieluga, Dolgoi, Bolshoi, Elovoi,* and *Goloi.*

But it was sea otter that determined the further exploration and colonization of The Great Country by Russia. Catherine II became Empress, and Great Catherine found sea-otter skins most becoming to her peculiar type of beauty, and sea-otter skins she would and must have. Those Russian-American governors who wished to curry favor at St. Peters-

burg—or, indeed, to live long in the land!—saw to
it that Her Imperial Majesty was well provided
with sea otters! Because a certain Virgin Queen
possessed a sweet tooth and coveted "the Sugar Islands," little England had once begun her western
empire-building; and because a pretty lady with a
whimsy for furs happened to sit upon the throne of
Great Peter, Russia came to possess a colony in far-
away America. It is impossible to overstate the part
played by the now almost extinct sea otter in the
early conquest of Alaska. Bancroft says:

Little would have been heard of them (these first
Russian discoveries in America) for some time to come,
if ever, had it not been for the beautiful furs brought
back from Bering Island and elsewhere. Siberia was still
sufficient to satisfy the Tsar for purposes of expatriation,
and the Russians were not such zealots as to undertake
conquest for the sake of conversion and to make religion
a cloak for their atrocities; hence, but for these costly
skins, each of which proclaimed in loudest strains the
glories of Alaska, the Great Land might have long
rested, undisturbed.

The first score years of Russian rule were so full
of atrocities and massacre of natives that the tale is
now impossible to tell; and it is little wonder that
for generations after, *all* white men were feared and
hated by the natives, and, whenever possible, revenge
for early cruelties was swiftly taken. The very name
for "rifle" in the Aleut language is "Russu"!
Some love to call this period the day of high romance in Alaska, and mourn its passing, but for the
native population it was a dark and bitter chapter.
"Booted Russian adventurers looted fur, hewed
down majestic Sitka spruce, and worked out rich

copper deposits with native slaves, while the tribes fought helplessly, hopelessly, for their homes and hunting grounds." When Lieutenant Allen ascended the Copper River, Nicolai, " the most intelligent of the Midnooskies," told him something of the massacre of three Russian expeditions which had previously attempted the Atná. The Russians had forced the natives to draw their sleds up the river, in winter—driving with whip and gun, killing those who rebelled, allowing *no sleep*. But while the Russians slept and one alone kept watch, this armed man first and then the others were all killed. It was done but to repay unspeakable cruelties and to escape a savage slavery. As the Copper River Chief who killed Semoylof and his party is reported to have said: "We did not wantonly kill, we executed. The Russian men are murderers." And the natives knew only a Mosaic law of eye for eye and tooth for tooth. The Russian and Indian contests were not opera bouffe wars but very real, and many an innocent pioneer later lost his life before this black page of history was completely turned. The common saying during those Russian days was, " Heaven is high— and the Tsar is far away!" Empire was indeed slowly building here, but under a rough scaffolding.

Some of the men sent out from Russia were real builders, however, iron men of destiny; and this was necessary, for capricious Catherine did not have a clear field in Russian America. It was not a case of to have and to hold, but rather to get and to keep. The Spanish were not long in hearing the news of goings-on in the North Pacific, and Spain remembered well that Balboa had waded out waist deep into the waters of this ocean and claimed *all* the shores washed by it. So there were Spanish ex-

peditions galore, outfitted from Mexico and California, and little cities and great bays along the south
coast of Alaska resound to-day with Spanish names
put there by Perez and Quadra. If the Spaniards
had but guessed the El Dorado that lay hidden
behind the glacier-thundering coast range, how completely the entire history of our Pacific Northwest
might have to be rewritten! But George Carmack
was not yet born, and all that ever reached California from Alaska in these far days were a few inferior
sea-otter pelts which the Romanof disdained, monas-
tery bells for Franciscan Missions cast in bronze at
Kokiak, and shiploads of ice to cool the hot wines
of New Spain.

But the Russian exploration in Alaska did make
the Spaniard "look down his nose"—and up the
map—and take the only real interest he had so far
shown in holding the land to-day called California.
To meet the southward-sweeping Russians, Spain
occupied and outfitted San Diego, Monterey, and
Yerba Buena on San Francisco Bay. California's
pastoral period of the great missions paralleled the
numbered days of Alaska's Russian colonization, and
California grew up side by side with Alaska—
neighbor children of widely different parentage but
of the same age. And though their home folk were
not any too friendly (and the grasping far-sailing
Russians in the North were feared in California's
early days only second to the grasping far-sailing
Yankees in the East), the children of the households
would play together, as neighbor children do.
Mother Spain was always ordering these sons of
Russia away, but they always came right back; and
even Spain, that still great naval mistress, could not
keep the little Russian ships of Baranof's colonials

from San Francisco Bay—from trading there and swapping jackknives with her own children.

Baron Rezanof, "Chamberlain of the Russian Court and Commander of all America," appeared in Sitka in these days to investigate the doings of the Russian-American Fur Company, study Alaska with a view to extensive colonizing schemes, and establish trade relations with Japan that lay so close below the Aleutians. He was the first of Alaska's real " boosters," for he saw the latent bigness of the country and it appealed to his own big empire-minded imagination. Baranof had flogged with the knout a settler who brought him gold quartz, for *he* was there to get out furs for Catherine; but Rezanof sent out mining engineers to search for that Island of Gold the natives told of—perhaps the golden Treadwell on the Gastineau. Ostensibly to get fresh foodstuffs to relieve some of his Russians who had scurvy, but really with a view toward extending Russian claims down the Pacific as far as Mexico, he made a trip to San Francisco Bay, taking with him in the *Juno* a shipload of furs and bronze bells from the spiritual outposts of the Emperor Paul, to trade with other spiritual outposts at Father Juni-pero Sera's California Missions. It is supposed that a bell found only recently near Los Angeles, in an orange grove at Camulos by Mrs. Harriman the campanologist, is from that very cargo brought down in Alaskan bottoms by the romantic Rezanof; and this may very well have been " the first Mission bell to sound the tintinabulation of Christianity in the West." Its Russian inscription reads, *"This big bell was cast on the Island of Kokiak in the month of June, 1796* (about the time when George Washington was deciding that he did not choose to run again as President), *by Eugene, Arch-abbot of Russia. . . . Baranof."* Some old friar has chiselled into bronze the added line of Spanish— *"De San Fernando."*

Arriving at Yerba Buena, the princely Rezanof found that the vice-regent of Mexico had forbidden all trade with the Russian-Americans. But Rezanof stayed on and spent many months in that little town now known as San Francisco. Nor was he idle. His amiable and courtly ways not only won the Governor, but he courted too the Governor's daughter, Doña Concepcion de Argüello, and the story of that wooing has been told by Bret Harte, you will remember. But one day when the Governor's back was turned, Rezanof loaded up his little ship with all the grain and foodstuffs he could cram on board her—fanegas of wheat and oats, pease and beans, large quantities of flour and salt and tallow—and sailed back into the North. Returning to St. Petersburg from Sitka that winter, by way of Siberia, to report on Alaskan conditions and recommend a more enlightened and forward-looking policy for the new-world colony (and also ask his friendly sovereign's permission to wed the lovely Spaniard) his horse broke through thin ice just forming, while crossing a stream, and he was forced to camp in the snow. Rezanof was half frozen from the exposure, and this gay Russian cavalier—an empire builder with a dream—died with his work but half completed.

Some iron was smelted and some coal and copper mined for local use during the Russian régime, and German coal miners were put in charge of one mine, it is said, where fifteen hundred feet of tunnel was driven. But the only real search for gold under the

Russians was directed by an Imperial mining engineer who, after two years' work, reported adversely on Alaska as a mining country!

The Russians were good boat builders, and they built and delivered at an early date a fine vessel to the order of the Friars of Dolores, and the very first steamboat to ply inland California waters was a product of Sitka's Alaskan shipyards. The Russian colonists were craftsmen, too, and made the plows and hoes for the Spanish Mission in Monterey. They carried grain from the Sacramento Valley to Sitka, in Russian bottoms, to be ground in Russian-built mills (for the Russians were "faculized" where the Spanish, as a rule, were not) and returned again with flour. And, because the flour took up so much less room than grain did, they took along an extra cargo of ice for ballast. But, alas, the one thing the Russians did *not* like about California was its climate, and there were no California Chambers of Commerce then to give these statements the lie. Russians of Sitka, the Russian capital of "frozen Alaska" (as the world so falsely calls it) wrote back long accounts of the "vile weather off the California coast." They actually did!

Sitka was the queen city of the North then, and it remains to this day one of the loveliest towns of Alaska, though shorn of its capitoline prestige by modern near-by Juneau. The first settlements of Alaska, as of New England, were all concentrated upon the coast and on the lower reaches of the one great navigable stream, the Yukon; and they are still distinctly maritime in character, as civilization continues here her old-time way of following arteries made by geology. Sitka on Baranof Island (with the Twins, or Dvoini bratef,—twin brothers,—the

islets at the entrance to her harbor) was once a
Thlingit stronghold and later was made Baranof's
city; but while the Iron Governor made New Archangel, as she was formerly called, Sitka had and
has her own touch of natural and heavenly beauty.
Her National Park is uncommonly quaint, with its
sixteen totem poles donated to the United States by
the modern Indians of southeastern Alaska, who feel
that this old stronghold of their ancestors is the
fitting place in which to preserve their totems; and
her islands, her extinct volcano, her snow-topped
mountain 'cones, green valleys and island-studded
bay blend in a charm incomparable where little
friendly waves slap upon gray-green rock in Sitka
harbor.

Here was the Governor's castle rock, where Baranof in the coat of chain mail which he always
wore beneath his cloak (no idle gesture this, for his
life was often threatened) lorded it over northern
land and sea, for at that time Sitka was the chief
port on all the western coast. Cruel in many public
acts, as were also our own Stuarts, the Russian rulers
were often charming socially; and in the early nineteenth century there were formal balls in Sitka finer
by far than anything then going on at our own
Charleston or Philadelphia, and quite as cere-
monious too,—though warmed by Russian love of
pageantry and color,—led by those men and women
reared in a rich exotic court that knew the height of
luxury in living. Jewels and candle light were here,
velvets and fine music; and through it all the tragedy
of that mythical Princess who, forced to marry
against her will, disappeared during her wedding
banquet, took poison, and now—poor ghost—haunts
in her rustling silken bridal garments the northwest

Photograph by Merrill of Sitka.   From a print in Harper's Weekly, 1867.

OLD SITKA AS IT APPEARED IN THE RUSSIAN DAYS.

WAMPUM TRIMMED INDIAN COAT—AND MITTENS THAT CAN'T BE LOST.

TÁNANA INDIAN WOMAN IN HER BEAD-TRIMMED MOOSE-HIDE DRESS.

chamber of the castle, wringing her lovely bejewelled hands, and leaving behind the perfume of wild rose wherever she may pass. This same room is said to have been used by Lady Franklin when she came North in the middle of last century, in forlorn hope of tracing her intrepid husband, lost in a fruitless search for Northwest Passage. This room was also used, they say, by Secretary Seward upon the occasion of his visit to the newly acquired American territory.

Here in the Russian Cathedral of St. Michael the Archangel, before the ikon of Our Lady of Kazan, it is hard indeed to believe that, as is often said, " the Russian Church is the treasure house of Alaska's cash, the prison house of the native's soul." Pierpont Morgan is reported to have offered $25,000 for this fine Byzantinc piece—and been refused. Inside the church are paintings, banners, color, rich embroideries, and the deep ritual chants of the Greek Church, so unlike any music of the West. Outside, the golden-green curly spire and dome bespeak exotic eighteenth-century Russia, making one feel as blatantly Saxon as Hengest or Horsa. Outside, too, in the old town, hand-hewed log buildings, the fine workmanship of Baranof's men, seem like a Russian ballet set and make one think that Russian dancers in high color costume might any moment outburst from these doorways, low lintels under moss-green roofs, to whirl and stamp in wild and glamorous abandon.

And why not? Russia set the tune upon this coast for nearly a century and a half—a period of history quite as long as many eastern colonies knew before the American Revolution. Young Alaska was born a cub both of The Great Bear and The Bear That

Walked Like a Man; and any bear must dance to tunes if he wear an iron ring in his nose. Baranof forged that iron ring and he forged it right here in lovely Sitka, historically the most significant town of all Alaska.

Practically all the early settlements center around the work of this Iron Governor, usurper and user of power. At first he was an independent trader on the Anadir, then agent for the Shelikof Company, and later the driving autocratic manager of the Russian American Company which exercised practically an absolute sway over Alaskan destinies for sixty-seven years—even more so than the Hudson Bay Company in its domination of the early Canadian Northwest. Bancroft pays this unstinted tribute: " Alexander Baranof was no ordinary man. . . . To him was due, more than to all others, the success of the Russian colonies in America; by him they had been founded and fostered, and but for him they would never have been established, or would have had, at best, a brief and troubled existence." Baranof built savagely but he built securely; though undoubtedly unscrupulous and arrogant to a degree, he was yet far-sighted and extremely energetic—and he needed to be, for he must face the world's greatest naval power as rival. Had Russian supremacy under Baranof failed in the late eighteenth and early nineteenth centuries, then England's very active efforts to obtain the territory for herself would undoubtedly have been successful; and if England had once secured Alaska, rest assured that Uncle Sam could never have bought his attic, at any price.

England sent her most famous navigator, Captain James Cook, to sail up the western coast of North America in 1778 and secure there either a northwest trade route or another New England, to offset the losses already well begun at Lexington and Concord. He made his first discovery on the present Alaska coast near the present site of Sitka, and he named the cape and mountain at the entrance to Sitka Harbor after the mouth of Plymouth Harbor—Edgecumbe. Here was a new pilgrim for a new Plymouth with a vengeance, a Captain Miles Standish type and one accustomed to success.

But Cook, though he sailed north up to the ice-pack of that insuperable paleocrystic sea; and though he left his British names of sweethearts, friends and rulers upon the headlands, bays and rivers of Alaska to carry a remembrance of his exploits; although he skirted westward and reëstablished the fact that there was no direct land touch between Asia and North America; now he flung himself down the globe to winter at the Sandwich Islands, which he named in honor of the Earl. Then, in a moment, all was over with the great voyager. He lay upon that far Hawaiian beach, still and slain, to the despair of his wondering men. Here was one of our own kin and one most memorable; take him for all in all, a man among the noblest of his kind. It is well that his name, too, is written into the cartography of The Great Country.

Trained as midshipman under Cook, George Vancouver now took up the work, sailing from England in 1791. A careful navigator, he painstakingly filled in the reconnaissance sketched so grandiosely in a big salient way by his predecessor, and named some of the outstanding mountains of our western coast for his own sturdy British admirals. Upon the explorations of Cook and Vancouver, England based her claim to all of northwestern North America.

But the Russians were on the ground, with colonists and an iron rule, and not even Great Britain could budge them.

"Manifest Destiny," however, had begun to march. In 1789 Captain Robert Gray, a Yankee skipper, sailed out of Boston round to the Pacific Coast, and three years later he discovered and entered the mouth of a very fine large river there, which he named Columbia in honor of his own good ship. By virtue of Gray's discoveries and those of the Lewis and Clark land expedition to the Pacific coast, in conjunction with the rights acquired from France by the Louisiana Purchase in 1803 and from Spain by the Florida Purchase in 1819, the United States laid claim to a vast area on the Pacific coast roughly known as the Oregon Tract. In 1824 Russia agreed to make no settlement south of 54° 40′ and the United States agreed to make none north of that line, while in the next year Russia and Great Britain came to a similar agreement, thus settling the boundaries of Russian America. The United States was becoming a great power in her own right. Extensive actual settlements by American citizens in the Oregon Tract after 1832 made Uncle Sam's claim perfect up to the forty-ninth parallel, and above that we had no valid claim, except perhaps as against Russia.

And then, just after the Civil War, we bought Alaska from Tsar Alexander for the cheapest song in history. There was more back of this purchase, on both sides, than the history books usually tell; but in the memoirs of the Russian Court, in the reports of Hudson Bay officials, and in the biographies of such American statesmen as Seward, Blaine and Franklin K. Lane, the inner and perhaps more interesting story may be read. The Russian Government initiated the matter and undoubtedly desired more earnestly to sell than the United States, deeply in debt after a long hard-fought war, desired to buy. But why did Russia wish to sell this hard-won province of Baranof? And why was the United States, even at bargain-sale prices, willing to pay out $7,200,000 in gold for another northwest, " a vast area of rocks and ice," when our nearer northwest was as yet undeveloped and gold was still at a high post-war premium? The answer is the old X to many a problem—" *Tertium quid.*"

Tsar Alexander was not only " stony broke " and wanted very much to sell something, to somebody, but he also mistrusted England. Might not this too-distant Asia-touching province of his be seized one day by England, from closely-adjoining Canada, and be used for a base against him as another Crimea? Having in mind a " Slavic drive to the south which might bring him again in collision with the Mistress of the Seas," why not turn a penny honestly, right now, in friendly barter with a friendly Uncle Sam, as Napoleon had done earlier with Louisiana, rather than run the risk of having the goods taken later, willy-nilly? The gold rush of '49 had brought to the Pacific coast of the United States and the British Canadian provinces a hardy pioneering people, and it became increasingly evident that the Russian Government must either invest a great deal more in its non-contiguous Alaskan province to hold it securely, or soon this might indeed become a British possession. Eyes were certainly being cast in that direction. Besides, the sea otter were going fast, were almost gone even then, as he well knew; and the Russian American Fur Company had already

fallen into the discard. And, too, Uncle Sam owed
Tsar Alexander a favor; and so Alexander would
put the matter up to him, and urge Stoeckl to push
it through before the British got wind of the affair.
Why not?

During the War Between the States just finished
there had been some very dark days for " Mr. Lincoln's Government," and one of the darkest clouds
always overhanging had been the lowering attitude
of Great Britain, complicated as it was by the close
contacts of many southern planters with England and
the close interweaving strands of King Cotton's kingdom of trade. In those very darkest hours, when we
were " enacting a history which no man yet thoroughly comprehends," and when the North had need
of friends as seldom before, a strange partnership of
interests had led the Russian Tsar to send his fleet
on a mission of good cheer and encouragement, to
visit his democratic friend Uncle Sam; and British
sympathizers with the South, enthusiastic over the
success of the *Shenandoah,* had found their spirits
dampened by a simultaneous display of friendly
Russian men-of-war in New York Harbor and San
Francisco Bay. General Banks said: " Who knew
how many more there were on their voyage here?
From that hour France on the one hand and England on the other receded, and the American Government regained its position and power."

However, Alaska did not really cost $7,200,000
but only $1,400,000. Prior to the Civil War there
had been some dickering about a possible purchase
of Alaska. The British Hudson Bay Company
(backed by tremendous capital, the " Standard Oil "
of that day, a great trust to exploit natural resources)
had already leased the coastal strip for fur trade, and

for many years Great Britain had been coveting the Panhandle of Alaska. Both Russia and Uncle Sam knew this. What followed is described in his " Letters," by Franklin K. Lane, a war Secretary like Seward, but of our own day:

During the war the matter lay dormant. We had more territory than we could take care of. When England, however, began to manifest her friendly disposition toward the Confederacy, and we learned from Europe that England and France were carrying on negotiations for the recognition of the Southern States, and possibly of some manifestation by their fleets against the blockade which we had instituted (and which they claimed was not effective and merely a paper blockade), we looked about for a friend, and Russia was the only European country upon whose friendship we could rely. Thereupon Secretary Seward secured from Russia a demonstration, in American ports, of Russian friendship. Her ships of war sailed to both of our coasts, the Atlantic and Pacific, *with the understanding that the expense of this demonstration should be met by the United States, out of the contingent fund. It was to be a secret matter*.
The war came to a close, and immediately thereafter Lincoln was assassinated and the administration changed. It was not longer possible to pay for this demonstration, secretly, under the excuse of war, but a way was found for paying Russia through the purchase of Alaska. The warrant for *$1,400,000 was the warrant for the purchase of Alaska, the warrant for $5,800,000 was for Russia's expenses in her naval demonstration in our behalf;* but history only knows the fact that the United States paid $7,200,000 for this territory, which is now demonstrated to be one of the richest portions of the earth in mineral deposits.

And that is how the Bear Cub became a ward of Uncle Sam, and that is how Uncle Sam showed his gratitude for Russia's once friendly turn. Then it could not be told, nor yet for years thereafter; but Sumner and Seward knew, and Sumner and Seward pushed the purchase with all the might of two dominant personalities. Through them Uncle Sam was able to keep his gentleman's agreement and save the honor of his word. He handed Russia the seven millions—and none too gracefully accepted title to "Seward's Folly," "Walrussia." Thirty years of neglect followed, and then a leaky wooden tramp steamer came limping into that sawmill town of Seattle,—which now, thanks in good part to Alaskan exports, is the commercial metropolis of the Northwest,—and the wires of the world hummed to an electric word, "Gold!" But not until George Carmack and Indian Kate went fishing that day up Klondike River did Uncle Sam do anything but wish himself well rid of "a bad bargain."

Of those thirty years I shall say nothing, for there is nothing to say which any sensitive American can read with pride. Our Government having made a bargain, as it were against its will, promptly forgot about Alaska. Worse than nothing was done to build a stable government here, and the land sank back far beyond the point to which Baranof had raised it by his energy and thrift. The best we can do is to pass quickly over those years, remembering only, when we weigh Alaska in any balance, that *nothing Uncle Sam can do to-day to open up the North generously and sanely can over-compensate for that critical period of slight and neglect,* at the time when the new land most needed help and guidance. Alaska is young, but in her formative years she had no friend at all, and even her legal guardian forsook her. Heaven was still very high,

Alaskans found, and Washington was quite as far away as ever St. Petersburg had been. "Then was then and now is now; but hungry generations cry out for the same liberties and against the same restraints, nor will they be put off with soft answers —and hard taxes!" Accustomed to the liberties and privileges of citizens of the United States, American residents in Alaska were very naturally discontented with being a "crown colony" and wished "dominion status." The only excuse for this great sin of listlessness on the part of our government was that successive Washington administrations were passing through their own Tragic Era of reconstruction in the South, with all the complex attendant problems. These were for Alaskans "the years that the Locust hath eaten."

Presidential messages were sent to Congress each year, drawing attention to the fact that Alaska had not yet been granted the protection and civil rights guaranteed in the treaty with Russia. Innumerable petitions were forwarded from the new Northwest. Over thirty bills were drafted in Congress to give a civil form of government to Alaska, but with no result. In 1882 American colonists threatened to unite their cause with that of the Russians who had remained, and make an appeal to the Tsar. Since Uncle Sam had just severely lectured several foreign governments for their failure to protect the Jews, Armenians and other dwellers within their borders, undoubtedly the Tsar, if anywise human, would have relished a chance to memorialize our government on similar subjects.

So, in 1884, a bill providing civil government for "The District of Alaska" was finally enacted into law, and Alaska later became a Territory with the

passage in 1912 of what is known as the Organic
Act. The people of the Territory had no representation in the National Legislative body until 1906
(nor does this delegate have a *vote* to-day) and no
local self-government of any kind until 1912, when
an elective legislative assembly, but with stout strings
running back to Washington, was authorized by
Congress. Only this legislative department, however, is under the control of the people of Alaska,
and then only in the matter of selecting the members. All *acts* of the Alaska legislature are subject
to veto by the Governor (who is appointed by the
President, as New England's colonial Governors
were appointed by the King) or to nullification by
Congress. We have here, you see, the old, old question of popular assemblies and royal governors. No
governor of Alaska has been or can be really " popular " until he is elected by popular vote, and, as in
the days of Andros, the people have " caught at
everything to lessen the prerogative." We American citizens of Alaska are not yet considered to be
of age; we are held as wards in chancery.

And yet, with the stores of Uncle Sam's resources
belowstairs, that once seemed limitless, now beginning to be numbered, he may well soon turn his eyes
with a quite different look up to his well-stocked
attic. As Burke once said, moving for conciliation
with another too-lightly-prized colony, who knows
but that, with suitable nurture and in suitable time,
" This child of your old age . . . with a true
filial piety, with a Roman charity . . . may put
the full breast of its youthful exuberance to the
mouth of its exhausted parent? "

XX

The Glint of Ancient Bronze

WE have, so far, only glanced at the most obvious of all the parallels between early colonial days in Alaska and in New England—the fact that early discoverers, fur traders and later colonists upon both the Atlantic and Pacific coasts had to deal, not with an empty and unpeopled continent but with one already inhabited, though not by any means "settled" in our Saxon sense. In both cases the real work of extending the frontier was not a mere peaceful penetration into an untenanted "wilderness." First comers found a proud and independent native people, with whom they must contend for possession of the land.

As in all eastern colonial narrative, so also in Alaska, the ofttimes tragic mask of the Indian, cast from the native matrix of the soil, emerges out of the dramatic background of old stories as a picturesque element, of some interest to travellers and students but too little considered by his white neighbors. His villages are practically all separate, his mode of life demands seasonal migration to summer fish camp and winter trap line. As the white men came in increasing numbers, both in New England and in Alaska, a desire for expansion back into the continent and a desire for village sites at favorable bays and river outlets naturally led settlers to adopt a more and more aggressive attitude toward the natives. But the natives were few in number when spread upon the vastness of this terrain, and after the first few years their influence upon the whites became almost negligible because there were so few real points of contact between them. Their modes of life, their thoughts, their customs and aims were far apart, their plane of living was dissimilar, their roots twisted back into a very different soil. But in the early days, "as friend or spying enemy," James Truslow Adams says, "he was constantly in and out of the little villages as he is of the pages of the early records. Although there was, unluckily, little that the white man could teach him that was of any service, he, on the contrary, taught the colonists many a useful lesson. He showed them how and when to plant, trapped their game and gathered in their stock of furs, guided them through the almost trackless forest, and in a multitude of ways gave them knowledge of the land which they had entered and of the products it might yield." We read a great deal in history about Indian Wars, but we don't read half enough about Indian help and friendliness.

But cruelty and misunderstanding developed cruelty and misunderstanding here, as in New England. For twenty years after Bering's first discoveries the fur hunters treated the natives to extremes of torture that proved "bloody instructions, which being taught return to plague the inventor." Moving along the coast, from the first contact with the Aleuts to their next contact with the Thlingits and Haidas, the Russians found themselves facing a warlike people, capable of swift, vengeful and concerted action. There were reprisals and counter reprisals, just as in our eastern Indian wars. When the United States bought Alaska, the land was looked upon in governmental circles merely as another Indian Ter-

ritory. In spite of Sumner's high-sounding words
in the Senate about the great blessing we were about
to confer upon this God-forsaken country by extending to it our mild laws, no laws at all were enacted!
The United States *Army* took over Alaska from
Russia, ran up our flag, received the keys, and remained in nominal charge until 1870. "The with-
drawal of the remaining soldiers in 1877," says an
official report, "was regarded by the few white residents of Alaska as a boon, especially to the native
population who had suffered in many ways because
of their presence." From '77 to '79 there was no
government of any description in Alaska, but late in
'78 trouble arose in Sitka between whites and the
Sitka and Hoonah Thlingits, who outnumbered the
settlers three to one. Notice of serious impending
trouble was sent to Washington but brought no
response; so an urgent appeal for help on behalf of
the whites was made to the British Admiral at Victoria, who dispatched the *Osprey* at once, and probably by his swift action prevented the total destruc-
tion of Baranof's once proud little city. In April
'79 came our own *Alaska,* and later the *Jamestown*
under Captain Beardslee; and the *Jamestown was*
the United States in this territory during the stirring
period of Joe Juneau's gold strike. One lone naval
officer was all Alaska knew of U. S. government
until 1884.

When Washington was yet a territory, with General Nelson A. Miles commanding The Department
of the Columbia, " in view of the fact that so little
is known of the interior of the territory of Alaska,
and that the conflicting interests between the white
people and the Indians of the territory may in the
near future result in serious disturbances between

the two races," Lieutenant Allen was dispatched on his quest into the inner land to learn:

especially their disposition toward the Russian Government in the past and toward the United States Government in the past and at the present time, and toward the whites who are making their way into that region. You will further examine their (Indian) modes of life and their ways of communication from one part of the country to another, the amount and kinds of *material of war* in their possession, and from whence obtained. You will further obtain such information as may be practicable as to the character of the country or means of using and sustaining a *military force, if one should be needed in the territory* . . . and any other information which would be important and valuable to the *military service.* . . . In no case will you move in any section of the country where you cannot go without provoking *hostilities* or inciting natives to resistance.

Back of the cold and formal diction of this military order one senses the lurking danger, the copper blade pointed at this " distant and uncertain expedition." And small wonder, when no less than three Russian parties had been slain when setting out upon a similar investigation.

The Tánana Indians of the Interior had a bad reputation even among neighbor tribes. In 1882 Mr. Simms, the missionary, had started with a few natives up the Tánana in a canoe but had got no further than the mouth of the Kantishna, for the Yukon natives, through fear of the Tananatánas, had refused to go further. In 1883 Schwatka had heard from the upper Yukon that Tánana Indians were great fighters, were always opposed to any travel through their country, and were determined that no whites should ever enter their hunting grounds.

From all they had heard and seen, they certainly
hadn't a good report of the Russians—and how were
they to know in what ways "the Boston men" dif-
fered from those of Baranof? Allen tells again and
again in his account, of how very proud and sus-
picious the Inner Indians were in act, how scornful
of his trials, his ignorance of the country. Allen
succeeded in his quest, but the natives were not at
all impressed by any majesty of the United States,
through the efforts of his ragged struggling party.
As one native said, of the first United States official
whom he saw and who proved an unskilful cook,
"Why, the United States doesn't even know how to
bake biscuits!"

Geographically speaking, there are four quite distinct native peoples in Alaska, inhabiting our four
major land divisions; and these native peoples have
evidently come at different times with different back-
grounds, and have reacted differently to white in-
cursion and settlement. The first group, composed
of Thlingits, Haidas and Tsimpseans, all live in
Southeastern Alaska, though they are distinct tribes
linguistically speaking. The Tsimpseans (who
emigrated from British Columbia with Father Duncan, that strange Yorkshire apostle to the natives)
are settled farthest south at Metlakatla. Next to the
north are the 500 Haidas, with only two towns,
Kasaan and Hydaburg. The Thlingits beyond and
around them are by far the most numerous of these
Southeasterners, 4,000 in the last census, and have
their villages at Yakutat, Klukwan, Haines, Juneau,
Douglas, Hoonah, Sitka, Angoon, Killisnoo, Kake,
Wrangell, Klawock, Ketchikan, and Saxman, all
Thlingits talking the same language but each town
keeping a different accent. This group occupies the

section roughly corresponding to Alaska's First Judicial Division.

The Eskimos occupy the far north and northwest and are more numerous than all the Indians put together. This section comprises most of Alaska's Second Division. Then there are Aleuts, from Controller Bay across to the furthermost western island touching Russia; and most of our Fourth Division or Interior Indians are Athapaskan "Tinneh," (or "Taná"—the word is variously spelled) to the number of about 5,000. So you will see that we can no more speak about the natives of Alaska as one simple unit or question than we can speak so of the country's climate or white people. All combined, the native races form a little less than half of Alaska's present total population.

Whence did the Indians come? Some say from the South Seas. One scientist has pointed out that there is a marked resemblance between them and the Maoris, others a similarity between them and the Hawaiians. Some say they were first driven out on the Aleutian Islands by Mongol invasions. Another says, "There is no doubt in my mind that the first emigrants crossed to America from Asia." The Tsimpseans have a flood legend and tell that before the flood they lived in "a beautiful country with lovely sunshine, large trees, and gorgeous flowers." Everything they say about it sounds as though they were describing a tropical Pacific Island, and some of their strange totem birds are said to have South Sea cousins. A friend, who is herself an officer of our Alaska Chapter of the D. A. R. and a *Mayflower* descendant, is married to one of the outstanding leaders of the Alaska Native Brotherhood, William Paul, the attorney of Ketchikan. She writes:

I am not prepared to say with any authority where these people came from, racially. Certain ones clearly have the almond eyes and other facial characteristics of the Oriental; but in the cases that I have investigated, these can easily be explained by a more or less recent admixture with outside peoples. It is quite within reason that many Mongolians have been blown or drifted across the ocean. On the other hand, most of the high-caste families, which are likely to be pure blood, show almost a Greek profile, a clean-cut, beautiful grouping of features. Their own legends tell of many days marching across the tall grass; then there is the story among the Wrangell people of having come from under the Stikine Glacier; the main Wrangell family has a name that arose from the camp that was made after this migration, " the upland owners," while another group took the name of "outside owners," and the family name appears in Tongass (Ketchikan), Sitka, Hoonah and Chilkat. There is a great deal of white intermixture all over southeastern Alaska. Among the Haidas there are many bright red heads. How far back this mixture began I am unable to say; but it is a long way, because I have been told that in the ancient graves on the Queen Charlotte Islands, from which the Haidas originally came, long since deserted, the skulls have red hair. Among the Tsimpseans there is quite a bit of curly hair. Of course, in this modern day, there are some red heads produced by henna! There seems to be no history of a longer subjugated people; that is, their legends tell of no people already occupying the land when they came into it.

These folk had a patriarchal system, that is, each village did not have a head chief except in time of war, when some chief (in Wrangell Chief Shakes, one of the Nani-ayi family) led them to battle. Otherwise each family was a unit to itself, in its own community house, and the father of the family was the chief. When he died, the name and title and property descended to his sister's son. These family chiefs owned everything; all the young men trapped and hunted and fished and turned over everything to the chief, and it was his duty to guard the family honor. When the house became too crowded, some young man would build another, retaining his family name, and in time new families were originated in that way. In fact, that is how William Paul's family got their name. They really belong to the Kiks-uddy family which has branches in many towns, but long ago there was a quarrel over a woman, and a part of the family moved out and built themselves temporary quarters of cedar bark, hence Tee (cedar) -Hit (house) -Ton (town), now shortened to Tee-ton.

The names stay within the family, and all within the family are of equal caste, although if they do something to disgrace the name they then become out-cast. There seem to be some families that are low caste just for the same reason that some white people are low in the social scale—too shiftless or feckless to work for either financial security or honor! The villages located on the trade routes and near the fur supply were the strongest, most feared and most honored—Sitka and Hoonah on the coast, due to fur-seal migrations; and Chilkat, Taku and Wrangell on the rivers. Certain families in each village had the " big " names, some of the family names like Kok-won-tons, Kiks-uddy, Kuck-la-wady being present in many villages. There were other villages where there were no high-caste families, and these were looked down upon by the entire district.

There is considerable Russian intermixture at Sitka and Juneau and Hoonah, and in fact quite a large percentage of natives now living near old Russian settlements show traces of this ancestry. For, while it was distinctly to the interest of the Russ in Alaska, as to the French in Canada, that the Indian remain in his original hunter state, both French and Russian accepted the Indian as he was and intermarried freely. The French and Russians had none of that racial contempt for " the heathen and the savage," which Saxon settlers so often showed both here and in New England—especially when the Indian " possessed lands coveted by the Saints of God! " In New England, the Fathers stoutly pushed out a dozen or so stiff Old Testament texts to hide behind, in warring with their tribal adversaries; but to-day (as recently in Fairbanks) a citizen merely says, "I refuse to serve on a committee with a native! "

When the early fear of the " savages " passed, dealings with them gradually sank to a lower ethical plane. Indians in Alaska to-day (except for Metlakatla) hold their land under the Act of Congress which says that Indians and others in the Territory shall not be disturbed in the possession or occupation of land used or claimed by them, but that the means of acquiring *title* shall be left for future legislation. As regards Indians, that legislation has just been passed in the last year or two; so that in all the original Indian towns there are certain tracts of land which are called Indian lands, but are not yet subdivided into lots. The only evidence of ownership is the building and fences. When an Indian family living next to a white man comes back from a summer's work at the cannery or a winter's trapping, it is a common thing to find that their fence has moved over a foot or two; there are instances where fifteen and twenty feet have been stolen in small lots that way. These petty injustices are very common, and that is why the Native Brotherhood in Alaska have worked so hard to secure the right to hold deeds to their houses and lots, as well as full-time schools for their children, abolishment of the fish-trap, and the right to vote as citizens. Some of these questions are now partly solved for them.

More and more the intelligent natives come to realize that the white man will never think as they do, and therefore it is necessary for them to think as white men and act as white men, if the two peoples are to remain side by side in the same wide land. Otherwise, the Indian will remain a copper-tinted, sometimes lurid, slowly-fading background to the Alaskan story, as he was in that of New England. The Northwest Indian has always been a good trader, and he is willing to buy to-day the white man's best. Perhaps he asks too much when he asks for justice. Who knows? Of New England's founding it is said:

To have expected sympathy, understanding and justice in the situation as it developed in the seventeenth century, is asking too much, both of human nature and of the period. Indeed, it is questionable whether, in the competition between races of higher and lower civilization, when the former intrude upon the lands of the latter, justice in its strictest sense is ever possible.

If we truly wish to Americanize the Alaska Indians, then we must realize that to steal from helpless wards is unfair and that such dishonesty always reacts. And we have stolen—a nibble here, a nibble there—whenever we wanted what he had. We could do it because he hadn't a political organiza-

tion sufficiently strong for social defense, or an
economic ability developed along lines that could
compete favorably with ours. We destroyed caribou
and seals and sea otters and whales, we brought the
liquor traffic to him and the " flu." As the Turk
said when reproached about the decimation of the
Armenian race, *"Where* are the American Indians? "

In Alaska, Indians to-day have rights as citizens
only when they give up all tribal customs and merge
with the body politic. Otherwise they are wards,
without any rights. The Government by this policy
has asked the natives to give up everything they have
previously held precious, and "put in" with us.
Can we blame them if more and more they are looking to this method as the only real solution of their
problems, since only so can their voice be heard?
In 1929 at Klawock, for the first time in the history
of Alaska, an Indian community has undertaken to
organize a legal municipal government.

What are the "tribal customs" our Alaskan Indians are being asked to give up in order to become
American citizens, and what survival value have
these customs? Like many of our own, some are
excellent and some are not so good; and as among
our white selves, there are some still backward communities and some very far advanced in civilization
and outlook.

The Indian has traditional communal ideas of real
estate very different from ours—ideas which he has
tried to hold, but cannot any longer against the white
man's fixed laws. In early days white men "bought"
Indian sites, such as Manhattan, for a few trinkets.
Of course the Indians did not know what they were
doing, because they themselves had no system of

deeds or real property transfer; and so the parchments to which they put their mark were "as ethically invalid as a child's sale of his inheritance for a stick of candy!"

Slavery was perhaps the worst of the old customs, but slavery is something we ourselves gave up not so very long ago. In fact, Lady Simon in her authoritative book published in 1929, states that there are over four million slaves in the world, this moment! Lieutenant Allen found slavery still practiced among the Indians of the Copper River as late as '85, but slavery among the Southeastern natives had generally ceased by 1890, and the last authentic case of which I have any knowledge was brought to light in 1898. Slaves were acquired either in war or by purchase, but mostly by raids to the south. That is why a Thlingit sees red when he is called a Siwash! " Siwashes " to the Thlingits were merely the Flathead slaves they got in raids. These slaves were not badly treated, came and went with perfect freedom, hunted and fished. But—in the feasts incident to totem-pole raising or the building of a new community house, the builder acquired honor in proportion to the number of slaves he could afford to sacrifice, and they were dropped (sometimes alive) into the hole in which the totem pole or the corner posts of the house were placed. Sometimes slaves were ransomed, sometimes they escaped without ransom. In the latter case the "unredeemed name" follows down to his descendants, who conceivably may not know their ancestor's history. On one occasion a rather prominent man in another village made an insulting remark about William Paul (or Shgindy, his Indian name) which his stepfather overheard.

" Long ago," he said, simply but with profound effect, " Shgindy's grandfather had a slave, and that slave's name was the same as *your* name.   He ran away, but he never redeemed his honor by sending back the ransom."—And that closed the incident decisively!

Father Jetté of Tánana, that ripe old scholar descended from a noble French family of Quebec, has commented at length upon the absolute democracy of the Athapascan Tinneh, our Interior Indians of Alaska.   He found in his long life-work here, both as priest and ethnologist, that "public opinion alone governed."   Among the southeastern tribes there is a very rigid and extensive caste system based both upon family prestige and personality.   Frances Paul tells me:

" One has to be born high caste, but he has also to achieve it.   The oldest son of a man's sister was his heir, as a usual thing; but if a younger nephew displayed more ability, he became by common consent the heir to the name and property.   One of the big reasons for a so-called potlatch was to elevate such heirs to their caste; it was the custom to pierce the ear for each feast, and my husband's father had four holes in his ear, representing four feasts his mother's father gave before he reached an age to put a stop to it.   This grandfather gave twelve feasts in all. High-caste children could marry only within their caste; for that reason most families are related all through the villages, in the search to find a husband or wife of equal caste.

" A low-caste family might originate from the marriage of a slave into even a high-caste family; that did not elevate the slave, but lowered the high caste."

This constant stress upon the stain of serfdom, upon blood, rank, achievement, and family honor, in all the Indian tales I've heard, reminds me of nothing quite so much as the purely personal aspects of our own early Frankish days of feudalism, developed in the Dark and Middle Ages of Europe. These people have known a somewhat similar social system, the two great differences being that serfs or slaves did not belong to the land here, and that descent among the Indians was traced back on the *mother's* side, interminably, instead of through the father's family.

A chief among the Indians does not inherit his position. It comes by merit, as he exhibits qualities of distinction, and discernment and good sense are his best qualifications for office. I have heard a story of a chief who took two missionaries, with his own leading villagers, to a great council. On the return trip the war canoe with thirty-five men in it began to labor in the heavy sea. One little missionary weighing only about a hundred pounds, sitting in the bow, called to the other, a man weighing over two hundred seated in the stern, to pray. The Indian chief raised his paddle in the air—the signal to wait—and cried out: "*You* pray! *Big* man *paddle!*"—There's real leadership for you.

The illicit liquor of the natives is known as hootchinoo, and it and its effects are not to be trusted, for white men who sample it call the stuff "volcano juice!" But in judging the matter of contraband trade here, we whites have not a very clear record ourselves. Medicine men and witchcraft are other phases of the "old customs" which, with slavery, it is well to see pass, for much of this was bigoted and cruel.

These people carry far in totem symbol their conviction of a life in all nature. Like the Egyptians, the Indian seems to brood a great deal upon a future existence and takes great interest in genealogy, to which he erects his totems crowned first of all with the symbol of his mother's family. I have myself an Indian charm which I greatly prize, given me by a very ancient Indian woman of Fairbanks, one of the wisest and kindliest of friends. I was starting on a long journey and " Grandma " came to me, bent and brown, and put a little package in my hand.

"You keep him. You good girl. You come back."

"What is it, Grandma? " I asked, looking down curiously at the beaded strip of moose hide, fringed at one end and in the other end an insert of a worn, stained, crooked tooth. "What is this tooth, and why shall I come back if I take it? Is it a story of your people? Tell me."

My old friend did not usually speak of her people's ancient beliefs, for they are very sacred to her. But the moment was pregnant, since we were parting for no one knew how long and we had been fast friends. After a hesitation, at last she said: " My mother give him. My mother mother give him. Long time. Maybe before Russ man come. He one porcupine tooth. Porcupine always take care himself, even with big brown bear. You take him, you take care self, even with big brown bear. You come back."

When people tell me there's no warmth of friendship possible between white and red, I open up my treasure chest and show them Grandma's precious token. I think a porcupine tooth is a better " luck charm " than a rabbit's foot, for rabbits run away from "big brown bear"—but a "porky" always puts up a fight! I think there's better fortune in bristling than in running.

The Indians all over Alaska are great sticklers for etiquette, and everything must be done according to form and custom, with all the proper observance. Only those who know and follow this, get on well with natives. "Face" is as important to an Indian as to an Oriental, and must be saved at any cost. One of the most characteristic old customs is the potlatch, which the missionaries are trying hard to abolish, for they say it needlessly impoverishes the natives. But the custom is rooted very deep and is not likely soon to pass.

Thrift—the disposition to lay up to-day for to-morrow's necessity—seems to be a very late trait to develop in human consciousness, and many of the most sophisticated members of white nations are still quite as incapable of real thrift as are the Tánana Indians! The desire to possess only that one may give away, can still be found among these primitive people, and by potlatch they dispose of excess possessions. It's a Carnegie-like plan, to win praise for themselves and escape the cares of too much wealth, in one magnificent gesture. And yet we praise the canny Andrew but blame the poor Indian. Pride in the ability to give back even more to his people than he has received, can still be seen in the native potlatch. These folk are stone-age communists and practice religiously the old group-pattern which they preach, and there is no article of our Christian faith these Indians can better understand than that "it is more blessed to give than to receive." The potlatch is a matter of pride, of saving face, of establishing prestige; and, because marriage is so strictly regulated among the Thlingits by totem, when William Paul's mother was brought back as a small baby from Victoria by *her* mother, a potlatch simply had to be given and a totem erected, " to wipe out the stain of having a *white* father."

Tattooing is a custom of the Haidas but is reserved for high caste, though it has been adopted by the Thlingits who live next to them; but the farther north one goes the less there is of this, and none, I believe, among the Chilkats. Tsimpsean women of rank used to wear a labrette of bone or shell, on dress occasions. For one does wrong to think of these people in their primitive state as continually taken up with the quest for food. Like the Eskimos, they kept themselves fed and sheltered (when their natural resources are not tampered with) and had plenty of time left for leisure and the arts—more time than we in our too busy civilization. Leisure time was taken up, as it should be, with social life and education—teaching taboo, folk way and legend to the younger generation—learning old tales of the supermen of their people, heroes, demons and gods. Drawing, etching, carving of totems and much decorating had to be done, for the totem mark must be on everything. Art, literature, and religion came close home and were very real, in the old tribal life.

Allen tells of the copper bullets of the Atná, their bows and arrows of " tempered " birch, all skilfully hand made; and I have a fine set of arrows done by Chief Thomas' son, with six different shapes of steel and bone heads for different purposes of killing or merely stunning. One finds silversmiths at Sitka, and coppersmiths among the Chilkats near Lynn Canal; and though there was no knowledge of metal tempering, they were good engravers. Before the white man came, copper was their main metal, as it was found in nuggets on the White and Copper Rivers or pried out of matrices. Long copper knives are still common along the Tánana, and are unpleasantly deadly. Embroidery with porcupine quills is an old, nearly a lost, art. The Chilkat blankets are as distinctive as the Navajo, but little known and rare. Made of the wool-like under fur of the all-white Rocky Mountain goat of Southeastern Alaska, they have something the effect of Navajo blankets in texture, but the color harmonies are entirely different, being black from hemlock, flat yellow from a lichen dye, and a pale bluish green from copper stain, the total result being grayish, soft and truly exquisite. Woven by slow laborious process on hand looms and with great ceremony—for it is a religious rite and one must fast for it—this art is rapidly passing with civilization, although a fairest flower of American life.

All over Alaska one may find fine basketry and wicker work, but from furthermost Attu of the Aleutian chain come the most lovely, rare, and sought-for of them all. Few of the old basket weavers are now left on Attu, for there is little food upon these treeless islands, and disease and semi-starvation have done the work which the Russians left off when they decimated the Aleuts. Made of the finest straw, woven in rich color, these Attu baskets are the gems of the collector's fancy; but few whites go so far to find them. For twice the Attu price you may pick up good baskets at Dutch Harbor, if you are lucky, when the Nome boat puts in. But by the time the few remaining baskets reach Southeastern Alaska and the tourist shops, you may have to pay as high as two hundred dollars for a fine

CHIEF THOMAS OF THE TÁNANA WITH HIS WIFE AND SON.

THE SON OF OUR TANANA CHIEF MAKES VERY FINE ARROWS.

Photograph by Fisher, Ketchikan.

ONE OF THE OLD BLOCK HOUSES BUILT IN
RUSSIAN DAYS.

A CACHE SET ON HIGH STILTS TO FOIL THE
THIEVING BEARS AND WOLVERINES.

specimen. But it will be well worth that, both in painstaking toil and in great rarity.

Yakutat baskets are done in slender spruce roots and vegetable dyed grasses so that, when old, genuine Yakutats take on a mellow and almost Etruscan color.

In Southeastern Alaska the women make a holiday picnic of root gathering for their baskets, taking a lunch along and all the children. The roots are peeled, scraped, boiled, and then left in water to soak, after which they are scraped with a clam shell until glossy and smooth. The Haidas make grass baskets and grass hats for dances and potlatch. The best Interior baskets are of birch bark, pliable and tough, the older ones embroidered in a solid design of porcupine quill, exceptionally fine. The Lower Yukon baskets are large and coarse, of salty sedges woven like raffia but serviceable, and often decorated with a dab of fur or with an animal tooth or bit of old ivory worked in as a handle. Such art-craft is a racial characteristic.

How much of all this native culture is to remain? Will the natives of Alaska acquire only useful white learning from us, such as the principles of correct food and sanitation? Or will they lose their own strong traits only to borrow of our worst and weakest? Will they attend our schools, for which they now are asking, only to come out of them listless, sullen, maladjusted to the world? Or will they really learn to become useful American citizens? Will they follow old chiefs in the old tribal potlatch way, or will they follow younger leaders into new and socially constructive ways? The Alaskan native is a primitive but not, to-day, a "savage" and ethnically his stock is high. Will the ownership of land, for which these people are so pathetically hungry, prove a blessing, or will all those past millennia of communal land-holding refuse to be abridged in one generation? Can the tribal mind take on the Saxon pattern, and if so, how and when? Or must it still be protected from its own inexperience? These are some of the problems which cast dark shadows into dusky corners of Uncle Sam's attic.

Let us open doors, let us encourage peculiar gifts and native crafts, let us tear down barriers of prejudice and old distrust. Above all, let a proud and highly-civilized people deal justly with a proud and primitive people, co-dwelling in our midst— deal justly both as a nation and as individuals. We are of a great brotherhood, a human brotherhood. We are blood brothers of the same wanderers' totem and clan. Is this Alaska ours, or is it theirs? Does it belong to both of us, or to whichever of us can use the land more justly? They came here, as did we, from another coast, the whence and where unknown. We know something of our own whence and where, but both of us as races are alike the guests of the Great Country. To earlier comers than ourselves we owe some courtesy, surely. To ourselves, as more advanced scholars in the school of civilization, we surely owe the dignity and courtliness of true *noblesse oblige.*

Alaska is to-day a white man's land and will be so, increasingly. But we must prove our right to it, as we must prove our whiteness, by our acts. If we talk white—but act yellow—then we shall lose our own just claim to go up and possess the Great Country.

XXI

Traps That Caught an Empire

THE first serious interest taken in Alaska concerned Alaska's fur; and just as John Smith's 1614 voyage and return with a profitable cargo of fish and furs gave title of New England to the northeastern wedge of America, so Bering's men, returning with sea-otter pelts, made Catherine claim her fur-piece in the northwest segment of the continent. Fish and furs still continue, and have long continued, two of the main sources of the Great Country's richness and revenue.

Fur trade in Alaska has been cut to the same pattern that determined the early chapters of New England and inner Canada. In 1600 Chauvin obtained exclusive rights to the fur trade in "The New Land"; in 1634 Nicolet the fur trader, under Champlain, worked his way up the Ottawa River and Great Lakes into Wisconsin. In 1670 Charles II granted a charter to Prince Rupert and seventeen other noblemen and gentlemen, incorporating them as the "Governor and Company of Adventurers of England Trading into Hudson's Bay," securing to them "the sole trade and commerce of all the seas, straits, bays, rivers, lakes, creeks and sounds, in whatsoever latitude they shall be, within the entrance of the straits," and with this grant went complete overlordship and entire legislative, judicial and executive control, within these vague limits. In almost the same words, more than a century later, Catherine

249

II by Imperial ukase gave a charter to the Shelikof-Golikof Company granting exclusive trade and exclusive control in the regions they already occupied, and in 1799 the feeble-minded Paul I created the Russian American Company, which owned Alaska and ran it as a great fur factory. Up to the purchase of Alaska and for more than thirty years thereafter, traffic in furs was the chief intent of the new territory. Mining was incidental, for Alaska's great mineral wealth was unguessed and unknown.

The Shelikof-Golikof Fur Company in Alaska was merged with several other independent companies and individuals who had been trading in the new world—"promyshleniki", Russian freebooters and *coureurs de bois* who hunted on their own account and at their own risk. Thus was formed a great monopoly like the Hudson Bay Company, with similar delegated military and civil powers in the colony. Several members of the Russian royal family, as well as the Imperial Government itself, were heavy shareholders, and this company held unbroken grip on Russian-American trade until just before Alaska's transfer. In sea otter Russia had found a fur precious enough to colonize a continent; for Alaska is a continent, as well as a peninsula—as Europe is a peninsula of Asia.

Several of Captain Cook's officers and men had traded trifles from their kits for sea-otter peltry, with the natives of Alaska. On their way home after his death they sold these skins in Canton for ten thousand dollars! The mandarins, too, for their state robes, as well as the fair Catherine, had a keen eye for the beauty of these exquisite seal-like pelts, with fur of silky wool that dropped so softly, dense, varying in color from pale gray and rich brown to deepest

A TRAPPER'S CABIN IN THE FAR-FLUNG FUR LAND.

THE GOVERNMENT FARM NEAR FAIRBANKS IS UNCLE SAM'S NORTH
WINDOW-BOX.

ON TRAIL FROM IDITROD TO ANCHORAGE, ALASKA.

DOG-POWER MAIL SERVICE WAS SLOW AND NOT ALWAYS SURE.

POTATO DIGGING AT HOLY CROSS MISSION LOOKS LIKE BRIGHT-
COLORED ITALY

black. Their heads were like sable caps of velvet,
when swimming, their fur was sprinkled unevenly
with frosty hairs in points, their pelage gleamed like
lustre of old silver upon antique bronze. News of
these fabulous Chinese prices went flying around the
world with Cook's far-sailing men, and Winship,
Cleveland and Rowan, Meares, Portlock and Dixon,
Quadra, Martinez and Caamaño,—" republicans of
Boston and America," as Baranof called them,
" King George men " as well as " Russ men," and
others under the Spanish, Swedish, French or Por-
tuguese flags—scoured these bays and inlets and
warped into every cove for the sea-beaver, *morskie
bobri,* most valuable fur in the world market. During the closing years of the eighteenth century and
the opening decade of the nineteenth, it is estimated
that from eight to ten thousand sea-otter skins were
taken to Asia each year from the southern waters of
Alaska. Hence—Baranof, the Iron Governor!

Under him, redoubts—odinátischka—were built,
and fleets of hundreds of bidarkas combed the
sounds. As the Russians said: " When the cod are
all gone from Archangel, then the *morskie bobri*
may go from Alaska." To-day, by federal law, no
sea-otter killing is permitted in Alaskan waters; but
to-day there are practically no sea otters left to kill.
I doubt if a hundred white inhabitants of Alaska
have seen a sea-otter pelt. I doubt if ten have seen
a live sea otter. The animal is almost extinct, thanks
to those bucko mates who " traded with cannon, shot-
ted with grape." Dr. Stellar, the ardent naturalist
who accompanied Bering, told that in his day " they
covered the shore in great droves. . . . We
killed upward of eight hundred of them, and if the
narrow limits of the craft we constructed had per-

mitted, we could have killed three times as many."
To-day the sea otter is a scattered fugitive and almost a myth, where once it was so thickly plentiful about the broken reefs and kelp patches. Sea otter was to the Russian Court what ermine has been to other princely European powers, and sea otter built the early Russian churches of Alaska. A single pelt has been sold for five thousand dollars, and sea otter provided the golden fleece of Alaska's first argonauts. For sea otter in early Alaska days took the place of beaver in the early Northwest, of sable in Siberia— "an immediate worth-while prize of trade and wealth."

The Alaskan Indians had not considered it highly, before the Russians came. They made some garments of its warm soft fur, but hair seal and sea lion had a better meat, and *their* hides were better raincoat material for the moist and drippy climate of the southern coast. But Catherine found the fur "monstrous becoming," and sea otter were soon rated at a premium above gold in Imperial taxes. To-day its pelt is truly more than worth its weight in gold, and you cannot walk into even the best of fur shops and say, "I'd like to see a sea-otter skin." If you do, they'll probably smile at you—and call the manager! The only pelts I've seen are either precious keepsakes of Russian émigrés, or dangerously poached and smuggled skins, two of which I was once shown in a lonely beach cabin of Alaska—behind locked doors, under a pledge of absolute secrecy.

For many years the transfer of Alaska to the United States merely changed commercial fur managers for the country. The Alaska Commercial Company secured a lease of the seal islands for twenty years, took over many of the old Russian-

American trading posts in middle and western Alaska, and continued the rule of fur, discouraging settlement by whites.

It is claimed that a hundred thousand seal skins were taken from the Pribilof group in a single year under this lease, and in 1885 Lieutenant Allen found that the Alaska Commercial Company was furnishing scattered traders on the Yukon with supplies at twenty-five per cent. above San Francisco prices and charging a fixed amount for transportation up the river. In return the traders must agree to transfer to the Company *all* furs they could obtain, and at prices about one half of the San Francisco prices. The Indians had to take out *their* price in trade, so that here again was handsome profit; and half-breed Russians, who could see how the natives were being cheated and overcharged, led frequent revolts. The whole western part of Alaska and the vast Interior were for long years under the thumb of a great monopoly which, as Father Kashevaroff says:

recognized no law but its own gain. . . . Volumes could be written about the abuses practiced, the oppression akin to slavery meted out to the natives and the people who came under its rule. The poor people, who heard of the transfer of the Territory to the United States and expected better conditions, were sorely disappointed. The first taskmasters under the Russian rule were unscrupulous in their treatment of the people under their control. Having come from the ranks of exiles, criminal and political prisoners, they knew no mercy to the weaker ones. They kept the people in ignorance and slavery. The second masters, the American monopoly under the guise of successors to the Russian Company, were very little better.

The fur seals which make their home on the

Pribilof Islands in Bering Sea belong to a species distinct from any other fur seal, and this Alaskan herd comprises, it is safe to say, ninety per cent. of all existing fur seal in the world. The number in the Pribilof herd when Alaska was purchased has been estimated at from two to five million. During a period of forty years, following upon 1870, the right to take fur-seal skins here was leased by the United States Government to a private corporation. Pelagic sealing, however, soon developed into such proportions and was pushed with such greed and lack of foresight that the very existence of the herd was threatened. It was evident that unless something very drastic was done, fur seals would go the way of sea otters and become practically extinct.

Four nations were interested, and for many years had been keenly interested, in the fur-seal industry and the very moot question of " pelagic sealing." This term, which has been the subject of such hot international dispute centering about Alaskan waters, should be defined, I think. " Pelagic " sealing means " the killing of seals *while they are in the water,*" and those familiar with Greek will recognize here the old root word meaning " open sea." While the United States permitted the killing of seals by its leasing company when the seals were on the islands for purposes of breeding, Great Britain, Russia and Japan had been killing seals in open Bering Sea and the North Pacific, where a large proportion of the animals killed were not secured, but lost. Also, when killed in the water, both males and females were taken, and this was economically wasteful. The young were born upon the Pribilofs, and remained there while the mother mammals went to sea, hunting for food. If the mother was killed while absent, the pup was left alone upon the islands to starve to death, and thousands of seal pups had been so starved to death there in a single season.   On the other hand, Sovereign Powers claimed their perfect right, under the law of nations, to hunt and kill seal *in the open sea*.

At the suggestion of Lord Salisbury each of the Powers concerned in this pelagic controversy named two arbiters, and the President of France, the King of Italy, and the King of Norway and Sweden each named one.   The sittings of the tribunal began in Paris in 1893, and the United States argued here that:

Seals had some of the characteristics of domestic animals, and could therefore be the subject of something in the nature of a right of property.   They were so far amenable to human control that it was possible to take their increase without destroying the stock.   Sealing upon the land was legitimate sealing, and the United States being the owners of the land, the industry was a trust vested in them for the benefit of mankind.   On the other hand, pelagic sealing, being a method of promiscuous slaughter, was illegitimate; it was *contra bonos mores* and analagous to piracy.   Consequently the United States claimed a right to restrain such practices, both as proprietors of the seals and as proprietors and trustees of the legitimate industry.

The final result of this discussion was a four-power treaty, entered into between the United States, Great Britain, Russia and Japan, entirely prohibiting pelagic sealing in the North Pacific and Bering Sea. When the second sealing lease expired in 1910, the United States Government itself took over the entire management of the sealing industry on the Pribilof Islands.   The size of the herd has now increased to nearly a million head once more, only three-year-old males of the best fur-bearing age are killed, and then only at the most favorable time of year. A quarter million skins have already been sold by Uncle Sam himself at the St. Louis fur market, and the profits turned into the United States Treasury—a certain fraction of this sum being divided between Japan and Great Britain to compensate them for their "hands off" agreement. The only open-sea hunters now allowed are the Pacific Coast natives, who are permitted by the treaty to "carry on pelagic sealing in canoes or undecked boats propelled wholly by paddles, oars or sails, and not transported by or used in connection with other vessels, and manned by not more than five persons each, *in the way hitherto practiced* by the said Indians, Aleuts, or other aborigines, and *without the use of firearms."*

The Pribilofs are the natural chosen breeding grounds of the fur-seal herds, and here each summer their young are born. After the breeding season is over, the seals leave the islands in the fall on their annual sea migration, going south—some as far as southern California. The fur seal is a strong believer in polygamy, and the breeding males are huge, five hundred pounds in weight, while the cows average less than ninety pounds. As the males do not breed until they are seven or eight years old, and the females bear their first pups when they are but three years old, it is easy to see that it is a great saving of animal life, and a very simple matter when regulated, to select the animals that are to be killed from the young male seals, which do not associate with the breeding animals but keep to themselves in care-free bachelor groups in separate parts of the islands.

The adult animals are of a grayish-brown color, but the new-born pups are jet black and do not turn grayish until after they take their first swimming lesson, when about six weeks old. They grow so rapidly, however, that they are well able to leave the islands in the fall with the older seals, on their going-south journey. Strangely, the only place in Alaska where the fur-seal herd ever comes ashore is on these Pribilof Islands. Between times they ply the North Pacific sea-lanes. In early summer, about a month before the cows come north, the males proceed to the fog-shrouded breeding islands, where each bull seal establishes his plot of land, much as settlers did in the famous land-rushes of the West. He squats on it, and he fights for it! Free-for-all scrimmages and torn and ruined pelts are the order of the day, just as soon as the cow seals begin to appear, and for this reason the skin of an old bull seal is worthless as fur.

A harem selected, fought for, and established, housekeeping is next set up, pups are born, are fed, and the youngsters taught to swim. This takes all summer, and all this time the young bachelor crowd are kept jealously sequestered to one side, where they spend their days in light-hearted sports, tumbling, flipper-cuffing, and fancy diving. Their healthy youth, their fine fur all unblemished of scars, one hapless day will bring a swift tap on the head by Uncle Sam's own agent, and soon you or I have a lustrous coat, made of eight or ten of him—a fur that will stand wear and tear, year in and year out, and a more permanent investment than is almost any other pelage. After the skins are removed they are preserved in salt; and when thoroughly cured, they are packed in barrels and shipped to the public fur auctions where, before sale, they are dressed, dyed, and prepared for making into fine garments. More than a hundred distinct processes are used in treating each pelt, and the *least* time required is two months, so that the result, which perhaps seems costly, is a dressed skin of the greatest beauty and durability. Many of the processes and formulas involved in dressing, dyeing, and machining the skins are closely-guarded trade secrets, and only a very few groups of fur-workers in all the world know how to handle these pelts in the way which best brings out their remarkable qualities. The fur is dyed either a black or the now more fashionable (as it was in my mother's girlhood days!) log-wood brown, *" Bois de Campêche."*

To many people Alaska is still looked upon as a vast fur farm (which it is—though it is so much more), and as most of my friends who have visited me in Alaska have asked first about the typical Alaska furs and how to select them, I'll suggest a few of the most distinctive skins to be sought in the Great Country. Each type has special qualities, for service or beauty, which sometimes only the experienced fur-wise person realizes.

Climbing partly out from the water on Alaska's fur scale we come to muskrat, or " musquash," as the English people prefer to call this hard-service, relatively durable fur. Only far northern " rats " have the deepest, glossiest coats, southern rats are far less beautiful in pelage color, and western rats do not wear so well, I'm told. Assure yourself, if possible, that you have true northern skins before you invest in a muskrat coat. I have one that I have worn continuously each winter for twenty years, and recently I was offered more than I paid for it originally—which goes to prove that in selecting furs it pays to buy only the very best. The compact body of the muskrat in his native northern haunt is completely covered with a dense, soft, gray under-fur, guarded by shiny, long and dark brown water-hairs. Pluck those long guard-hairs, shear the under fur evenly, dye it black, and you have " Hudson seal "— but a less durable fur than true sealskin. The muskrat will never be found far from water, and many a distant corner of Alaskan forest echoes to his splash as, with a leap and fling, his flat scaly tail strikes upon the stream.

The water-hairs of beaver are either cut level with the rest of the fur (unplucked) or entirely removed (plucked beaver). Here is an extremely durable fur, heavy-skinned and long-wearing like all aquatic pelage. Deeply-furred pelts are most prized, and such are found in this far corner of Uncle Sam's attic, for they are evidence of hard winters sturdily survived. You would expect " the engineer " to have a well-built double-service coat, as well as his cunningly contrived two-story house, and these he surely has.

Land otter is another far northern fur, and common land otter—as distinct from the rare and costly sea otter—is found all over Alaska except on the extreme north and west coasts. He, too, prefers a combination of timber and stream. With a rather large skin, of dark and richly glossy dense brown fur, he has a deep layer of fat under that strong hide which feeds the thick pelt and also protects him from the cold when swimming in his ice-cold waterways. A handsome, sportive fisherman is Otter—" The joyful, keen, and fearless otter "—with a sturdy gentlemanly pelage, extremely durable.

Fox ranching is the latest game in Alaska, and white ("Arctic"), blue, red, cross, black and silver are all to be found here. The fox farmer can have no close neighbors, however, and if he has not an island all his own he must go to the expense of putting up costly woven-wire fences, that must go down as well as up, for " foxes have holes! " In general, the colder the climate the longer and denser the fur, and Alaskan foxes are also said to be the largest in the world.

The lovely red fox wears all the colors of burning autumn on his coat—yellow and orange, red and brown, black on leg and white on big fine tip of brush. Aside from the special white and blue fox, any fox not actually red or black (silver) is a " cross fox," and a fine cross can be a superb pelage of softly blended color. Prime silver or black foxes are next to sea otter in pelt value, and while $2,625 is a record price for a black pelt, $34,000 is said to have been paid for a live pair destined for fox farming. Foxes are always fashionable fur, for if the tan shades are being worn, then red and cross and beige-dyed Arctic are the rage; while if blue and gray and black are reigning colors, then Arctic, blue (real or taupe-dyed), silver or black foxes will be desired. Fox fur is fragile, because the long guard-hairs are brittle and easily broken. The further north you go, the larger grows the brush which Reynard tucks about his nose and pads at night when he curls down to sleep, and his coat, too, is developed by the cold.

The Alaska fox is clever, but another Alaskan animal is the very symbol of alert observation. The most beautiful building in Washington (a city of beautiful buildings) is, to my mind, The National Academy of Science, a subtle harmony of white marble and eruginous green. In deep relief about this building, composing the copper *chéneau,* are figures of the owl of Minerva typifying wisdom, and of the lynx, symbol of that sharp-eyed observation so necessary for scientific research. Alaskan lynx carries a very lovely robe indeed, and seems to me the finest of Alaska's furs for tailors' uses. Some dye it black to imitate black fox, but its natural soft tones are so beautifully blended and harmonize so graciously with almost any color, that to dye this fine northern species of lynx seems to fur lovers a crime. Lynx is found all over Alaska, except in the extreme west. He is catlike, soft and furry, is very large, and his enormous feet are really snowshoes, packed with hairs between the pads. His ears are marvelously pricked and high-tufted, and he wears a stately bib of long white fur under his throat, and very feline whiskers! Fine lynx is a pelage long neglected in the fur markets, but now fast becoming justly popular.

Wolverine is an Alaskan fur animal of extraordinary power for his size, a small bear in vigor and intelligence but far more "ornery" in disposition! He is truly the scavenger of the North, "the glutton," following bears and wolves to eat their table leavings. Fine wolverine fur is blackish brown, with paler brown bands that begin at the shoulders and meet on the tail, skunk fashion, making a striking design. Seemingly this fur never wears out, and in my opinion it is fully as beautiful as most fox pelts. He is a tireless ranger, can live on one good meal a week, and, say old hunters, "a mother bear *may* attack, a mother wolverine *will!*" A wolverine will attack anything, of any size, and "lick its weight in wildcats!" Wolverine is found ranging the entire

mainland of Alaska, wherever stands of spruce timber are found. He is a difficult beast to trap, a terrible camp robber, "devilishly clever," "a pest."
Trappers hate him, for he ravages their trap lines.

But Eskimo women prefer wolverine above every
other fur, for it is the only fur, they say, which will
not frost with moisture from the breath. Wood-
brown wolverine frames becomingly the copper faces
of all Alaska's Eskimos, within their handsome
parka hoods; and Muk-pi's necessity is the luxury of
Fifth Avenue, for I have seen stunning wolverine-
trimmed coats in the windows of the very finest shops
there.

As we approach the aristocrats of furdom, surely
mink must be considered first—generation-wearing,
always coveted by fashion. Fur workers call it "an
honest fur," for its life and quality are long. Fur
trappers call it "dependable," for there is always a
ready and eager market for fine dark mink skins.
One of my trapper friends said to me not long ago,
"We caught plenty of big dark mink this year, because the salmon canneries at the mouth of the Yukon
have been closed." Perhaps you ask, "What on
earth have salmon to do with mink?" The answer
is, "What have oats to do with horses?" Old trappers believe that the rich oily meat of the salmon, in
forest-bordered rivers of Alaska, is to the silky coat
of Alaska's mink what oats are to the blue-ribboner
of the Horse Show. As a bay horse, well fed and
well cared for, will have a smoother, oilier, darker-
appearing coat than that same horse turned out to
rustle on scrubby range—rough-haired and sun-
burned dry—so the gloss and the glow of health and
well-fed vigor, essential to fine mink peltries, seem to
depend in good part upon diet. The trappers say:

"No salmon—no fine sable mink!"   Fish diet has other by-products than brains, in the far North!

Darkly-wooded river courses, rich in fish—these are mink's solitary habitat, for he is a great fisher and a great ratter, diving, swimming, living in holes and banks and streams. Dark brown, darker brown on back and nearly black of tail, with sometimes a white spot on his throat, he looks like a large well-furred rat, with short, close and even under-fur protected by glossy and strong top hair. He, too, is amphibious, and his water sports make his pelt more wiry and more durable than marten. Mink are being ranched successfully in many sections of Alaska, as well as trapped over all of the forested fresh-water areas.

Marten has a heavier-seeming body and a far bushier tail than mink, and is arboreal in his habit. His lovely aristocratic fur is a soft, silky brown, shading into blackish brown on tail and legs, grayish of head, with a white or yellow or sometimes brightly orange spot on throat or belly. The underwool is close, warm and exceptionally soft, while the top hairs are fine and flowing. He lives all over Alaska except upon the farthest north and west unwooded coasts, for he is most at home and wears his best raiment in darkest, thickest spruce forests, which tend to make his coat dark and heavy, also. He doesn't like settlers, and resents and avoids the scent and mark of axe on clearings in his timberland.

"Sable," the last word in fur luxury, is trade name among fur men for the highest grade of dark-furred marten, and is the most expensive pelage, reckoned by square foot unit. But the word "sable" has been much abused by the trade. Because, though meaning merely "very dark" or "black" it still carries a connotation of Russian sable (and " Russian sable " is the trade name for darkest and silkiest of the marten family), dyed skunk has been ennobled by calling it in alias " Alaska sable "—an insult to both words! —and low-grade mink and yellow marten have been " sabled " or " topped " by tinting the long hairs with a dark dye, drawn through them on a comb. There are many tricks in the fur trade, and those who live where fine furs really grow are often amused and shocked to see the sports and subterfuges of the less scrupulous fur dealers Outside; but to most people the real fur world is unknown. A whole book could be written about fur substitutes and fur disguises, but two patent facts remain when all is considered: It is well never to buy furs except from an honest person or firm, one knowing fur; and—in spite of all the artifice and trading on the public's general ignorance, employed by the unscrupulous in both these trades—fine furs and precious stones remain among the choicest treasures of humankind, as they have for time immemorial and probably always will, so long as women love beauty in color and texture.

There is one truly regal fur found in Alaska which we have yet to mention, and that is ermine. This royal member of the weasel family is a turncoat, and yet this very quality is his claim to eminent distinction and not a stain upon his escutcheon. He merely adapts himself to his environment, does stoat, and in the summer merges with his drab and stony haunts by wearing a thin coat of tawn or beige. But when snow falls he dons a robe of sleek white samite. The tip of tail remains jet black year round, however, and when tiny ermine skins are made up into coronation robes for kings and symmetrically spotted over with black, the garment is said to be of miniver. The finest ermine comes from the far north, is always fashionable, but needs the care its regal formality deserves.

Before the discovery of gold, before the development of fisheries, came fur, and many of our interior sections of Alaska are to-day quite as much fur lands as were sections of the West a century ago. This long-time home of mine lies upon the vast inner highway of the waters, and here and now this section is passing through a transition from scattered settlement to seriously attempted colonization; and here and now explorers, trappers " out looking for fur tracks," and home-makers are alike at work building up a future state, in different sections of The Great Country. We inherit still that passion of all first comers for furs—a craving that seemed fairly to flame in our forefathers, too, even when the oldest West was the Atlantic seaboard itself. The quest for furs that led them ever deeper and deeper into the retreating forests at last made open and desirable an entire continent, even with inexorable death forever stalking close beside them upon the trail. At one time the vanity of empresses and of courts, to-day the vanity of shop-girls and of post-war millionairesses—all this vanity of vanities is serving, by the subtle mystery of demand, to develop the rich fur trade in our present colony of the North; and because of the far-reaching tributaries of the Yukon, pioneers will for years to come keep passing on and up its wide-spread laterals, striking boldly into the dim forests that border all its waters, with eager patience setting their remote trap lines.

XXII

Quintals of Fish

THE greatest fisheries are far from the tropics because, for one reason, in colder waters there is a rich supply of plankton—that floating and drifting minute pelagic life upon which sea-fish largely feed—and fish not only live under frozen lakes in winter, but even in deep waters under the Arctic ice.

In 1505 we know that there were fishermen from Brittany and Normandy on the Gulf of St. Lawrence; and the English occupation in North America began with fishermen who early sought the banks of Newfoundland, the nucleus of both French and English settlement in America. By 1578 there were a hundred and fifty vessels of France alone employed in the American fisheries. In the old days fisheries were known as the " New England silver mine," and Adams said, " If no precious metals rewarded search, if the beaver retreated farther and farther into the wilderness, if the soil gave but grudging yield, here, at least, was limitless wealth. The industry, thanks to the combination of shoals and icy waters, became the cornerstone of the prosperity of New England, and in the colonial history of that section commerce smells as strongly of fish as theology does of brimstone! "

Sumner spoke eloquently of the " quintals of fish " to be found in Alaska; and this is still true, as the yearly pack proves. While there is much fiery brimstone of controversy (commercial but not theological!) in connection with the organization and regulation of Alaska fisheries by the Mother Country, yet the salmon pack alone each year is worth from six to seven times the total original cost of " Seward's Folly! " Less romantic than the search for gold, but a source to-day of greater revenue than even Alaska gold, the fish farmer on a large scale (who is also a miner of the sea) stakes out his claim with costly " traps "—because he wishes to prevent a strike rather than discover one! The only creature that can find his way out of this contraption of large piles, thousands of feet of strong wire netting and even more thick, heavily tarred mesh netting, is the canny seal; and he seems to know the combination, for he swims in at will, takes what salmon he wishes, and swims right out, never mazed or losing his way. Also interested in the canneries and traps that dot all of Alaska's southern coast are the ever-present gulls, which scream and wheel about the silver fish heads poured in pile. Herring and halibut, cod and clams, shrimp, crab and trout all add their quota to Alaska's fishy catch. One November more than a million pounds of halibut was landed on a Seattle dock from Alaska in one day, and the prospector of Interior Alaska knows no more hardship or privation than does the halibut and cod fisherman of the South Coast. Those who go down to these northern seas in little ships must be stout indeed of heart, for though the North Pacific is not winter cold in Arctic extremes, it is wet and foggy, and the life is truly a hard one.

The most important fishery in Alaska is for salmon, and while chinook or king, red or sock-eye, pink or hump-back, chum or keta, and coho or silver salmon can all, as Lieutenant Allen found on the Tánana, be taken in season in one day, the advance guard of each usually arrives in the order named; and ling cod of fine quality and size can be taken from our Tánana in the early fall, white fish and pickerel from the near-by lakes, and grayling as soon as the streams clear in early June. But salmon are the romantic fish, and red salmon or sock-eye is the best known, most valuable and most sought of Alaska's five distinct species of wide distribution. The "silver horde" of Alaska's streams leap waterfalls to reach their desired place, and surely there is something of this salmon trait in the typical Alaskan sourdough's make-up. He never seems to know when the heights are too great for him—and so, they never are!

What makes the salmon insist on overleaping those tumbling falls to reach their bourne? How do they know there is a lake above, where life may be ended in last rest, after long effort? Migrating seaward as slowly-matured fingerlings in the spring of their third year, they roam the sea, grow large and fatten for three seasons, inaccessible to man. Then, upon reaching sexual maturity in their third sea-summer, they return, leaping high in the air with flashes of silver as they first taste fresh water again—*return to the same inland water in which they were hatched*— a strange and short life history. They are not taught the way but they come back, unaided, at the very end of life-span, only to seed again their native stream, then perish. Why, then, this frantic lunging effort, with death the only goal?

Of the great cannery industry of Southeastern Alaska, and of the regulations concerning fisheries promulgated by the Federal Bureau of Fisheries, there is this to say: The organized salmon industry was undoubtedly at one time courting complete disaster by the methods employed, and could only be saved by being subjected to close supervision under well-devised regulations.   To meet this emergency Congress in 1924 enacted a law (The White Bill, favored by the majority of Alaskans) granting very wide powers to the Bureau of Fisheries, and looking to the protection of fisheries in Alaska: " for the purpose of preventing further depletion of the salmon runs and of restoring them as nearly as possible to their former condition of abundance . . . to insure year after year adequate spawning in each of the multitudinous streams through the vast extent of Alaska."   As there are more than a thousand salmon streams here, and Alaska furnishes more than two-thirds of the world's canned salmon, the magnitude and complexity of the general problem are apparent.   Almost insuperable difficulties have arisen in the way of just local administration, however, and it is very hard for any mere layman to decide just who is right.   Very often one faction will assert a thing to be an incontrovertible fact— but this assertion will be denied with equal assurance by the other side!

The controversy in Alaska regarding fisheries seems to hinge on the fish trap.   The large and mainly non-resident cannery interests strongly support its use, while local people generally favor its prohibition.   The arguments supporting the use of this appliance for catching salmon are, first, that salmon are delivered by the fish trap as needed, not too many or too few for the capacity of the cannery; second, they are delivered in better condition; third, seines cannot supply the quantity that the industry demands; and, fourth, a fish trap will not go on a strike, whereas fishermen may! The argument that trap-caught fish are cheaper is no longer seriously pushed, for the testimony on this point is very conflicting, even as gathered from cannerymen themselves.

The arguments against the fish trap of course follow along the lines laid out by its proponents: first, the fish trap, because *too* efficient, is depleting the supply of seed-salmon, which soon will be insufficient in quantity; second, the condition of the salmon when delivered to the cannery is entirely within the power of the buyer, the canneryman, to control; third, at one time no fish traps were used in Alaska and yet the seines and gill nets furnished an adequate supply of salmon; and, fourth, conceding the argument of cannerymen as regards the possibility of strikes, fishermen assert that as a matter of governmental policy this is not a legitimate argument, one not used against other lines of industry.

To those who claim that the salmon pack of Alaska could not be put up without traps, the anti-trap men point out the Province of British Columbia, adjoining country very similar to Southeastern Alaska in topography and weather. No fish traps are allowed there, and yet a large and steady supply of salmon (one and one-half million cases) is annually obtained from seiners and gill netters; while to those who claim that a better quality of salmon is obtained from traps, Alaskans point out that British Columbia does not use traps at all and yet secures a better market price for her product.

Granted that the fish in these colonial waters exist solely to provide (as both French and British ministers in the old days claimed for the Newfoundland banks) a maximum present food supply at cheaper cost, for the *people of the Mother Country as a whole,* then most of the Federal rulings and regulations, though admittedly arrived at by methods of trial and error, are well devised to meet this end. But if you grant (as do all Alaskan natives, most local white fishermen and many of the cannerymen themselves) that the seine is a better conserver of fish supply than the fish trap, and if you grant that it is the instinctive wish of American colonials and natives alike to be "masters in their own house"— then the industry as now organized is in a position highly inimical both to colonial sentiment and settlement.

One of our most truly representative Alaskans said to me only last night: "The present rulings leave out the human and typically Alaskan element, entirely. Expensive fish traps, catching a maximum haul, are only possible to big concerns; while traps are in operation, the individual, the native of Southeastern Alaska who has always depended on salmon as his main source of food supply, is simply left to starve. The United States Government asks the native Alaskan to live as a white man, and elevate himself and his children to the white man's standard of life—based on cleanliness, health, education, and responsible work. In the same breath the Government, by allowing commercial fish traps on the main salmon streams, takes from the southeastern Alaska native the one occupation he has been trained through centuries to follow, and colonial cousins have always met a cool reception when they come asking for 'rights'!"

The whole trouble is that there are at least three sets of interests at work here—commercial fishing,

game fishing, and plain family " grub " fishing—and
one man's meat is often another man's lack of meat.
British Columbia can well be studied in this connection and its policies may one day be adopted here, *if*
the single end of developing Alaska as a future state
of our Union shall ever be the purpose of our home
government.   British Columbia, a self-governing
province, has built up careful policies which appear
to be satisfactory both to its cannerymen and fishermen; whereas Alaska is now in the midst of a bitter
controversy, with relatively impotent territorial citizens on the one side and financially powerful non-
resident cannery interests on the other.

" The trap destroys itself by its very devilish
efficiency," say my Southeastern Alaska friends.
" Gold dredging is efficient when the dredge takes
out *all* the gold, but the proper gear for catching
fish is that gear which will allow enough fish to
escape, to seed the creeks properly for the coming
years.   It is part of the Magna Carta and of all
reasonable fish legislation that people who live on
the upper streams have an equal share in the fish
catch with the people who live on the lower end of
the streams.   But the fish which come into Inian
Passage and go into the traps there, are on their way
to spawn in the Chilkat River; and the upland
owners on the Chilkat believe they are entitled to
some of the fish that ' God told to come back and
spawn in our river.'   But as long as the fish traps
flourish unmolested in Inian Passage, the natives
simply will not get any salmon, and the traps are
as surely driving out the fishing white population
from the Territory as they are starving out the
Indians.

" A trap can hook one end to the shore, run out

into the ocean a thousand feet or more and stand all summer; but a seine fisherman cannot hook one end of his *net* to the shore for ten minutes without danger of prosecution and jail. In British Columbia even the canners admit it is against public policy to use fish traps, and the B. C. catch is 100 per cent. movable gear; but to-day practically no white seiners are left in Southeastern Alaska. The prospector used to make a grubstake by fishing and then go into the hills in winter. There are no prospectors near here, now. The Scandinavian seiners have gone into trolling, but with the new regulations affecting that, they are reduced to hard straits. Only the Indians are left to seine, and they—poor souls—cannot leave the country! If it is the Government's policy to depopulate this section of the colony, then they are going about it very efficiently under the new fisheries rules—yet the home government constantly twits us with having a small population! The canners buy all their supplies outside Alaska, and hire three-fourths of their help outside Alaska under the yellow-dog contracts; a large percentage of such help is Asiatic, hired at slave's wage and paid off—not in Alaska but in Seattle or San Francisco. They bring nothing to the country and they take all they dare from it.

" Doesn't Uncle Sam realize that the residents of this Territory have a greater interest than any one else in the perpetuation of the fish business? Then why doesn't he, who should be helpful to us, give up this harsh attitude toward his colonials—or is that too much for us to expect, from any Mother Country toward a new, raw land? But surely our Uncle Sam can consult vitally interested Alaskans *before* he issues regulations regarding our major industry here,

and not just talk to our commercial clubs. What do
the business men of the towns know about practical
fishery? Nothing. And the Government holds fish
hearings in Seattle, and then says, 'The public had
an opportunity to present its case.' How many of
our native or small white fishermen, do you think,
can afford to make a trip to Seattle and talk there
to Uncle Sam about this trouble? We believe as
thoroughly as any one—and more so—that the industry should be stabilized, and because of this
belief we all supported the White Bill; but we do
not believe that this should be done at the expense
of Alaska's population. We too are interested in
industrial efficiency, but we are even more interested
in living! We want to conserve both fish *and* population, but the Fisheries officials say frankly and
openly, 'The population of Alaska is no concern of
ours.'

" Until the Fisheries take the human element here
into account and look on us as a colony of human
beings—as *Americans,* not merely as a fat fish-pond
—the people of Southeastern Alaska will feel the
same bitter enmity that our own ancestors in Boston
felt when they dumped tea overboard, one night,
until it spilled like seaweed on the beach! Back in
Washington they apparently do not understand why
the feeling against fish traps is so strong, here. Apparently they do not understand that with large
groups of our people in this section it is a question
of starve or not to starve. There is nothing else these
people can turn to for a livelihood."

Who are to be heard in this matter, and what end
is to be sought: optimum present pack, optimum
future supply, or optimum colonial development?
Years ago there was a notion of government for

colonies called " The Mercantile Theory." Under it the ideal empire embraced the home country (" the source of credit, the seat of manufactures, the selling agency to the world for the whole empire, the center of administration, and the protective power to guard the system ") and the colonies, planted where they could send home raw products and existing for this purpose solely. " Such a system," Adams says, " presupposed that every part would be willing to subordinate itself to the theoretical needs of the whole. . . . But its logic, seemingly so perfect, left out of account the fact that colonists were human beings (who would surely develop their own local interests, troubles, aspirations) and *not insensible parts of a great machine*. . . . New England did not fit into this elaborate and delicately adjusted trade-machine."

Because New England didn't—and couldn't—men like " Sam " Adams and John Hancock talked about Stamp Acts and Tea. But the Alaska Native Brotherhood to-day talks about seines and weirs, gill-nets and fish traps, " the hook-off " and " the dead-line."

XXIII

Pastures of the Wilderness

IT'S a farther cry than Lochaber, in most places, from frost to farms, but not so in Alaska; for here, as we already know, agriculture is in part dependent upon frost for its success. In the Tánana Valley the sub-irrigation formed by melting frost coming up through the turned and opened soil is one factor making our splendid crops possible.

But my experience has been that, while Outsiders will believe any statement we Insiders make on the subject of frost, they are very skeptical about our farms. When we say "farms" in the same breath with "Alaska," they snort at us and merely think we're joking. On no phase of Alaska's many resources is it so difficult to get a serious hearing as on the really basic subject of agriculture—except with those relatively few people who possess both intelligence and open minds.

What, then, are the facts and how deep is "bed-rock" truth in this foundation matter of agriculture, upon which a permanent population must eventually be built?

Alaska has the largest glaciers on American soil, but she has also the longest summer days. In some sections of Alaska that day is three months long and very warm indeed. At Matanuska there were 126 "growing" days in 1921. Any farmer knows what this means, and any farmer in the States knows too that an extension of actual sunshine to 22 continuous hours per diem would increase *his* crops; and he also knows how much a summer of relative briefness may be compensated by intense sunlight. Only two per cent. of Alaska's land area is covered with the perpetual ice and snow of high mountains and glaciers, while, on the other hand, in the great valleys of the Yukon, Kuskokwim and Tánana of the Interior, and the Susitna, Matanuska and White River valleys of the south, there are wide areas of already proved agricultural possibilities which could support an ever-growing population. Some of Alaska's valleys are covered 10 to 20 feet deep with a black chocolaty loam from old river deposits, and I have looked on plains of wild red-top grasses 40 miles long and extending as far as the eye could see. On the South Coast humidity combines with extra sunlight and fertile soil to create ideal growing conditions for certain garden crops and dairying produce, while in the Interior almost continuous summer sunshine plus the sub-irrigation of frost waters living under us, make wheat and rye and other similar crops a known and tested success. As Jack Underwood says, " Spoiled child of Nature, Alaska has been endowed with about everything that could be desired by way of climate." Professor Georgeson of the U. S. Department of Agriculture, who did pioneering work in Alaska for many years, declares that " there is *no possibility* of the failure of the country in agriculture."

In farming land Alaska is so far superior to New England that there is simply no comparison. Official Department of Agriculture experiments demonstrate that 100,000 square miles of Alaskan terrain are capable of being turned to various agricultural uses and can produce all the hardy vegetables, forage plants, grains, garden truck and berries needed for a heavy population. The possible farming area of Alaska is equal to that of Massachusetts, Connecticut, New Hampshire, Pennsylvania, New Jersey, Delaware and Maryland, combined. There is more agricultural land in Alaska than in all the Scandinavian Peninsula, which supports to-day a farming population of more than 3,000,000; and this acreage is exclusive of the wide reindeer grazing lands extending north of the Yukon to the Arctic. Altogether, government agronomists estimate 32,-000,000 acres of arable land that can be cleared and cultivated, and a similar area suitable for grazing certain types of live stock. A large portion of Alaska lies in the same latitude as Norway, Sweden and Finland, has a better climate, a more fertile soil (as all my many Scandinavian friends in the North vehemently assure me) and taken as a whole is larger than all three, as well as Denmark and Iceland— which for a thousand years has supported *its* population on a less highly mineralized, less arable soil.

It is my belief that Scandinavian colonists will make of Alaska in the future a great productive state such as Peder the Victorious and his kin, those "Giants in the Earth," have already made of great sections of our nearer Northwest. Those who express surprise at farming as a possible major industry in the far North, forget that sections of northern Europe have been agricultural for centuries. The myth of "Alaska, the land of icebergs and polar bears, Eskimos and ice-worms," is in a fair way to get a death blow when Seward's Ice-Box is really opened up and people see what goodies lie inside. Serious settlers may one day do for Alaska the work the Mormons did for Utah. The wheat yield at

Fairbanks is sometimes at the rate of 33 bushels to the acre; and strawberries "half the size of golf balls," as one tourist described them, are grown along the line of the Alaska Railroad. The Spaniards started north from Mexico to find the fabled golden cities of Cibola, and found instead the cattle and wheat empires that stretch from Texas to the Dakotas—though they didn't have vision enough to realize it. Begotten and flowered upon paradox, even so Alaska may one day well be famous chiefly for its exceptional potatoes and strawberries, for we are learning that one acre of land in certain parts of Alaska will raise more vegetables than four acres in certain portions of the States, and do it in half the time. Metals and fur and fish are natural frontier products; they were the things sought first in New England, too. But as we live here longer and spy out the land further, we begin to read what is written in plain script upon the hills and valleys:

" Is this an empty land which you have reached? The North is not stretched out over an empty space nor is the Earth hung upon nothing. You see my cattle grazing on a thousand hills. You see their pastures on the plains. They feed and they are filled here. Beasts of the field are not afraid, for the pastures of the wilderness do spring. Why, then, should any child of man do less? These are not barren grounds but fertile prairies. Dig, and do eat."

The plentiful moose, mountain sheep and caribou of Alaska are all pasture animals, and surely they are Nature's pictographic way of telling us that this is truly pasture land. Maternal Earth broods here, as ever. Stefansson says, "Where land animals are plentiful, one needs no further proof of vegetation!"

A pioneer farmer of the Northland writes:

Yes, I have a farm in Alaska and, what is more to
the point, I like it. It is located on the east side of
Glacier Bay at Strawberry Point, just where the ground
begins to rise toward the mountains. I have never been
as well satisfied any place I have lived, as I am here; I
don't have the dust storms characteristic of the country in
eastern Oregon; I do not have to dig a hundred feet for
water to drink, and I do not need to build an irrigation
ditch to get water to make things grow. I raise barley,
oats, rutabagas, potatoes, etc., and they grow well.
Meat is running wild about the shores and I do not even
have to feed it.

Birds? Yes, lots of them—ducks, geese, snipe,
ptarmigan, grouse—plenty of them; and if I want a deer,
all I have to do is to go over to Pleasant Island, about
two miles south, and get one and have venison for my
table. I don't kill many. If I get as many birds in two
months as is allowed to a city sport, who kills his limit
in a day, I can have a bird twice a week.

Berries? Well, I should say! The woods are full of
them. That is why the point that sticks out in the bay
is called Strawberry Point. Just walk over it in the last
of July and the air is full of the scent of the berries. We
eat until our appetites are satisfied, put up for winter use
all we want, and leave the rest to rot on the ground.
Strawberries, salmon berries, huckleberries, currants,
nagoon berries grow in any quantity. We feed nearly all
our produce to the stock. We keep horses, cattle, pigs,
and chickens and they do well. We catch enough fur-
bearing animals to pay our grocery bill with the skins, so
make a living and that is all most people do in the city.

These men were only beginners, just as men once
began to settle on the bunch-grass sections of the
West and grew to be giants in the earth there,—prairies that ox teams crept across on the long road to

Willamette,—land long considered fit only for horned toads and rattlesnakes. That was the time the cry was raised, " Go West! " To-day it's changing; and to-morrow, when men realize the frontier still extends and is untaken, and that a hundred and sixty acres of Uncle Sam's farm land is theirs *for* the taking, almost anywhere in Alaska, another covered-wagon saga will begin. But before this is possible our old men must dream dreams and our young men must see visions. There is no haste, Alaska knows long patience. But they are coming.

We have our forests and our mines, of which Denmark has practically none to-day. But take a globe and trace your finger round it east from Sitka, and you'll find Denmark lying at the same latitude. Denmark is composed of a peninsula with islands, fifteen thousand square miles, once forested and moss-grown with tundra until cleared now for pasture land. To-day Denmark, one-fortieth the size of our Alaska, supports her two and a half millions of people and more cattle to the acre than any other country in the world. Danish butter is shipped to New York City at a profit, and Iceland markets quantities of butter in England; for a ton of butter will pay for distant shipment, and the best dairy products in the world come from regions similar in climate to southern Alaska.

" But these Alaska beginnings are just first steps, general outlines, visions," I hear you say. " What has been actually done to make the dream come true? What actually can be raised there, and how do you know it can? Be definite, be factual. Colonists aren't fed on theories, but on crops."

While it is true that some of the earliest Russian colonists were purposefully recruited from agricultural districts, with a sane view toward securing the type of settler that would be most successful in the new possessions over seas, when they arrived in Russian America the pressure from home upon the governors was so great, in the matter of securing furs, that these first families of two hundred souls were widely scattered, were driven to get out a big fur yield and not a yield of crops. " The two ideas did not mix well, for agriculture is an all-year, occupation and the Russians were primarily concerned in trade. Much of the agricultural work of the early settlements such as Kodiak (as much of the pioneer work by Catholic Missions, such as Holy Cross) was done by natives, under the instruction of the clergy. But the natives were by nature fishermen, hunters and trappers, and the Creoles were mostly agents for the company."

Russian masters were either directing sea-otter hunts, building ships at Resurrection Bay, or stealing down the coast to poach on Spain's possessions, though Khlebnikof in 1838 stated that about a thousand bushels of potatoes were then raised in Sitka, and " there is hardly a cleared spot that is not used for kitchen gardens." In 1790 Three Saints Bay had gardens growing potatoes and cabbage, in 1818 the Siberian cattle brought to Kodiak numbered five hundred, and there were ten cows in Sitka, hay being cut by natives and brought in by canoe. But all through the Russian days there were no individual settlers as such, but only employees—practically indentured servants—of the fur company; and at no time was an able-bodied man whose wish and care might be to get out and develop a few paternal acres, to call his own and hand down to his children, ever allowed to do so.

Nor was there, from Alaska's purchase in 1867 down to 1898, any attempt made by the United States to reward in any way the initiative of those who might see undeveloped agricultural possibilities here. In place of too much government, as under the Russians, there was now no government at all. But something happened in 1898—not in Alaska but just across the border in " Y. T." Hungry swarms of men poured over White Pass and Chilkoot and down the Yukon, packing all their grub with them; for no one had ever told them—because no one knew —that anything vegetable would grow here. Then one day a discouraged miner in Dawson, opening a package which he thought contained beans, found he had been sent assorted garden seeds by mistake! To him, at the moment, hungry and scurvy-worn and blue, it seemed the cruellest stroke Fate could have foisted on him. With a curse he strode to the open door, cast the rattling, dry and useless things in handfuls out upon the spring mud of the south hill-slope, rushed off to town, struck a pal for a grub-stake, and " beat it " for the creeks.

A month later he returned, the story goes, and found a miracle! The little melting trickles of water from the hill, the slippages of spring mud, had buried those discarded seeds. The long-stretched early summer days of drawing sun had warmed and quickened them and, by no will of man, they had become food for the hungry; for his hillside was now a mass of vivid shooting green, a strangely Dolly Varden patterned garden of helter-skelter, but actual and edible. He sold his first " sass " to his scurvy-ridden mates for a fat poke of precious " dust " ; but he had made a strike and a discovery that was to outlast Klondike gold itself.

That is why, when disappointed Klondikers hiked over into Fairbanks after Pedro's find here, they brought the thought of growing things tucked into pockets of their minds. That is why, when Alaska's gold-camps began to "pay big" and a determined group of American citizens began to settle here, Uncle Sam himself began to plant some window-boxes in his own high attic.

In March of 1903 an act was passed providing for the entry of agricultural lands in Alaska. Thirty years ago the first agricultural experiment station was established at Sitka, and since then four others have been started in various sections of the big land favorable to varied farming undertakings—Kodiak, Rampart, Matanuska and Fairbanks. These stations have done pioneer work, each specializing in some different phase of agriculture; have literally cleared ground and now have gathered a set of facts, a library of literature, and have perfected a technique of possibility and limitations. What they have done is to suggest those lines of farming which can be undertaken with known success, until the farmer stands securely on his own feet and can then afford to experiment for himself. Mistakes are fewer, results more sure, because of this system. Some Federal help was necessary, for prospectors are not by nature farmers. They tell a story in one section of Alaska of an old-timer who admired his neighbor's garden truck extravagantly, and "borrowed" frequently, especially the fresh green peas.

"Why don't you plant some for yourself?" he was asked. "Why, I did, but nothing grew," he answered. Further questions elicited the fact that it was *canned* peas he had planted!

I have told you that my own very first sight on

reaching Fairbanks, when I first came in by boat, was the sloping grain fields of the Government Farm. But I can never tell you what that sight really meant to me, in wonder and security, in sense of home and permanent settlement and well-being. A wheat field is the white man's bread, a surer meat than moose upon the hills. And it was then that text from Joel jumped into my mind (you see, I am a parsonage-bred person) and ever since then it has stuck with me: " Be not afraid, ye beasts of the field; for the pastures of the wilderness do spring."

The Tánana Valley section of a thousand square miles has proved exceptionally favorable to grain growing and the cultivation of hardy vegetables, particularly potatoes. (The Rampart Station was found to be duplicating much of the Fairbanks work, under similar conditions, and so was discontinued, the cleared fields being used now as a landing place for planes.) Here, under the very Arctic Circle, our Farmers' Association have built a flouring mill and both grow and grind native wheat. Indeed, it looks as though an empire of wheat is going to be developed here, to supplement the golden empire of the past, the copper empire and the silver horde of fishes of the Coast, the fur and reindeer empires of both Alaska's past and future. The soil here has been found to have the same qualities which make the wheat of Manitoba famous. Once Manitoba was considered ridiculously far north for consideration as an agricultural province, but now we know better; for it is a recognized principle that the farther north wheat grows and matures, the better quality is the resulting crop. Farmers are forever pushing their work-stained shoulders against that ever-retreating "wheat line," rolling it back further north. No one now dares to prophesy the north-most limits of wheat growing, for this grain has great powers of adaptation. It almost seems as though it has no limits, given intelligent breeding of the right acclimated strains.

On the mild south coast at Sitka topographic and climatic conditions are not favorable to wheat growing; but at Matanuska oats, barley, wheat and rye are grown, and at Fairbanks ruby wheat seeded May 20, heads June 28, blooms July 5, and matures August 5. In one recent year the average yield of wheat in Alabama was 10.5 bushels per acre, in Iowa 19.2; but an average of the yield of wheat in the Tánana Valley was 25 bushels per acre, *over a five-year period*. Barley matures by July 30 and yields as high as 32 bushels, a strain of Canadian oats seeded May 27 was ripe August 4, and yielded 35 bushels per acre, while Wisconsin Pedigree No. 7 produced 40. Peas drilled May 18 bloom June 20, and mature 40 days later, yielding 10 to 16 bushels. "All varieties of yellow-flowered alfalfa seeded in June came through the winter well," says one report; "and vetch seeded five years ago has produced a fine crop this year, with plants over three feet high."

Why shouldn't the wilderness pastures grow? There are ten thousand acres of wild rye in Alaska —then why not cultivated crops? Dr. Smith of the Department of Agriculture says, "The soil seems as productive as the best soils of Minnesota and Wisconsin." Oats grow at Unalaska. A number of hybrid barleys now mature early in Alaska, and some, having no beards, can be used for hay and feed for farm animals without being threshed. Winter rye and wheat can be successfully grown in the

Interior wherever the snowfall is deep enough to protect from the low winter temperatures. Rye has proved hardier than oats. A very sturdy and prolific strain of spring wheat has been developed, and more than forty tons were ground at the local flour mill last year.

The Tánana Valley Agriculture Association is a lively coöperative enterprise born in 1917, and composed of farmers living near Fairbanks. It is the selling and distributing agent for local farmers, and all farm products are pooled by it, production is regulated, and profits distributed pro rata. The Association owns its own warehouse and warm storage plant and operates the flour mill—an outstanding coöperative success. As " W. F." says, " It has grown greater with the years that have passed into history, until it is the biggest thing in this camp to-day." M. D. Snodgrass (an early member of this Association, once connected with our Fairbanks Agricultural Station, a former member of the Alaska Legislature, himself a " dirt farmer " and in touch with agricultural work at Kodiak and Matanuska) is now in charge of colonization projects for the Alaska Railroad, and I can think of no man more intimately informed upon this phase of Alaska's life. The Association holds an agricultural fair each September in Fairbanks, gives a big banquet each winter when local products alone are served,—and people nearly commit felonies to secure tickets to it!—and puts on an annual picnic some time in the summer. " There is no man, woman, or child in the Fairbanks district," says " W. F.," " who does not know the baking and eating qualities of our home-grown and home-milled graham, white and whole-wheat flour."

Sugar beets grown here are found to contain the

highest known percentage of sugar. The cultivation of all the hardier vegetables has been thoroughly demonstrated throughout most of Alaska. Radishes, turnips, kale and lettuce can be grown nearly anywhere. Carrots, parsnips, parsley, peas, cress, cabbage, cauliflower, Brussels sprouts, onions, spinach, beets, potatoes, and rhubarb may be matured not only along the Coast but also in the Interior of Alaska on garden sites that are sheltered and sun-exposed. Potato growing has developed into a real industry, especially near Fairbanks, and potatoes as well as cabbage, peas and turnips have been raised successfully even as far up as Coldfoot on the Koyukuk, 68 degrees north.

In Fairbanks local celery is earlier on the market than in Boston. The white Jerusalem artichoke is grown at Sitka with success, and all hardy vegetables flourish luxuriantly in that climate,—from turnips at 15 tons per acre to rhubarb which grows exceptionally well there,—and all these are also grown in Fairbanks. In fact, I can think of no major garden product, other than corn, which I have not seen growing in some Alaska garden; I have seen corn grown and matured here, but in local hothouses, as are tomatoes, cucumbers and a score of other tender plants. Indeed, because of the quick uninterrupted shooting up to which the long suns force these gardens, plants grow especially crisp and tender, and root vegetables are without woody fibre.

I once heard a child born in Fairbanks say, upon returning from a trip Outside: " I didn't like those Outside vegetables. They haven't any taste." You can see that Alaska's future is safely assured when her little children—who are proverbially truthful—begin thus early to boost the home product!

The Sitka Experiment Station has specialized in horticulture, and has made a great success of the hybridization of strawberries, crossing cultivated varieties with the hardy and sweet native wild strawberries and producing a result that's sturdy and yields large berries of excellent quality, retaining the fine flavor of the wild but taking on the size and color of the best cultivated products. These hybrids now grow lustily in almost any section of Alaska. Raspberries and strawberries grow plentifully and well at Fairbanks. An official report states:

In 1903 a test orchard of apples and other fruits was planted at Sitka, and in 1911 the fruit of five varieties matured. The difficulty with apple growing has been not the winter cold but the fact that the summer temperature (on the Coast) was not sufficient to ripen the fruit, and the temperature in the autumn was such as not to cause the wood thoroughly to ripen before freezing. In the Interior of the Territory the summers are warm enough, but the winters appear to be too severe for the trees to survive without protection.

Peaches, pears, plums, and cherries are grown at Sitka, although no one ever believed this possible; and there is a new gravel walk laid out there, between a strip of sward leading through apple orchard and flower beds, which if you'll once walk down it, will convert you to the possibilities of the North more quickly than a library of books! Ketchikan, Sitka, Juneau and Haines have all demonstrated their ability to produce apples. In Juneau the Sisters at St. Anne's Hospital make a fine amber jelly of their apple crop, made possible through the care of Father Rocatti. Berry and vegetable canning is developing as an industry at Anchorage and other points on the South Coast. In 1928 fine jelly made of Matanuska currants was given away at the Tánana Valley Fair, and Alaska's berries are famous among those who know them. Jonas Lie, in his "Second Sight," remarked: "The learned say that the intensities of color and fragrance in the far North are due to the power of light which fills the air when the sun shines without interruption day and night. Therefore one cannot pick so aromatic strawberries and raspberries or so fragrant birch boughs in any other clime. If a fairy idyl has any home, it is certainly in the deep fjord valleys of Nordland in the summer."

I am no gardener, but even I can raise anything here I've tried to! The Sitka Experiment Station has found the Japanese sweet crimson *rosa rugosa* an especial favorite. Annuals grow luxuriantly at Sitka, baby-blue-eyes being the first to blossom and balsam the last, while in between come candy-tuft, clarkia, chrysanthemum, cockscomb, centaurea, lobelia, larkspur, mignonette, nasturtium, phlox, pansy, Santa Barbara poppy, Shirley poppy, scarlet sage, scabiosa, snapdragon, stocks, sweet peas, verbena and zinnia—almost an alphabet of posies!— while perennials by the score bloom profusely throughout the summer and nearly all bulbous plants so far introduced have been successful, including crocus, thirty-seven varieties of "glads," narcissus, English and Japanese iris, and tulips.

The first-coming Russians early recognized the possibilities of Alaska for stock-breeding purposes and imported cattle from Siberia, and when the United States purchased Alaska, cattle raising was still in progress at the principal Russian settlements. Indeed, some remnants of the original Russian stock

were still in evidence when the first agricultural experiment station was established in 1898. But the
animals were small and slim, with a narrow head
and thin upright horns. They were dark brown or
red in color, and poor both in milk yield and in
beef production. Obviously, since Alaska imports
more than a million dollars' worth of dairy products
annually and over half a million dollars' worth of
beef, Uncle Sam thought he would try his hand at
raising cattle locally—real cattle, and not the type
of the scrawny Russian herd remnants.

But first he began to inquire about forage, and he
found that, excluding the heavily forested region of
Southeastern Alaska, the remainder of the Territory
was largely a forage-producing area, that certain
favored valley sections were eminently suitable for
farming, and that, *given a stock adapted to the
climate,* there were unlimited possibilities. He saw
grass in abundance, and where there's grass in summer there's grass in winter—and what is winter grass
but uncut hay? Perhaps he could find some animal
rugged enough to withstand the cold of winter,
warm-coated, a good " rustler," and one that was not
pampered and stall-fed but had hoofs for pawing
through light snow—and wasn't afraid to use them!
He found one such animal in the reindeer, suited to
sub-arctic prairies, " barren lands," the Bering
coastal plain, and " the slope of the lonely water-
shed that borders the Polar brim." But he hunted
further, and made some very interesting experiments. Indeed, he *made* an animal, to order, to fit
the country.

In 1917 cross-breeding on the coast was begun
between Galloways and Holstein-Friesians, to create
sturdy, general-utility cattle that would be suitable

for southern Alaska, and in this cross we have a hardy animal that is capable of giving all this part of the country desirable herds. The Matanuska Valley is now essentially a dairying locality. But the really fascinating experiment has been at Fairbanks; for here we have crossed Asiatic yak with Galloway cattle and have produced a curiously-fringed bovine that can be used for meat, milk or domestic service. Cattle and yak are commonly crossed in Asia, where it has long been the domestic bovine of Tibet and adjoining India, China, Mongolia and Siberia. The yak can endure extreme altitude and extreme temperature in either its wild or domestic state, and is not fussy about forage. It stands on short stout legs and has a very heavy long coat of hair that drops down like black chenille. The hybrids produced from this cross are sturdy, stocky animals though of an odd appearance, and are perfectly adapted to the native pastures of both sub and supra-arctic circles.

A herd of fifteen bison from South Dakota were brought into Alaska two years ago and were liberated on the range of the Delta district on the upper Tánana. The entire herd, including a calf born this year, are now grazing near Jarvis Creek, are in good condition, and evidently quite at home here. Domestic sheep are also kept in many sections, and when Senator Warren (who was called " the greatest shepherd since Abraham ") visited us in Fairbanks and we took him out to see something of our valley, I was interested to hear him exclaim: " What a land for sheep! It reminds me of Wyoming, when I first went there as a young man." Recently a twenty-year lease has been granted on Sitkalidak Island, which is to be stocked immediately with a thousand head of

sheep. Sheep do well at Kodiak, and the Cordova
Daily Times said in 1923, when a thousand sheep
were shipped to Unalaska:

> Sheep raising in Alaska!
> Can you beat it?
> Even the thought of such a thing a few years ago,
> before gas wagons succeeded malemutes and horses, and
> when dance halls and yellow gold were in flower, would
> have caused old sourdoughs to have pinched themselves
> to see if they were strictly sober! Regarding the grazing
> lands—acres and acres and miles and miles of them—
> there never has been any doubt, for in early days sheep
> were driven in over the trail and allowed to fatten on the
> luscious grasses of the Tánana before being slaughtered
> for winter consumption. The main trouble was to keep
> malemutes from destroying the bands!

The wool from these flocks brings a high price in
the western market, and in the fall of 1929 the first
shipload of mutton was exported from the islands.
Sheep are raised to-day at Matanuska, too, and " the
flock when turned at large is afforded protection
from the weather by standing timber, and seeks the
open sheds only on stormy or extremely cold nights "
—the January mean temperature of Matanuska being higher than that of Bismark or Duluth. Shear-
ing is done early in May, and one ram fleece recently
weighed fifteen pounds while the average weight of
the famous Lincolnshire fleeces is but twelve. In
other sections hog raising has been profitable.
Stoney of Salmon Creek is a hog-rancher, and Stoney
says, " When I started in the business every one told
me it was impossible to raise hogs in Alaska, but I
don't pay much attention to pessimists." Stoney sold
nineteen hogs to local markets last year at slightly

over $67 per head and, as Stroller says, "You know hogs! They're among the best sellers. A hog will run an Alaska prospector a close second when it comes to living off the country, and he grows like a head of cabbage or a rutabaga. In March he is a small bundle of short bristles, but in October or November he is ready for the market."

It's hard for me to leave the farm and go a-foresting, but a word must be said of this other great natural resource of the Great Country—for much of Uncle Sam's attic is truly built of logs, though except in the south the timber is not large. Trees are heavy drinkers and do not thrive well in frozen ground. Much of Interior Alaska is timbered, especially along the streams, but the trees here cannot send down tap roots into the frozen gravels and so they spread out a mat of fine roots instead, which, with the overburden of moss, support them. But high winds or burning off the moss topples them over. Interior Alaska timber will not likely furnish export outside the Territory, but is needed here for home consumption, on the Yukon and Kuskokwim basins. Of the estimated 150,000,000 acres of Interior forests, probably only half bears timber of sufficient size to make it valuable for cordwood, saw logs, boat building, mine timbers and farm use. There is a forest along the entire line of the Alaska Railroad, except over Broad Pass itself. These Interior forests are all in the public domain, and, although their present commercial value may be small, yet in any consideration of a forest policy for the nation these extensive woods of Uncle Sam should not be overlooked—for Alaska may well be a state, one day, and then she'll want her own trees. These interior forests have already played an im-

portant part in the pioneer development of the
country. Uncle Sam owns forests here that extend
up beyond the Circle, on the Chandalár and Porcupine. The inland forests are comparable to those of
Maine and eastern Canada as to species, though inferior as to quality—white spruce, white birch, balsam, poplar, black cottonwood, aspen, black spruce,
and tamarack or larch—white spruce and white
birch being most common. Timberline in the Yukon
Basin is roughly 2,500 feet above sea level, and tree
growth is slow.

The best Alaskan timber is comprised in the twenty
million acres of Tongass and Chugach National
Forests and the two million acres of similar character lying in between. These national forests are
about to become important factors in a new industry,
for they include seventy-seven *billion* feet of timber
suitable for lumber and pulp. Southeastern Alaska
is surely going to break into newsprint, soon! It is
estimated that this territory can produce a million
and a half cords of pulp wood or a million tons of
newsprint *each year,* and do it, too, by holding the
annual cutting down to an amount which will be
annually replaced by normal tree growth. If developed carefully under Forest Service supervision,
the annual cut strictly held down to annual growth,
these two national forests can supply a wood-pulp
industry indefinitely.

The two principal tree species in the south are
western hemlock and Sitka spruce, usually found
growing together, also with scattered stands of
western red cedar and Alaska or yellow cedar. Sitka
spruce is far and away the finest tree of Alaska. It
reaches a great size—10 feet in diameter and 250
feet in height—and its clean-limbed columnar trunk,

extending up through a dense surrounding of dwarfed hemlock, stands like a hero's shaft. Its wood is good for many things, from boxes for canned salmon to airplanes and newspaper. Hemlock is fine for the piling used in fish-trap and dock construction, and it, too, is a paper-making wood. Western red cedar is a shingle wood. Alaska yellow cedar, "the slowest-growing tree of North America," is excellent for boats, telephone poles and furniture, and there is a growing demand for it in Japan where it is valued for its insect-resisting qualities. The wood has a peculiar odor, shows remarkable resistance to decay, and the Indians like it best for paddles. Alaska birch, too, is an excellent furniture wood, and pieces we ourselves have made of it for our Fairbanks home not only fit well with old pieces of mahogany but are often taken for mahogany! Its drying and cutting qualities are good, and it is a little softer and a little closer grained than is the eastern paper-birch.

All the ties and piling used on the Alaska Railroad are native timber, largely from Kenai Peninsula and Cook Inlet—spruce and hemlock cut from the right-of-way, suitable for piling and ties, also being used. Most Alaska towns are built of Alaska logs and lumber, and before we opened up our coal seams our fires were from Alaska's forests. The builder of Alaska's new capitol at Juneau, a Nome sourdough now a Chicago contractor, is said to be planning the use of Alaska lumber, wherever possible in its construction, as well as Alaska marble, cement made from Alaska limestone, and Alaska labor.

Forests tie in with water power, and the first unit of the paper mills about to be erected on Gastineau will be powered, it is reported, from a lake hitherto unknown but discovered accidentally near Taku Inlet by this summer's Naval Alaska Aërial Survey. This hidden lake lay tucked away in the hills, its natural storage reservoir of power unguessed until picked out by the navy's cameras. Its discovery will, it is estimated, save hundreds of thousands of dollars in shorter transmission lines, for it lies only three miles from tide-water and within twenty miles of Juneau. Even Alaska's trees and white coal stand indebted to her trackless air ways, unlimited.

The streams of Alaska have always been important factors in her youthful growth. Like New England, she has a fall-line near the coast, with power available in many places. The success of the placer workings in northern and central Alaska has depended primarily on the water available for sluicing, hydraulicking and dredging, and water power has long been used by mines, canneries, sawmills and other industries in Southeastern Alaska. The future of mining and lumbering plants, of fisheries and wood-pulp manufacture, as well as of electro-chemical products, hinges upon that falling water.

Mention the wealth of Alaska and it is likely that the average person will think instinctively of gold. Yet in the years to come it's very probable that other natural resources of the land—wheat, cattle, fruits, timber and water power—will bring more wealth and certainly more permanent population than fabled gold mines ever did. Gold is a fleeting harvest; once taken, it is gone and unrenewable. But these are harvests of perpetual pastures, upspringing in our mis-called " wilderness."

XXIV

The Social Arctic Circle

SPEAKING for the Alaska town I know most intimately, I'm sure our " best " people would resent any implication that a social set exists here. We are of the frontier, and artificial and arbitrary social distinctions do not flourish upon frontier soil. You are just as good as I am: I am just as good as you are. We are all colonists, upon an equal footing. Time has not broken into first and last divisions the warm human solidarity of our on-marching ranks. All alike are shock troops, here, holding the thin, red, fighting line of civilization in hand-to-hand combat with reality. In any successful hand-to-hand fight it is every man for himself; and no official salutes or forms of delicate approach are desirable or in keeping with the stern work to be done—the work of subduing Nature to human habitation and human habituation.

If people only interest you when they are poured in formal molds, if you relish only the social contacts of set occasions, if manners rather than innate qualities seem to you the better basis for judgment of your fellow man or choice of your associates, then you will only be bored in any frontier community. Reflections in The Mirrors of Fairbanks will show you more mackinaws than " claw-hammer coats "— and though the latter are not lacking and are worn with ease and grace upon occasion, they are not *de*

rigueur, even upon the most formal " set occasions."
At any of the big town dances which literally every
one attends, from court and clergy to restaurant bus-
boy and grocer's delivery clerk, you will see all raiment from Parisian creation to glorified simple house
dress, everybody knows everybody, and all are having
an equally fine time. All types are here, for as early
New England was once a microcosm of seventeenth-
century society, so our contemporary colony is a re-
flection of all phases of the twentieth.

What makes true " social position " ?   Is it real
property?   Then that bus-boy is your social equal,
for he happens to own one of the most promising
claims upon one of our richest gold-bearing creeks,
and we know that he is working in the café this
winter to get a " stake " which will enable him next
summer to open up that rich new lead which he discovered late last fall. Next year "The Company"
will very likely buy that claim, on which they already
hold an option; and if they do, they may take out a
quarter million from it.   But real mines are not
found, but made—by hard development work; and
large mining corporations have to be shown. They
don't buy mere prospect holes. A wildcat must be
tamed—and with a drill—before it works for pay!
Is social caste graded by the car you own, as some
one recently remarked?   Then that laundress in the
fluttering muslin frock is an aristocrat, for she drives
as fine a make of car as any in our district. Is it
" family," as others claim, and " blood will tell " ?
That man in mackinaw over yonder is a younger son
of one of the oldest British lines of blue blood—a
rolling-stone adventurer who finds a fillip in the life
of the frontier and outlet here for old, repressed, inherited traits, come down to him from ancestors who

sailed and fought with Drake, and built an empire on distant raw, new soils.

But you are of less superficial temper, and you say: " These things are not the test. Society, in any real meaning of the word, implies a congregating of persons trained in the same school of thought. There can be no true society unless you have both men and women living the life of the mind, and having respect for that life." To you who really know, then, I would say this: Not long ago we thought to organize a university club, and among the thousand-odd people wintering that year in Fairbanks we found without any trouble, or without exhausting a list of possibilities, over sixty with degrees from universities ranging from Göttingen, Upsala and Oxford, to Old Nassau and Stanford. If there be kinship in the ways of mind, then certain root of friendliness is here.

The differences you will find in social Arctic circles are the differences of relative time and place, and not differences of people. The town of Fairbanks is not, at this writing, yet thirty years old. Except for children born here since 1902 (and most of those who have attained majority are now away at college, for seventy-five per cent. of our highschool graduates do go to college) every other person has *come* here—from other far sections of the world, for some specific reason. When I first came to the North a woman said to me, " Every one has come to find something, or to forget something." The differences between social life here and elsewhere lie buried in the implications of that very true statement.

What brought us together here—the individuals who, collectively, form our society? Among those who came to forget something there is, first of all,

the " race of men who don't fit in." Some few were
frankly misfits and failures seeking refuge in the wilderness—men with the requisite physical hardihood
to survive the early rough conditions of pioneer life
but who by temperament were unsuited to the existing social order Outside, as they saw it. Many of
the early New England Pilgrims brought with them
that same feeling of non-conformity, a preference
for a smaller, a more remote community, where men
would count for more as individuals than they did
in seventeenth-century social England. To-day these
are the alone-goers who wish to remove themselves
from the poisons, strains, depressions and mechani-
zation of what they consider a too-crowded civilization and have, to this end, sought out America's last
frontier, hoping to secure here a fresh start, a new
environment, a more even " break," and association
with new and perhaps truer individuals. These have
come to get away from pasts—historical pasts or personal pasts—and are not much interested in old roots
or old conventions, for they are themselves uprooted
and unconventional. One such has said to me: " For
God's sake don't waste your time digging up stuff
about Alaska's past history! We came here to *escape*
history, if that's possible. The old ways are all bad.
Let's forget them, and start afresh."

There is a grouping of similar-minded men on
any frontier line, in any far colony—men not interested in reading or thinking history, but men who
are themselves, without realizing it, making history;
for of such is the groundwork colonial pattern composed. As individuals they may be " lazy as sin "
or perfect models of industry; but as citizens they
have certain definite qualities that can always be
counted upon—inherent qualities rooted to this en-

vironment as truly as the city type is set in concrete. Intense optimism is one such characteristic, practical ingenuity is another; versatility, a certain religious and social tolerance, a firm belief in the creed that " a man's a man for a' that," will always be found in this class of frontiersman, no matter how else riotously combined with conflicting discords of characteristics, or how else colored by racial or national origins.[1] If they live here long enough, Scot, Kanuk, Jew, Negro, Jap, Swede or Montenegrin will all bear the stamp of the last frontier. Their minds will be Alaska-made, for this brand of *thought* is the first manufactured product of any frontier state, long before it reaches economically the manufacturing stage. Our people are all non-conformists, in the wide sense of the word, and a community of non-conformists is never a stagnant spot. After all, it's only non-conformists who have amounted to much— the Copernicus type who would not conform astronomically, the Columbus type who would not conform geographically, the Jefferson type who would not conform politically, the Edison and Rockefeller and Ford types who refuse conformity in matters of invention, organization and sales pattern. These non-conformists have done the most interesting of the world's jobs, and perhaps we are beginning to realize that no one ever gets far ahead of the crowd by herding very closely with it.

The new forty-niners of Alaska, the founding fathers of a new forty-ninth state, are essentially individualists with a strong feeling for and tenderness

[1] Many personal sketches and true stories of Alaska's people will be found in *We Are Alaskans,* by Mary Lee Davis.

toward individual liberty. They really believe that
men were created free, that men were born equal,
and that the rights of the individual should never be
unwholesomely abridged. Because they believe this,
they act upon it. Hence we have on the frontier a
rare assortment of vivid personalities, a complexity
of manners and types, a grouping of intensified qualities. Those who are scamps by nature become more
and more raw in their manners after they scamper
to the frontier; but those who are decent and clean-
hearted find here more useful outlets for their virtues, and these virtues grow with daily use. The
frontier does not segregate the scamps and saints, it
juxtaposes them; and that makes life exciting and
zestful, morally strenuous and testful. Danger and
isolation in the early days, freedom from restraint
in the middle period of Alaska's past,—combined
with opportunities for financial success with little
or no capital, as in placer mining,—naturally attracted " the adventurers, the restless and the con-
tentious," just as Adams has described the settlers
of early New England. Having come, having cast
off the old, they have stubbornly refused to let go
in their wrestling, without a blessing. They wouldn't
go back and face the folks back home without " a
full poke."

Even those who have not been financially successful here have come finally to have their reward in
seeing that, even in Alaska, life can be well lived.
They have found a more natural and more unhurried
pace, restful and as yet not highly mechanized. Here
the absence of crowd infection and a relative lack
of germ density make for health. In proof—when
Stefansson came down from his five winters spent
in the High Arctic, up on the roof of the attic where

he had been all that time entirely free from "colds," and got to Herschel Island (which we Interior Alaskans consider the jumping-off place!) he caught a severe cold, a cold which nearly killed him. When men such as my Scotch friend from the relatively lonely Kantishna, or Fannie Quigley, come to the "crowded town of Fairbanks," they almost always catch a cold. When we go Outside from our relatively uncrowded town to the city of Seattle, we almost always "catch a cold." Like cold itself, colds are apparently a matter of something more or something less, not something stable or fixed, inherent in one's biological chemistry.

Perhaps it is because we know each other better that we are more trustful here. Honesty is the very best insurance policy, and Fairbanks is the only town I've ever lived in where I did not carry burglar insurance. When I first came here many houses had no keys, ever. The house on Front Street, which we rented for the first two years, had no key to the front door when we took possession, and the man who owned it thought me mighty queer when I asked for one.

"What do you want of a key?" he said. "No one in Fairbanks ever locks a door—except, perhaps, *when the boat is in.*"

There you have it, for the boat brought strangers; and it's always the stranger—not people whom you know—who is distrusted. Or, as Peter Dow put it, arriving in Seattle from a mining camp at the head of the Koyukuk River where he lived for twenty-five years:

"What's it done for us up North—this rotten civilization? In the old days we had justice in our camps. Everything was settled in miners' meetings.

Gold was left unlocked in miners' cabins and never a grain stolen. Food was always handy in cabins along the trail, for any traveller. Then the United States came with marshals and their deputies and they brought a civilized class in, and now we have to lock our doors at night!"

Our Town is in a social transition, now that we have a railroad and airplane service. We are neither a frontier nor a city, at present, but have something of both. This change was shown dramatically in the famous "moccasin case" which agitated our court one spring. A man had sent his children to school that winter in moccasins, which he claimed were both cheaper and warmer than leather shoes. The teacher claimed that the heat of the room brought out essential odor of whatever kind and the not-too-delicate odor of native-tanned moose hide in special! She and many of the pupils were offended in the nostril, and so an order was issued that shoes were the proper foot-gear for indoor wear at school. The father, a pioneer and therefore of course an individualist, felt that his liberties were being abridged—and who was this Outside woman, this cheechako, to say what *his* children should wear? Feeling ran high and the matter finally came to court, giving us a spicy and dramatic spring session, a grand social pow-wow beaten upon that persistent resonant village drum of small towns, the local court-house, until (as was inevitable with a sourdough jury) the individualist had his way! The case was a good sample of the only two real differences between our social life here and elsewhere—the fact that we are pioneers and the fact of the northern climate.

Locality influences our accent, so that a different and a typically Alaskan vocabulary grows up out of this rich soil of shared experience; it also influences our perspective and preoccupations. Changed mechanics of living stamp a changed pattern on the mind. Mill towns think in different terms and symbols than do " cow towns," and mining towns have their own ethical and social pattern, peculiar to the trade men live by. We know an astonishing lack of tradition, incident to our recent immigration; but so, too, do many eastern cities. Many of the conventional props of city social life are missing; and untied instead of united qualities, as yet unsmelted, bring strange juxtapositions. We have no really " untouchable " castes on the frontier. The human strata are not laid down smoothly as in the old communities, each in its own ordered place, but are opened, exposed, tilted and weathered here, so that any one with an eye to human geology can read the story. Buried strata are no longer buried, for the strange upheaval which tossed us here has brought up into the open all that the older lands keep hidden. Any one coming directly from the east would perhaps most notice that nothing underlying need be taken for granted—on the frontier! Matters of social hiatus not talked about elsewhere are bandied between goody and gossip, tongues are vastly more free and things are said, names named, spades denominated. At first this startled me; but later it greatly interested, because it meant a social order so vividly changeful and chock-a-block with variety.

The circle of human contacts deepens as it narrows to the shape of a small community, and one gets to know revealingly well almost all the people whom one daily meets. My own years in the North seem to me a post-graduate course in essential human nature. There are no giftedly idle here, no fash-

ionably great, for all are equally busy. Mrs. H——
may be the wife of the bank president, and Mrs.
I—— the wife of the man who runs the hoist at a
mine; but if Mrs. I—— is a better cook in her own
right, then her parties will be more popular! For
we Fairbanks women are all our own cooks, and that
in itself is a social democracy. In the matter of self-
service we are all in the same boat, and that helps a
lot in understanding each other's problems. I don't
know any ordinary or uninteresting human beings in
Fairbanks, for the influence of the frontier has been
to individualize sharply. People do not dwell here
within the walls of fond memories, close-knit family
or "social" ties, parochial interests. They have re-
tained what they could of the graces and charms,
diversities and distinctions of their home places, and
these home places are so immensely varied that to
know them even vicariously is in itself an education;
but "freight is high" even upon mental baggage,
when one comes thus far, and here the ancient institutions upon which our kinsmen in the ancient lands
depend are either absent or haven't quite the same
meaning. "It is easy in the world to live after the
world's opinion: it is easy in solitude to live after
your own." Frontiersmen retain of "world's opinion" only that which they can put to immediate use,
under the pressure of new circumstance. The North,
as Professor Turner said of the West, "is a form of
society rather than an area."

There are some who define social life as a matter
of parties, hospitalities, and sports, and Fairbanks
life is very full of these pleasant diversions. Our
Town hasn't a golf course, but most major sports,
both winter and summer varieties, are enjoyed here.
The hospitalities of the northern towns are famous,

and Fairbanks—because it is farthest north, more so than even Dawson or Nome—has in its frontier stage been especially open-doored. There came a time in colonial America when, as Hall wrote long ago of the American colonies, " the mere name of stranger has ceased to be a passport. The country was civilized. There were taverns." So in the North, there are now comfortable " taverns " in all the major towns where numerous travellers are summer touring guests and where many of the creek population live in winter, if work on the claims is not possible. But wherever there are no hotels, then the frontier open-handedness is still in evidence and the stranger is taken within the gates, gladly.

As to houses, I have told you of our first log cabin in Fairbanks and that it was well fitted and commodious. After two years the owners returned and wished to live in it themselves, and as it was difficult to rent another (since practically every one owns his own home here) we were fortunate in being able to buy one. In a letter written the year after we moved into our new home, I described it to a friend:

Our new house is, in a way, a bit of the history of the country. Tourists coming here wonder how such a large, comfortable, really pleasant home ever happened to grow up in a town so remote—so, as they think, forgotten, distant, and primitive. It was built, in a way, on a bet, as a wager, in an odd manner.

A man who had been a wanderer, an adventurer, made quite a little fortune in Dawson in the early days, married a young wife who loved the bright lights of the city and its ways, and then came to our town to live. The wife longed for 'Frisco, but the husband—for reasons which I suspect, but which he alone knew best—did not care to leave the North. He proposed a compromise, so I have been told. If she would remain contented in Alaska for

ten years, he promised to build for her the finest house
that the Territory had known! She considered this.
Having had, perhaps, some former experience with the
futility of masculine promises, she went to her attorney
and had him draw up the plans and specifications of a
house such as her fondest dream had imaged. It was
to have a real lawn, first and foremost—that unknown,
luxurious thing in a land of moss; and it must have a real
fireplace, a thing until then unknown in the Interior. It
must have hot-water heat, even though a man had to
come from Seattle to install it, and an oak floor (another
import!), oak trim and doors, a large porch all screened
and roomy, a double garage, and the best plumbing
obtainable, with all-porcelain fixtures. This house was
to be really warm—not a log cabin to be chinked anew
each year, to sag in the corners when the frost moves,
and "with cracks you can stick the stovepipe through."
Oh, no! This was to be one frame house set inside
another frame house, complete, with six full inches of
sawdust in the space between the outer walls and also in
the ceilings, making it absolutely frost proof in winter
and heat proof in summer.

She knew what she wanted, and he, poor man—as
many another—signed on the dotted line! The house
was built, as per specifications. Before it was really
finished, in a sudden tragic moment this wanderer was
thrust unwarned out on his last long trail and the widow
left with her super-home—a house as seeming out of
place in this far land as a lovely Georgian mansion of
brick and elegant façade would have been anachronism
in seventeenth-century New England. And we—my
seven eighths and I, needing desperately a place to lay
our heads,— snatched upon this house as heaven-sent, and
bought the place, though we could ill afford to. But we
have found that a truly Alaska-built house has its advantages. My father, as you know, lives in an eastern city
famed the world over for its mild and equable winter
climate, for it lies where the Gulf Stream can touch it.
He occupies a house there of much the same cubic con-

tent as ours here; but last winter he burned twenty-five tons of coal to heat his house, and I burned nine to heat mine! It pays to build a house like an ice-box.

And so, you see, we live in comfort and at ease upon our pioneering venture. Guests who have come from the east have been quite as surprised at its comfort as were, I have no doubt, travellers from England who ventured to New England in colonial days and were entertained at your Salem in homes they thought remarkably comfortable to have sprung up " in the wilderness "! The cold has proved an ally, the air year-round a distillate of health. What more can I say, about " the discomforts of the North " which you seem to insist that we suffer?

President Harding said when he visited Fairbanks: " One who comes to Alaska from the States, even though measurably well read, usually has an impression that this is a man's country, that it is the home of the itinerant adventurer and prospector and sometimes of the roughneck. He does not stop to think, as I myself did not, of the charm of Alaska as a home country. . . . While Alaska is majestic and boundless and mighty, an empire in itself, it is also strikingly a home land; and that is the finest thing that may be said of any section, of any nation."

Song is a social agent, and music forms an important factor in the life of the North. Alaska, with its large quota of Russian and Scandinavian music lovers, is rich in music creation as well as music appreciation. Orchestras, bands, choruses, study clubs and choirs are found in nearly every town, and thirteen of these organizations are affiliated with the National Federation of Music Clubs. Take Ketchikan, for example: it has a rousing community orchestra presenting concerts annually, the Normanna Male Chorus of thirty-five members, the Ketchikan

Music Club which in 1929 presented Charles Wake-field Cadman in three concerts; and the Ketchikan City Band. The very oldest musical organization of which I know in Alaska is the Metlakatla Concert Band of thirty native members, founded by Father Duncan in 1877. The large choir of St. Michael's venerable cathedral of the Orthodox Church at Sitka sing gloriously in Russian under the leadership of John Panamarkof. And Florence Tobin, District President of the National Federation of Music Clubs, tells me that Alaska now has more music-club members per capita than any state in the Union.

If groups of interesting people make for a social order, if home comfort and the possibility of pleasant hospitality make for "society," then one may surely find them here, in flourishing peopled towns and imminent cities of the Northland. Alaskans have their backs to disappointment and their faces set toward hope. As "W. F." says: "Come good, come ill, I would rather my children live all their lives in Alaska than that they leave and prosper exceeding great in a worn-out world. For here is the last Frontier, the greatest that has been, and it is on the Frontier that a man has the chance to show what is in him—if it is! The Hi-carders, Hi-jackers, did not clutter up the Contribution Box with cheques. Those who came to the North solely because the North was then wide open, have went. The Sure-Thing Man went where It was and tied into It, from soda to hoc. Men don't grow big on coddling. Builders go forth to *build*."

It is not uncommon (in individuals such as explorers, in communities of pioneers, even in a whole nation) to see people who possess unusual resourcefulness in mastering *things,* baffled and unskilled in their human and purely social relations. But this does not seem to hold true in Alaska, where certain types of organization, especially the fraternal orders, are very strong and form really the most stabilizing influence. Watching their work, we learn that institutions are effects and not causes in true social life. The towns of the North are great get-together places, and when anything is going on, whether a good time or a peck of trouble, it is always a shared experience. The potlatch is an Indian affair, but if you are in actual need in the North, whoever knows of it will potlatch you to the limit of his stake!

I have spoken of the towns, for in the towns one finds truly social living—in all the word's best implication. But outside and beyond the towns lies that vast, almost empty, ninety-eight-per-cent-unclaimed, unmastered, real frontier. One realizes this when a man of seventy-three walks three days' journey to see a dentist, or when a family of five girls come to town, who have never seen an electric light. In Fairbanks we are not quite a city yet, nor are we quite the real frontier any more, but something in between, something in transition—meeting-place of wilderness trails and civilization, where both ends play from the middle. We live in the suburbs of melodromance and can reach out to either wilderness or civilization from this vantage coign, for recreation or change. It's pleasant to know that both are there, a stone's throw out on either hand. This helps us keep a telescopic vision, so that the immediate foreground of our own north end of Main Street— the sometimes sordid small-town stuff—does not obstruct the glory and the beauty and the proven worth of that great untouched hinterland lying just beyond the small town's limits.

Any town, of course, is not in itself the typical frontier, for town and frontier are mutually contradictory terms. The moment you begin to build a town you begin to push back the true frontier, which is composed of lonely men in lonely cabins and not of friendly groups living in clustered homes. One feels that presence of the pressing vastness all about, however, even when living in a so-called frontier town, and it modifies all thought and action. It draws us closer together, for one thing, in friendly coöperation whenever any trouble threatens. We are quite used to doing things for ourselves, and also for others.

Recently in Washington I was driving down Connecticut Avenue and came suddenly to an impasse. A five-ton truck, loaded high with bales of hay, had been struck by a street car and had overturned across the track, scattering a score of bales in an impassable barricade all across the avenue. In twenty seconds (for it was the rush hour when the United States Government is going home) hundreds of cars, it seemed, piled up on either side—honking and hooting a protest at this delay. But not one soul *did* anything! Every one sat his car there, impatient but inactive, waiting for the trained servants of the city —the police or the fire department—to come and remove the obstruction. The incident amused and re-instructed me in city ways, for I well knew it never could have happened in any western or northern town. There a dozen men would instantly have sprung from their cars, thrown aside the central bales and, in fewer seconds than it takes to tell, a free lane would have been cleared. But no one seemed even to think of this, here.

The friend who saw this with me was a Virginian

of gentle birth. When I said, "But look at all those men—why don't they *do* something?" she answered: "Why should they? They are not paid to; it's not their affair. That is the city's business, to keep the streets clear. There's not a man here has ever touched a bale of hay, I reckon. And, besides, many of these men, you must realize, are on their way to clubs or formal teas or dinners with their friends. How would it look if they came in all covered with hay, or with their hands all soiled and rusty from that horrid snaggy wire? Why, they'd be *laughed* at!"

And then I realized how far I'd travelled since the days when I was born in Jersey, lived in old York State, and was "educate in Boston town!" Where I'd been living lately, soil on one's hands or clothes was no disgrace, nor social service for the group a laughing matter. To me there's no more stimulating sight than people pitching in and doing what they've never done before—to help themselves or others out of a tight place. It's in a jack-pot that you see the very best frontier qualities rise to the surface, for then these super-individualists of ours knuckle down to superb tasks of coöperation, in a way that's "social" in the biggest, broadest, noblest sense of that abused word. We saw this handsomely when the great influenza epidemic swept in on us and within three days full nine hundred of our thousand then in town were stricken; but every able-bodied person jumped in and helped, with joyous uncomplaining, so that all were cared for and nearly all were healed.[1] Scarcely a person of our noblest help-

---

[1] *Grendel Walks Again* and *Bridges of Bread,* two chapters in the book called *We Are Alaskans,* by Mary Lee Davis, are stories of this great epidemic and the humorous resourcefulness of Alaskans in meeting it.

ers in that day could you have met at teas or formal functions in a great city. Few were of the priestly class and few were Levites, but they proved themselves Samaritan good saints of God when, of a sudden, faith and grit and courage were desperately needed. "Whatever makes a proper world, I do not know. But surely two elements are necessary— a common purpose and a common sympathy." In no group that I know are these two traits so notable as among those abiding in far places of the North.

Which are more truly "social": groups highly organized and stratified to function only in untouchable castes; or groups of individuals without caste, fluid and free, flowing in swift coöperation and compassionate service, as neighbor's need arises? It's an old query. Two thousand years ago a certain clever lawyer put that question of eternal life to a contemporary who, by the test of time, has proved to be the greatest Sociologist. In one of the most searching stories of all literature, that lawyer got his answer; for he was shown that any man, although perhaps of alien thought or despised race, who meets with fellow man in trouble on a lonely trail and gives of his compassion, time, or purse in free-will service —that man is your true neighbor.

Of such true neighbors is the kingdom of the North, the social Arctic Circle.

XXV

Alaska as an Alma Mater

A LITTLE boy who had lived his short life in outlying creek camps was brought to Fairbanks not long ago and attended his first church service. Fascinated by all he saw in the ancient order of the mass, he nearly broke up the congregation by exclaiming in a loud whisper:

"Ma! Why do the kids in white parkas make a smudge in winter? There ain't no skeeters, around here now, is there?"

However, most of Alaska's citizens, both white and copper, are much more familiar with the inside of a church than was this little lad; for all of Alaska's white towns are church supplied, and many missions minister to the native population. I'm sure that numerous Americans, even as I myself, received our very first knowledge of Alaska from the lips of these returning missionaries, for many of the clearest and most detailed accounts of native conditions have been given by them. Father Jetté the Tánana scholar, Archdeacon Stuck the famous explorer, the Chapman family of the lower Yukon who have devoted two generations of life-work to the natives of Anvik, Thomas the brilliant sportsman and intelligent observer of the Point Hope Tigara, Ziegler the noted artist of Cordova, S. Hall Young the writer and Muir's pen-and-canoe companion, Bishop Rowe the effective organizer of frontiersmen—all these, our friends, have come to Alaska to teach and all have remained to learn in her post-graduate school. And you and I learned of Alaska from them—of different sections according to our different creeds. For many of our mission boards, early in this century, formed a gentleman's agreement not to poach on one another's preserves in the Alaskan field, but, wisely and for added efficiency in service, each to concentrate his work in a particular district.

That's why, if you are a Presbyterian, you are most familiar with Southeastern Alaska and the work of S. Hall Young and Sheldon Jackson; if a Moravian, then this oldest Protestant missionary body in Alaska will have told you of " The Society of the United Brethren for Propagating the Gospel Among the Heathen," and of their several missions established among Indians and Eskimos of the Kuskokwim and upper Bristol Bay regions, where they have been at work for so many years. The Baptists selected Cook's Inlet and Prince William Sound; while if you follow the Roman faith, then surely you have listened to accounts of the magnificent work at Holy Cross in real industrial education; the Methodist Church chose the difficult Aleutians and the Peninsula; if you are of the Episcopalian creed, then the Interior of Alaska and the country northward has been unfolded to you and the story of the Tinneh and their problems; the Swedish and Norwegian missions occupy Norton Sound and Port Clarence, and the Congregationalists hold posts along Bering Sea and Bering Strait. This agreement has to do with native and not white centers of population, for in white towns there are many churches. The various mission boards have done their work so well that they now supply the largest body of literature available about the native population of various sec-

tions of Alaska, and it is needless here to duplicate
that already well-told story.

Others have traced the thread of education in
Alaska through a national rather than a religious
maze of industry—the Bureau of Education. William Hamilton, assistant chief of the Alaskan division, says:

For the native Alaskans, the Bureau of Education
provides teachers, physicians, and nurses—trained workers who have at heart the welfare of their charges. It
maintains schools, hospitals, and orphanages, relieves
destitution, fosters trade, organizes coöperative business
enterprises, establishes colonies, and controls the reindeer
industry (a recent Executive Order has transferred this
control to Alaska's governor). . . . The 27,000
natives are scattered along thousands of miles of coast
and on the great rivers, in villages ranging from 30 or 40
to 300 or 400 persons. The work would extend to the
utmost limits of the United States, in terms of distance,
with schools in Maine, California, Georgia, and Minnesota. One of the school districts is twice the size of the
State of Illinois. Many of the 83 settlements in which
the bureau's work is located are far beyond the limits of
regular transportation and mail service.

We have seen that Sheldon Jackson, of the Bureau
of Education, was the man with a dream who introduced reindeer to Alaska—certainly a distinct constructive contribution—as is also the work of the
Training School at Sitka and the Holy Cross experiments in farming and herding.

Holy Cross is a Catholic Mission on the lower
Yukon, twenty-five miles below Anvik. Established
in '86, it has now a splendid plant built up by the
patient industry of a long-visioned Church. The

times I've been at Holy Cross and talked with the
Fathers there, it has seemed to me that they have a
different (and perhaps—I do not know—a better)
view of education for the natives than have some
of our Protestant missions.   True to our individual
ideas, we Protestants have tried to educate to a high
plane certain outstanding individuals among the natives.   The Roman Church seems to be trying to
develop a more complex, able and mentalized *people*
from the material at hand, rather than develop strikingly gifted *individuals*.   On my second visit to Holy
Cross I had a long talk with one of the Fathers there,
a talk which I have turned over in my mind many
times since.   He said:

Human nature is plastic, adaptive, impressionable.   It
reacts to environment, and we have tried to produce here
factors of environment which will make real building
possible, *in later generations*.   Our Church is a patient
Mother, and it is upon the known amount and degree of
change producible by man-directed agencies that She has
based her work here.   We take only young children, and
only on the condition that they shall stay a certain definite
time.   The children of our school (and their children,
for many marry here and grow up into our community)
become adapted physiologically and even physically to
better and better living.   We believe that we must have
three generations of wheat eaters if we are truly to build
a new civilization here, and that's why we are all farmers.   Heredity helps in making adaptation progressively
easier.   It's easier to see this in animals, because their
life span is shorter; but if, as you tell me, you broke
horses to city use and cars twenty years ago and have
done so recently, you'll see what I mean.   Colts seem
to come into the world, nowadays, with the auto idea
fixed safely and sanely in their little heads—as city babies
lisp to-day, I'm told, of gears and magnetos!   That's

what we're doing here. The white and copper races must become adjusted to each other—or the *copper* race will surely be lost. We wish to make its survival possible, by hereditary adjustments to the basic facts of civilization—to immunize our people to the dangers of civilization by inoculating them with easily-assimilable amounts of the new, at proper times. We believe that an over-exposure to our civilization, all at once, causes disease and fever, not a healthy mind or body. We believe that there is real danger in over-stimulation, in stepping too suddenly from the Stone Age to the Twentieth Century. As you or I would need time to adjust physically to a Stone Age existence, these people need time to adjust mentally to this strange new world of European Civilization.

Education in Alaska began with Gregory Shelikof, father and founder of Russian colonies in America, as he was the first man to do something for the Alaska natives. At Kodiak, in 1784, he began to teach some rudiments of reading and arithmetic, and his wife Natalia, who accompanied him on all his voyages, began to instruct in domestic science—possibly moved by the " servant problem," which must have been pressing in this new raw colony! Catherine II, that " liberal Empress," became interested in the work and sent out some helpers in 1794. The first school in Sitka was started in 1820, where the natives were taught Russian, trades, and navigation; while in 1840 Captain Etolin, a half caste who had been instructed in local schools, was made director of the Company, and both he and his wife did much in a school way. Veniaminof established a theological seminary at Sitka which continued until the transfer of the Territory to the United States.

We Americans talk much about our notable interest in education, and so it is a matter of shame

that from 1867 to 1884 the Alaska natives were left
school-less by our government, and even Russia's
rudimentary work was not continued until Sheldon
Jackson, that tireless pioneer, secured a small appropriation under the Bureau of Education. The Presbyterians had opened a school at Wrangell in 1877,
however, and at Sitka a year later, while Moravians
and Friends were at work at the mouths of the Yukon
and Kuskokwim and at Kotzebue Sound. In 1896
Senator Teller of Colorado secured funds from Congress for reindeer distribution, since grown so valuable, and the Bureau of Education and the missions
have worked loyally together in developing the reindeer industry. The school system of Alaska is in
four parts—municipal, district, rural and Federal.
The first three are under the general supervision of
the Territorial Commissioner of Education at
Juneau, and the last-named—the Eskimo and Indian
vocational schools—are supervised by the Commissioner of Education of the United States. Many
Alaska towns have excellent high schools, and in all
the " white " towns you will find educational facilities of a higher grade than in communities of similar
size in many outside states. I know of no Alaska
town without a public library and reading room.

A new continent means many different things to
many different groups of people. When Spain first
opened up a new world, when France first penetrated
the Saint Lawrence and the Mississippi, when Englishmen began to colonize the eastern coast, there
were among them all some few to whom the new
land chiefly meant new souls of " savages " to save.
To others, these were ports of new trade and barter,
new natural resources to be opened up and exploited
—the " fish and furs and mynes of Gold and Copper "

of Captain John Smith's account; or it seemed a place of new fame and new fortune, or a place to make peaceful and fruitful new colonies, secure from many types of distraction prevalent in the Old World. And the interests of these many different types of empire founders often clashed.

Here in Alaska, which is a New America, there has been from the very beginning a group whose main interest was and still is the welfare and education and Christianization of the native peoples, just as in New Spain, New France, or New England. Here, too, their interests sometimes clash with those of traders, explorers, and settlers; and there are two distinct schools of thought as to how the native population can best be helped and protected and put upon their feet—whether by educating them so thoroughly into our ways that they in time become completely absorbed in the body of our citizens; or the Father Duncan school, which holds that natives should be left to keep all their own culture and racial ways not actually brutal, and be given " only as much of our culture as is good for them and they can readily absorb." Different missions in Alaska are working differently upon this problem, and it is extremely interesting to watch the contrastive results.

One church concentrates on agriculture, herding, living conditions; another stresses medical missions, others preach the benefits of cleanliness or of common-school education. All are excellent ends, all are needed, all are doing good, in different ways and by various means. The problem is complex and is capable of many diverse answers, because the natives of Alaska are not of one race or people but many, stand upon different rungs of Civilization's ladder, and have their individual qualities, capacities and

temperaments. Some traders oppose the missions
because, they say, "The missioner teaches the native
to read and count." That is, the native can now find
out for himself the market value of fish and fur, and
is therefore not to be cheated! I have known other
traders who have given richly of their time and
patience to instruct and be big brother to the native
people. It's in the spirit, not the letter, that we
seem to meet most closely. But I, who have knelt
and received Holy Communion from the hands of
an Indian priest, cannot well thereafter look upon
him as an alien or a savage. Can I? Or is Robert
Lowie right in saying that we are all of us "savages"
very close under the skin, and " to say that we are
savage is to say that we are human " ?

But if the problem of native education is as yet
but a trail, and a trail of many conflicting blazes,
white secular education in Alaska has taken the
traditional American paved highway and is travelling at a stiff speed. High-school enrollments are
increasing at a faster rate than elementary schools,
indicating that the country is becoming more and
more stabilized, more a land of genuine homes.
Parent-Teacher Associations with memberships of
thousands have sprung up, and the last figures which
I can find show a total of a hundred and sixty-seven
schools in our Territory, three hundred and sixty-
four teachers, enrollment of eight thousand, and an
annual expenditure of close to a million dollars.
This, for our new and tiny scattered population,
shows a healthy growth of up-shooting children.
Yesterday's Fairbanks paper gave notice of a pre-
school private kindergarten to be started, pupils
leave Wacker for Ketchikan High School by stage
now that the fine new government highway has

eliminated distance, and more than half of Alaska's white high-school graduates are going on to college. Our Fairbanks High School of nearly a hundred pupils publishes a lively annual—the *Ursa Major,* of a hundred pages and many illustrations—as well as *The Vega,* a news sheet called "The Farthest North School Paper." Fairbanks boasts a school library of sixteen hundred volumes, a gymnasium, six new classrooms in the last two years so that now no teacher has classes of over twenty-five, both boys' and girls' basket-ball teams, a Junior High School band of twenty pieces, a Glee Club of fifty members, a separate manual-arts building and domestic-science rooms. In educational matters, we white folk are better off, by a good deal, than were New England colonists in old days. Twenty-seven years after the founding of Plymouth a Massachusetts law provided that every town of fifty families must maintain a teacher and each town of a hundred families a grammar school. Twenty-seven years after the founding of Fairbanks an Alaskan law provides that wherever there are six children of school age, a teacher may be requested for a coöperative "rural" school, while ten are the minimum number for a district school maintained by the Territory.

The Road to Higher Education begins in Fairbanks, too, and winds out from town four miles to the Hill of Birches which one climbs to "The Farthest North College in the World," a going concern for several years past. Everything here is farthest, you see, and so we are not content with merely a comparatively "higher" education, but must call it highest! The college seal shows the profile of Denali, the mountain which is faced across the wide Tánana from that Hill of Birches, and it bears the ambitious motto *Ad Summum*—to the very top. To live up to the rarified atmosphere of McKinley's summit may tax our poor human lungs; but here at the Alaska Agricultural College and School of Mines, the last of the land-grant colleges, we take our fling at it.

Massachusetts had John Harvard's little school only sixteen years after the Pilgrims came, but we of the North set in place a cornerstone for our Alaska College only thirteen years after the coming of Pedro, Barnette and Wada to this Tánana camp. Judge Wickersham said, as he laid that stone: " The Pioneers of Alaska are gathered here . . . on this beautiful birch-clad hill, where until to-day only the foot of the moose and the wild Taná hunter have trod . . . to dedicate to the use of our youth a college for the special study of the sciences connected with agriculture and mining. . . . Among those now gathered around this stone . . . are students from many lands and graduates from many colleges—from Yale and Vassar, Oxford and Harvard, and from the universities of nearly every state of the Union; while such are the blessings of free schools that not one amongst us, excepting alone the native Taná, is without at least a common-school education. This group is typical of any other which might be gathered in this pioneer land—it contains students of every color and tongue—but none of us are Alaska born. We are immigrants from distant states where schools of learning similar to that which we will erect on this spot gave *us* advantages which will be denied to *our* children, if we fail to establish them here."

Are we too ambitious, too o'er-leaping, do you think, to attempt to carry this ancient torch of learn-

ing " to the summit," to the top of this spinning old
world, and plant it there, Excelsior-like? Have we
less cause than John Harvard had (and to men new-
come from England I fancy *that* beginning appeared
quite as crude in the light of Oxford or of Cam-
bridge as our own of to-day) to keep faith with our
wilderness of murmuring pine and of hemlock, our
savannahs and our prairies, developing into something—we know not what, but something worth
while? Have we "our nerve"? Well, if we have,
so too had Pilgrim Fathers. They too believed
whole-heartedly, not only in their adopted country
but in themselves as pioneers. A pioneer has to be
cock-sure, so don't blame him for it. New lands
mean new situations. Immediate need for immediate action arises and there is not a precedent in
sight. Most precedents wouldn't bear transplanting,
anyway.

Those who lived back in old England blamed New
England colonists for being too cock-sure, and Washington officials do the same with us. Don't blame us
for cock-sureness, for we need it mightily as an
essential tool of our trail-breaking. And remember,
too, how Stoughton wrote in the sixteen-seventies:
"God sifted a whole nation that He might send
choice grain over into this wilderness." Cock-sure?
Rather. Yet Adams calls this "but a mild expression of what the New Englander thoroughly believed, and loved to be told."

You can't keep people who are like that, down.
They will make cracking-good ancestors—ancestors
to be proud of. Just give them a century or so of
time!

But I must remind you of another meaning to
Alaskan education—one which has not, I think, been

touched on and which is yet a most powerful reagent.
Teachers, priests, nurses, clergy, Jesuit Fathers,
deaconesses, Friends, Lutherans, Sisters of the Catholic orders, Presbyterians, high and low church
Episcopalians—all of whom I've met and known in
numbers in The North—will say in various ways
when you talk intimately with them about the life
here: " We came to teach, but though we brought
our best, the land has taught *us* more than we could
give." And my own observation has been that the
keener the mind, the more trained the intellect, the
quicker has been this stimulus and this response to a
great teacher's stiff discipline and humanistic cur-
riculum. Those less keen of mind than these good
teachers, perhaps because not equally trained to
recognize instruction when they see it, have not
equally given The North due credit as a school of
men. But many do and have recognized in Alaska
herself a great educator, caustic and admirably
skilled.

The North grades her pupils as a miner grades
his pay dirt: a twist of her wrist and new values
appear, before unseen and unguessed—the flick of
pure gold in blackest sands. In a pioneer life, as
Scott wrote of the Antarctic: " Every day some new
fact comes to light, some new obstacle which
threatens the gravest obstruction. I suppose this is
the reason which makes the game so well worth playing." Alaskan pioneers like frontier life for many
of the same reasons for which sailors like " dirty
weather." Alaska keeps you on your toes, keeps
grading you, and is always propounding new and
practical examination questions to test your fitness to
remain. She keeps presenting constantly to your
attention something chaotic, something adverse,

which calls for action and provokes high spirit.
Sudden turnings of the trail, events that come whirl-
ing at you out of space like stray disastrous comets
. . . and "sudden the worst turns best, to the
brave."

Often the pioneer is called upon to pit his mettle,
nerves and skill against the seemingly insuperable,
and in that test to force the spirit to prevail against
the material. If you can get any old Alaskan to
open his heart to you, this is what he will tell you
is the ultimate lure of the land—this spiritual value
far above gold, which Service tried to phrase con-
cretely in "The Spell of the Yukon." We have
spoken to the earth and it has taught us, not of itself
but of ourselves. Those who enjoy to the uttermost
that inner stir of sharp action, twisting swift corner
into unforeseen event (and only those who do are
happy on the real frontier), find Alaska teaching,
quite as much as she is being taught, and blessing
those "who are not born above instruction by surprise!"

There is a challenge in the frontier call to turn
one's hand and mind to many things. One learns
here of necessity to do almost everything, one gets
away from the specialized and dependent living of
cities, and learns by doing and by self-teaching—the
trial and error way of science. A man in the open
plain, free to move in any direction, cannot rise.
But give a strong man two walls, hemming him ir-
revocably before and behind, and he can climb to
heaven by the very friction of his surroundings and
the vigor of his own propulsive grip. A frontier
provides those walls. One dearest of Alaskan friends
wrote me, on her return to Ireland:

I have to keep constantly pinching myself, when talking to my old friends, to remember that they have not been in Alaska, so their sense of values has not undergone the complete change that mine has. I met an old friend on Sunday whom I had not seen for nineteen years. She said, " Tell me, Jessie, what did you do when you first came out there ? " I could not answer her; I just looked blank and said, "Well, I believe I have done everything it is possible for one woman to do. Just ask me if I have done any one thing, and I will tell you." Really, Mary Lee, do you realize how full our lives were there, from cooking to washing, from teaching to conducting political meetings, from entertaining to keeping up the moral code? Talk of your missions! If we were not missionaries, I would like to know who was.

It is part of Nordland reality sometimes to live in the deep-most places of shared human experience, and to this richness Alaska is an open door. By living we learn—by folk, work and place—but pioneer life intensifies and deepens the process and speeds it up. We are told by modern experts in education that the philosophy underlying all true education is this: That individuality should be respected, latent powers drawn out, and so a basis laid for satisfactory adjustments to life. Alaska is a great teacher, because she does all these things for us. She keeps a progressive school for she encourages observation, stimulates thought, and teaches appropriate acting, by *experience*. While doing all this, her scholars are also storing up a world of interesting useful fact, as well. And we are all scholars, in her various classes, —cheechakos in her kindergarten and sourdoughs and old-timers and pioneers in the upper grades,— digesting the great facts she teaches, learning to read the secrets of her spaces and her spawning silences, acquiring skill in answering the many problems of adjustment which she propounds. Crafts and accomplishments are to be studied here, there are arts to be learned and appreciated, joyful activities to be shared, as in any busy well-planned school: a school for quick minds only, for the rolling years pass quickly and the semesters run from equinox to solstice on swift feet.

You will find among the Alaska-educated plenty of people who lack tuition but are rich in intuition. You will find many who are well read in the book sense, as well as many others who read well the rivers, mountains, and the inner seas, who know the secrets of the passes and the trails to Nowhere and to Everywhere, and who have entered into the secrets of the frost. You ask if we have an Alaskan " culture." I ask, "What is your definition of culture?" The President of the University of Nebraska recently defined it in these words: " Culture is the appreciation, not mainly contemplative but active and efficient, of the non-economic values. It is not identical with morality, but involves that. It covers enlightenment, breadth, open-mindedness, chivalry, honor, generosity, magnanimity, justice, gentleness, devotion to principle, the courage of one's convictions, and the power to sustain." By this test, as well as in the unexampled opportunities offered for the study of humanics, Alaska has truly a culture.

On a frontier one gets to know people more intimately and thoroughly than elsewhere, and this is in itself a rich treasure-house of educational value. One has the time and the opportunity to establish both strong friends and strong enemies, and the latter often teach us more than friends do, both of human

nature and our own limitations! When an Alaskan
speaks of " My Alaskan education " he is usually not
referring to facts he has learned about the country,
but facts he has learned about himself.

A friend wrote me one winter from the Outside:
" In that great white silence is the human soul shut
in, or is the world shut out? " Both, and both are
proving ground of character. Most Alaskans have
a horror of getting behind the rest of the world, so
they refuse to let a mere geographic accident set
limits to world contacts. We ourselves have sub-
scribed to forty-seven magazines, and they became
stimulating real friends to us, not merely periodicals.
Of these, six were music and six were art journals,
friends sent me all their concert and opera programs,
and I had galleries send in their catalogs and notes.
We have a musical library of a thousand classical
records, and have frequently shared them with others
who enjoy true music. I spent eight years here
studying and teaching the history of music—a thing
I always wanted to do but never had an opportunity
to do, before. It was a pleasant pastime, not a way
to " kill time "—that horrid phrase! New York
shopping services provided us up-to-date clothes, and
books were ordered by the quantity, the lists based
upon reliable magazine reviews. A cousin coming
from New York to visit us exclaimed: " Why, you
are more ' up ' on what is going on in New York
than I am. *I* haven't the *time!* "

That's it—your time is not forced into a fixed pattern, here, but you design your own pattern. Some
people find this confusing, but most of us like it. In
many things, on the frontier, you make your own
rules as you go along. All the props of civilization
are more loosely wedged, all the fences of conven-

tion are lower and more easily leaped, all the restraining dicta of "Society" are of less effect. "Never a law of God or man, runs North of fifty-three." Men put pragmatic tests to institutions, and if they "work well," then they will be reëstablished on the frontier. If not, then the frontier will have none of them. Morality is one of the first things put to test on the frontier, but men soon re-learn the expediency of morality, and it's not long before a frontier community becomes as strictly moral as the best. For morality really works.

Coming back to the so-called centers of civilization and culture after years in the North, I was surprised to find that even in university towns most people seemed less truly educated, often, than had my less complex Alaskan friends. I noticed with real pain a sense of drifting, a lack of individual purpose in direction, in many people whom I met there. For the most part they seemed to be taking life at second-hand and to be dressed in mental cast-offs and hand-me-downs of thought, in scanty and inadequate emotions. They seemed to be living all their days under inverted commas! Only then did I realize the real privilege it has been to live in the North—the deepest privilege that has ever come to me, the blessing of this eight-year seminar I had been taking at the feet of a great Instructress—in the assurance of tested values which comes from life lived literally beyond the press of crowd-thrown barriers. The frontier always has developed individuals, and always will, so long as a frontier remains. As one wrote me recently from Ketchikan, "It is my belief that we live in Alaska the most interesting life possible to our world to-day."

" The world stands out on either side,
No wider than the heart is wide:
Above the world is stretched the sky,
No higher than the soul is high.
.   .   .   But East and West will pinch the heart
That cannot keep them pushed apart;
And he whose soul is flat—the sky
Will cave in on him, by and by."

On the whole, life on the frontier is more difficult
for a woman than for a man. I say it frankly, and
I say it hesitatingly, but I believe it true. My own
deep love for the North is not a blind love. I wear
no bandage on my eyes to make me oblivious to the
psychological hardships of the frontier—which are
more real to most women than are the physical hardships. Nor do I shut my eyes to many things in
Alaskan life which are not lovely or of good repute,
for there are many such—even as in your own state
or your own city; for Alaska is, after all, just another part of our human world. But many of these
unlovely aspects have been too much stressed in
words of other writers for me to need repeat them,
even when I believe them. And, too, so many of
the less pleasant features of Alaskan life are passing
with new communications and intercourse—new
lanes of commerce opening new lanes of thought—
that I can see no need to call further attention to
minor actors in our drama already taking their last
curtain call.

I myself have learned most from Alaska's people
who, on the whole, assay decidedly to the good. We
have our quota of the small-minded, the narrow and
the close-minded—as what community has not?—and
a few of the evil-minded; but not many, if any, of
these are among the old-timers who set the stamp

and pace. Of the others, as Nora says: " Oh, sure, 'twill pass! Would there be nought but blessed saints in the far-away, we'd lose religion! It's tricky men, it is, would kape us mindful of the Deadly Sins, and know the face of them! "

A woman, to be happy on the frontier, must be busy, and she must be good company when alone with herself. Content' is a matter of con'tent. " When thou journeyest out into the shadows," the old Egyptian proverb says, " take not sweetmeats with thee but a seed of corn and a bottle of tears and wine, that thou mayest have a garden in the land whither thou goest."

It seems to me that it is a necessary task of the pioneer woman, especially, to see in place and in a perspective the social and educational life of these communities—small and weak as yet and set precariously upon the dangling fringe of civilization. We need, even more than do the men of the community, to see all the material of our frontier life in the rousing terms of historical drama: the pageant of years and peoples and far places, the races of men as protagonists, the continents as a shifting yet continuing stage, the patient centuries as witnesses. Above all, we women need that vision of ourselves as vital agents in this world of great events; for days of disillusion and adjustment are bound to come, when a multitude of petty things drag and distort, as clinging barnacles warp course and cause leeway. But once let us regard all this in a large frame, focused to perspective, and then we shall not lose that feeling of the total picture, shall not know cringing or a loss because of petty happenings in any single day.

We cannot know the future, or foresee it, any more

than early colonists in New England could have foreseen the actual development of the present British Empire or of the United States, " the creation of each of which has been largely dependent upon economic forces and scientific inventions, largely beyond the vision of any seventeenth-century mind. . . . The leaders of each of them," writes Adams, " must often have dreamed of what the future might have in store for the little colonies in which they had cast their lots, but it is impossible to say what those dreams may have been."—We Alaskans, too, are in our dreaming stage.

Yet this country is not a lotus-eaters' paradise, to which we've come in entire forgetfulness or utter ignorance of America's colonial past, which is our inheritance equally with you. We remember and we look forward. We are not pioneering in a trance. That might work elsewhere, but conditions here make such a course mean death—not to move forward, not to have a sense of true or at least relative direction. We try to use any tradition which we possess to enlighten, sharpen and focus the life that we see, and we need all our best knowledge to explain and amplify our basic and enthusiastic structural faith. Alaska herself has taught us, both of her resources and our own:

> " We men of earth have here the stuff
> Of Paradise—we have enough!
> We need no other stones to build
> The stairs into the Unfulfilled—
> No other ivory for the doors,
> No other marble for the floors—
> No other cedar for the beam
> And dome of man's immortal dream."

XXVI

How High Is the High North?

IN early Dawson days the cost of even the simplest living was almost prohibitive, and only the actual fact of "grass-root" gold made the first camp really possible. The reason was, of course, the utter lack of adequate transportation.

Bringing in perishables was a riskish business, and even necessities were so scarce they fetched outrageous prices. There were no wharves at first in Skagway, goods and passengers were lightered on scows and often stranded on the tide-flats, horses were pushed off to swim ashore as they could, and supplies piled upon the beach in utter confusion. One big Swede pulled a four-hundred-pound sled over the Pass through snow and wind and slide; but most merely packed as much ahead as they could, piled it up above the snow on a few spruce boughs, and went back for more—in five or six mile stages, ten or twelve trips, forth and back. One woman drove goats to her sled, that held a laundry outfit she planned to set up—when and if she reached Dawson. Thousands of home-made boats were built at Bennett—in shapes and ways that would give any honest shipwright nightmare! Some of them got through but, when they did, the freight they carried often proved to be quite literally worth its weight in gold. Transportation was a gamble, and therefore costs hit the ceiling.

The same thing happened in other early Yukon camps. An item in the Yukon *Press,* published in Circle City January 15, 1899, reads: " John Snell of Sausalito, California, arrived at Rampart last fall with a large cargo of eggs. Constant worry over the perishableness of his cargo led him to commit suicide." During the winter of '97–'98, L. F. Persons freighted on the Dyea trail to Lake Bennett a shipment of general merchandise and building material. When the spring break-up came he loaded his outfit on a scow and was the first to reach Dawson that season. Before he even landed the goods, he sold his entire cargo on the basis of a dollar a pound (including nails!)—with the exception of eggs, which readily brought a dollar apiece. He cleared up thirty thousand dollars profit from this one scow-load, and cannily invested in Seattle real estate.

The first vegetable man in Dawson charged six dollars a dozen for celery *stalks*—not bunches—and fifty cents a pound for turnips, carrots, cabbage, beets. Sugar sold for seventy-five dollars a hundred-weight, flour for a dollar a pound; two hundred dollars were paid for a crate of *frozen* potatoes, and the winter rate for eggs (even such as disseminated a sulphurated odor of new-born chick) was a dollar and a half apiece. Those were the days, as " W. F." says, "when two bits wouldn't even buy a postage stamp in Dawson." In early days Frank Joaquin, a pioneer on the Kuskokwim, had trouble chartering a boat in San Francisco to bring in his supplies, for owners said, " The Kuskokwim? There *ain't* no such place." When he did get a schooner, he could secure no marine insurance. In 1910 two thousand miners were caught by early fall in the Georgetown stampede, and Joaquin brought three hundred tons of freight up river in *The Quickstep,* loaded to her guards with cargo, bow and sides covered with tons of ice. With every miner in camp lending a hand, the cargo was unloaded at double quick. And just in time, for *The Quickstep* went into winter quarters that grim November morning—in the middle of the Kuskokwim! No wonder grub came high that winter, or that one miner who had saved a few Chinese matches retailed them " one block to a man, four bits a throw," so I've been told, and " to ask a man for a light, *that* winter, produced the same effect as calling a red-head a liar!"

In Dawson's early days, one time when miners' candles ran short, some local Wallingford conceived a bright idea—and cleaned up nine thousand dollars on the trick, before he was caught and " jumped the line " over into Alaska. Having on hand a supply of candle-wick, which was used for caulking the little rough-made prospectors' boats, and several cases of condensed milk, he first put strips of the wick in candle molds and then poured in milk which almost immediately froze when exposed at forty below. It made a fine-appearing creamy " wax " candle—as long as it was kept outdoors; and he actually sold these at $150 a case, or $1.25 apiece— while the game lasted!

In Nome stampede days a steak cost seven dollars, an apple one, and a bunk five. In early Fairbanks, sandwiches were a dollar, tiny "tin" Yukon stoves fifty dollars, and baking-powder biscuit sold for two dollars a dozen. Nome, even with sea-freight, paid forty dollars a ton for coal in 1921, but when Fairbanks got the railroad and tied up with the Nenána coal beds, coal sold with us for nine dollars screened lump and seven fifty for run-of-mine. The railroad brought the local price of milk down from thirty-seven and a half cents a quart, to twenty-five.

When we first came to Fairbanks we found many pioneer business conditions still in vogue, and gold dust still being taken in open exchange at many of the stores. One of my first shopping questions was to ask about the fine sets of gold scales I saw on many store counters; and the second, I think, about the meaning of the leather cup and dice, then to be found at the cash desk of nearly all shops. So imbued was everybody with the gambling element in trade that, if you made a purchase, you could " shoot for it," if you wished to do so. If Lady Luck was agin' you, the shopkeeper was paid double his original asking price; if with you, then you merely picked up your package and walked out, paying nothing! No Fairbanks child had ever seen a coin smaller than a quarter, the local " two bits " ; and one Sunday, " when the boat was in " and strangers visited Saint Matthews, a little choir boy watching my treasurer-husband count collection after service, remarked excitedly on seeing a dime, " What's that? Cheechako money? "

That cheechako dime nearly brought on a lawsuit. When my husband took it to the bank to deposit with the rest of the church money, the teller refused to accept it. It would " ball up the accounts," you see, for the bank cleared only to the nearest quarter. If some one gave you a cheque for $76.13, the bank would credit your account with $76.25; but if the cheque happened to be for $76.12, you got only seventy-six dollars flat. Otherwise, it " balled up the accounts," and since the bank took its cue—or seemed to—from the old faro banks and believed that a liberal percentage should accrue to the house, they took—and still do—a two-bit rake-off on all outside cheques. So you can see that, when confronted with that cheechako dime, a matter of high finance was involved.

My disgusted cheechako husband (for we were newcomers that year) said: " But this goes to the church account. You'll have to take it. It's the offering money." The teller merely grinned, " No, you pocket it. That's the way it's done. You're entitled to your percentage, too! " Only a stiff reminder that the dime was legal tender, the bank a U. S. Depository and therefore bound to accept U. S. currency, and other caustic and pertinent remarks, made that teller accept the offending dime. But I think he cordially hated my husband ever after.

This was a hang-over from the early days, of course, and the bank seems to be about the only one of our local business houses which still holds to these primitive ways, all others having changed to meet changing and more modern conditions. With the coming of the railroad, Fairbanks graduated from being a " two-bits town." and now " coast prices " prevail. Before the railroad all goods had to be ordered on a high Outside spring market, shipped in by long expensive water haul in summer, and kept in warm storage through the winter. Goods sold in winter would very likely not be paid for until next year's cleanup on the creeks. All this made for terrific overhead, but the railroad changed all that. Now a business man can ship direct from Seattle each week of the year, taking advantage of better market prices, and no large stock has now to be kept on hand at high storage cost or with long tie-up of capital. The price of provisions took a tremendous drop when the railroad found its way to our camp.

In the old days, the little commerce that existed was extremely self-important. The storekeeper " had a cinch " on what little transportation there was, and he also felt that to keep a store at all, on the last frontier, was to do a favor to the community. It was a monopoly, it was an " accommodation," and it was a gamble—and the buyer had not only to pay for the favor, the monopoly and the risk, but he also had to " stand in " or the storekeeper would refuse to sell to him. Frontier salesmanship was always a type of hold-up. But the railroad changed that, also; for now, if the stores don't suit us (but they do, for they have changed their attitude completely —or disappeared) we merely send a wire to Seattle and ship in for ourselves all that we need, by next week's boat and twice-weekly winter train. Fear and favor have been removed from our town's business, thanks to Uncle Sam's good parcel post and Uncle Sam's even better Alaska Railroad. Only the bank clings to the old-fashioned monopoly-accommodation idea of " stand in with me, or do without " ; but, unfortunately, it's much easier to wire to Seattle for goods than to arrange long-distance credit!

"W. F." says, " The banks (of the camp's early days) were put in one Pot, and then the Banker abated himself. *More* trouble! " Fairbanks had some very unfortunate experiences with bankers in her early history, which may account for the fact that more than a quarter million is deposited in postal savings here, leading the Territory: and whereas the per capita postal deposit in New York is only $295, in Fairbanks it is $907. Indeed, Fairbanks ranks among the first fifty cities of the U. S. A. in postal savings. Yet our now one and only bank is a good sound bank, even if it does charge two bits on outside cheques and two per cent. a month as ordinary interest—" and you have to sign away your store teeth to get *that*," says "W. F."! It has resources of over a million and is under government supervision. But Alaska needs small capital in many lines rather than big capital in a few, at its present stage, and small capital is not always easy to secure outside the local bank.

It was just a century after the landing of the Pilgrims that a team was driven from Connecticut to Rhode Island. Here in Alaska, too, before the railroad came, land travel was as difficult as costly. Here, as there, the coast streams are for the most part so broken by falls that they were useless as a pathway to the Interior, though we had the Yukon and they the Connecticut as early fur routes. Always added to the high cost of ocean freight was the high cost of land carriage, from fifty cents a pound up to unconscionable figures. Sheldon Jackson tells that in '95 and '96, mongrel Indian dogs for hauling freight on the Yukon cost a hundred to two hundred dollars each, and twenty cents a pound was paid for a thirty-mile haul. Such conditions tended to localize and isolate us in our industries and our interests and to restrict the possible area of distribution. The only product which would pay for its own carriage Outside over the winter trail, was solid gold ingots from our mines. Water freight was slow and not always certain. Concerning the opening of navigation for Yukon boats, the *News Miner* announced one year: " Here's dope on boats. The first boat will leave when it does. The first boat will arrive ditto! " When our furniture was shipped in, it came 2,700 miles to Saint Michael by ocean freight and 1,200 more miles up the river—a greater distance and a longer time in passage than for the famous *Mayflower* load of genuine antiques. And the freight bill! For transportation and costs of living are one and the same thing, apparently.

But the ways of travel are swiftly speeding up and hurrying almost faster now than the historian's ink can follow. The Aleut bidarka, Eskimo kyak and umiak, the dog sled, shoe pac, river boat and pack-horse are past or passing chapters in the story of Alaskan transportation, yielding now to rail and motor and plane. A broad statement, but one that will, I think, be unchallenged by any open-minded Alaskan or any open-minded national statesman, is this: Anything making for better transportation and communication between colony and mother country, benefits both colony and mother country.[1] All students of history know only too well the misunderstanding which can arise out of colonial isolation, and surely no Alaskan wishes to see that chapter repeated here.

But there's another widely-growing class, removed as far as possible from tundra-plodding sourdough mushers, who also benefit by Alaska's ever-increasing transportation facilities. I'm told that 30,000 tourists came last year to some part or another of Alaska, and next year another twin-screw steel ship of six thousand tons will be added to the Alaska run, to help accommodate the ever-growing numbers coming up to see the last frontier, take a step out in space and back in time, and see for themselves the wide-raftered area of Uncle Sam's attic. Times have changed, and much of the last frontier can be viewed

[1] For further development of this idea, see "What Does Alaska Want?" in *Scribner's* for June, 1927.

to-day in comfort from a steamer chair, an observation coach, or an airplane. At first, Alaskan communities saw only that the tourists bought curios, furs and photographs, spent money at hotels, hired autos, gas boats and guides, and purchased hunting and camping supplies. This revenue is not inconsiderable, but it is quite the smallest item in the real value of tourist travel to Alaska.

The Territory has something more to offer than scenery and splendid summer climate, and those who come with open mind and eye will not be blind to that something more. The business man on a summer junket doesn't lay aside his habit of trained financial thinking, and he readily grasps the significance of business possibilities latent here; for Alaska as a swiftly-developing colony has much to offer the investing intelligent visitor, which he can't help but see and will surely ponder. More than this, however—much more—is the fact that seeing really is believing; and those who have actually looked upon Alaska (not only the fringe of coast, but have penetrated into the heart of the country) return as converts and missionaries of the far-away colony, remember its problems of size and distance and newness, and will in time build up a body of understanding political thought, back home in the mother country where it is most needed. While the superficial tourist will see nothing but scenery and beginnings, the keen-minded traveller will vision an actual empire in the making.

For the real Alaskan problem to-day does not lie within Alaska but outside of Alaska—and it lies and lies and lies! Speaking to the Alaskan-Yukon Pioneers, Maurice Leehey once said, " The Alaska problem is simply this and nothing more: How can

Alaska get *the same chance the rest of the country had?*" We know what priceless wealth Uncle Sam gave away in order to build the western railroads in the states, and so we know how relatively tiny was the sum he spent in building the Alaska Railroad "to develop the country and the resources thereof for the use of the people of the United States." Yet every so often pessimistic congressmen arise and with a harsh crake declare that, because the Alaska Railroad hasn't yet paid thumping dividends, it is therefore a failure; and they seem quite willing— some of them—to turn our Territory "back to the moose for reclamation." Have they forgotten, these near-sighted ones, when and how their own western railroads were made to pay dividends?

The only fly in the agricultural ointment in Alaska to-day is the matter of transportation. A trunk line is not enough, though excellent. Feeders are needed. A farmer must be on a road if his farm is to keep him—a road he can travel year round. Millions of acres are useless in Alaska to-day because they are roadless acres. Until the railroad came, large mining operations were all confined to the coast and open tide-water, so that the mineral wealth of the Interior was almost untouched, except for the richest placers. Now Uncle Sam's railroad has changed all that, and, as Alaska's governor recently remarked, "a very large part of the reindeer country may be made tributary to the Alaska Railroad, and shipments over this line would greatly augment the return from this investment."

Conditions for agriculture are never ideal in a pioneer country. All first settlers, be they Pilgrims, early Kansas immigrants, or Alaskans, are confronted with obstacles and discouragement. Production costs are high because freight and labor are high. The farmer here eliminates labor cost by making his farm a one-man proposition—doing his own work with improved machinery and putting into his own pocket the $125 he would have to pay a "hand." Construction expenses are high, $30 to $35 a ton freight on building materials from Seattle: the cost of distribution of farm products is high, for transportation is again a major problem here. The farmer also has to pay a high interest rate on all borrowed money, and high freight on all equipment and groceries. But—that very freight rate is to him the equivalent of a tariff wall, protecting his own products and raising their price locally. To whatever price hay may be selling for Outside, the farmer here can add nearly the forty-dollar freight rate from Seattle, supply the local market, and cheat no one. And that there is a local market is proved by shipments from the port of Seattle, before the Tánana farms took to supplying local needs (which they do not even yet completely do); 982 tons of hay, 1,187 tons of oats, 241 tons of flour, 4,674 cases of eggs, 20,000 pounds of cold-storage poultry, as well as beef, mutton, pork and dairy products. As "W. F." was writing not so very long ago:

Men who should know better go before Congressional Committees and break into print to say that Alaska can never amount to anything in an agricultural way, because of this and that; whereas the farmers in Alaska are probably the most prosperous workmen of Alaska. Everything they raise they can sell, and to date they have not raised as much as they can sell in this immediate vicinity. At that, they are raising larger crops every year, clearing and farming more ground and progressing all along the line. Their flouring mill, the only one in

Alaska, is grinding every day, and last year the farmers in the Tánana Valley alone cultivated 1,599 acres of land, cleared 141 new acres, summer-fallowed 180 acres and will cultivate 2,000 acres this year, and are adding from 400 to 500 acres to cultivation yearly. Last year they raised and sold at the highest prices the products were ever sold for in the open market:

VEGETABLES—500 tons from 100 acres.

OAT HAY—1,026 tons from 1,036 acres.

GRAIN—Oats and barley, 1,270 bushels from 28 acres.

WHEAT—3,516 bushels from 183 acres.

Their wheat this year averaged 19 bushels per acre and their oats and barley 45 bushels per acre. For the potatoes raised in this Valley of Silent Men they received $40,000, and such prices for other farm produce that we hesitate to give them, as farmers Outside have never received them and would not believe that they could exist anywhere.

" The ability to make a living and get a fair amount of comfort and enjoyment out of life really depends upon equality in the use of the land from which wealth is produced and freedom to move about and trade." On this frontier, equality of economic opportunity is almost complete, for nowhere else in modern society does real equality of opportunity become so actual. As Jefferson wrote in 1795 of the frontier of his day: " Labour indeed is dear here, but rents are low, and on the whole a reasonable profit and comfortable subsistence result." So, too, doughty Captain John Smith recommended the frontier of New England as a good place for " All they that have Great Spirits & small Meanes!"

In many ways it seems to me as though a man alone can live here as cheaply and comfortably as any place. Living in a cabin of his own (which he can himself build, with a partner—and nearly half the Territory is forested), the Government gives him a hundred and sixty acres of farming land for a homestead, or a mining claim for the staking, provided only that he lives and works on it for part of the year. By doing his own cooking he can live on less than forty dollars in cash a month. Many live on less, if there are two partners, which is the usual thing. Two-room cabins rented for but ten to fifteen dollars per month when we first went to Fairbanks. We rented a large log cabin on the main street. It had a spacious living and dining room, a room we used as a library, three bedrooms, a generous kitchen, a very roomy pantry, and a bath and cellar and porches—all for forty dollars. The house had a large yard and garden, was located on a corner, and was comfortably furnished—though we brought much of our own.

Average clerk's wage in Fairbanks is $175 a month, as against $80 to $100 for similar work Outside. And it is remarkable how closely the person who wishes to do so may and can live literally " off the country." Salmon, grayling, many varieties of trout and white fish are to be had for the taking; ducks, geese, snipe, plover, ptarmigan, grouse and partridge provide a seasonal game-bird supply; moose, caribou, and mountain sheep (that real delight of gastronomes) are to be had for a hunter's picnic; wild huckleberries, red and black raspberries, and currants, gooseberries, high and low-bush cranberries, salmon berries, strawberries, juniper berries and " Oregon grapes " grow wild for the taking and by the trillion; wood for fuel is waiting the chopper's axe; and " cash money " on two sure markets is awaiting the man who runs a winter trap line for furs or takes out even a little gold, from land which any one may " claim." We found when we went to Fairbanks that any person, over twenty-one, may " locate, hold or work—or lease, sell, mortgage or otherwise dispose of "—mining claims in the Territory. An alien, however, " secures no title or right of possession as against the Government, but his rights are paramount as against all persons except the Government of the United States." Each owner of a claim must keep up the annual assessment work, and in so doing he can usually take out enough gold to pay expenses and make a little cash, even with rather desultory mining. If he secures a patent on his claim, then it is his actual property. But no alien can secure a patent—that's reserved for Uncle Sam's own nephews and nieces.

You can readily see that the cost of living here is exactly what you wish to make it. There are many things which Outside people are tempted to spend money for, that we are not. There are other things which the city dweller is forced to buy or have done for him, which we can get or do for ourselves. The frontier dweller escapes the psychological dangers of poverty as well as the actual fact of it, for there can be no real poverty where natural resources are so free. That's why we have no classes and no masses—no degrading, grinding, soul-destroying pauperism of the slums—for as there are no very rich on the frontier, so too there are no very poor. Many a sourdough here might find a hundred dollars a large sum to raise in cash on a moment's notice; but give him a winter's trapping, a summer's fish-wheel catch, a good season on his placer claim, and he will meet you with four figures in his roll. With wood, coal, game, fish, fruits, building material and land to be had for the taking, and wonderful gardens to be raised for the planting (and Uncle Sam himself will contribute free seeds from his own attic-window boxes, the agricultural experiment stations), all that the sourdough need provide is the overcoming of gravity and a little sweat and muscle! If he wishes, even his clothes may be made from products of the land, and winter caps and coats of home-grown fur, sleeping bags of mountain sheep, and moose-hide jackets and vests, are often to be met in Fairbanks.

The pioneer is always a sort of Robinson Crusoe, salvaging that which has been cast up to him and always using first what lies closest at hand. A colonist especially is acted upon by and reacts upon his environment, and is molded in habit and thought by the physical circumstances and possibilities of his habitude. Land forms, climate, animal life, vegetation, are all bound to influence him. Not with impunity, not without change and re-shaping, have we ourselves ventured up past the long firths from the open sea and into the enclosed and silent valleys of the North. We in Interior Alaska have not outgrown that Crusoe stage, for we are to-day what the tundra and the spruce forests and those half-guessed and immemorial geological happenings have made us. We are pioneer landsmen, as actually dependent upon the earth in which we send down roots as were our New England ancestors. We have not yet achieved the industrial stage, when subtle and intricate organization will release us from our "definite patch of the earth's surface, by whose characters all our activities are controlled, to a dreamland, served by the dusky jinns of the coal mines." The dusky jinns are at hand and potent enough, but we have not as yet exorcised them into our bottle and made them slaves. In that we need more capital, and capital is reaching out to the frontier even now to accomplish this last miracle. But capital will only travel where there is adequate transportation.

For myself, I thoroughly enjoy the pioneer way, because of its very Crusoe challenge; and always, I believe, happy frontiersmen will be those who truly enjoy adjustment to new and shifting environment and look upon it as a test of their own manliness and quality. In this land, geography and economics have real and dramatic parts to play upon the rim of civilization, where, as Isaiah Bowman says:

> We find man and nature rather evenly balanced in the struggle. . . . When standards of living were lower, economics had less to do with life on the frontier, but . . . the economic limits of a frontier enterprise are now sharply drawn. That throws a new light upon geographic conditions on the frontier. We now need to know rather precisely the conditions of soil and rainfall and labor, and even the availability of roadmaking materials, in a region of potential settlement.
>
> The effect has been to place the pioneer lands of the world on a higher plane of scientific study. It is not enough to locate a promising territory where the white man can make a living by agriculture or ranching. He asks questions about it that the old-fashioned pioneer never dreamed of. He is not content to face the wilderness with a sack of flour and an axe and a pair of strong hands. He demands that his enterprises shall pay from the start. He wants to be tied to a railway or a motor road, and, if possible, to a telephone. Accepted standards of living impel him to ask what the government will do for him if he breaks new ground in the pioneer zone. Formerly he asked only that government should leave him

alone. But pioneering in our times is so unlike that
of the romantic era of western expansion that our
ideas of it have to be entirely revised.
      . . . Even the outer marches of the occupied
lands feel the spell of science in the present age.
. . . When the earlier pioneer left for the wilderness he left an animal-transport community; he
now leaves a motor-car community. To ask him to
pioneer without motor or rail transport is to ask him
to go back to the living not of 1900 but 1700, relatively. The conclusion of the matter is that the
remaining pioneer lands of the world—and they are
still of enormous extent—must be developed on a
wide front, by organized groups, with government
aid. Not direct subsidy alone is required but an
indirect subsidy, represented by the application of
science to the study of frontier regions.

This is the solid economic reason for our various
governmental bureaus and their thoroughgoing reports upon Alaskan facts, as well as for a government-built Railroad. Of what use is a farm, unless
a road winds past it leading into some town? Of
what use is a town, unless a road winds through it
leading into some port? Of what use is the veriest
golconda of opportunity, unless the necessary freight
of material equipment can be unloaded at its portal,
making its richness real? Farmers and miners need
roads and railroads, and all alike need the steamship
lines—and the better that steamship service, the better business for them all. For Alaska is as truly a
non-contiguous colony and dependent upon ocean-
borne freight, as ever was New England.

The *Mayflower* passenger list did not include John
Milton's name, and that's a pity. The Miltons of
our little colony, too, are for the most part mute, if

not inglorious.   Many books about Alaska have been
written from the Outside view-point, looking in, too
few from intimate understanding and with true outlook.   Would that Alaska had an epic voice, a
" chanter of pains and joys, writer of here and
hereafter," to give us our needed strophe of transport, to ring against men's minds with clangor!

O Pioneers!   I sing the far edge of the world's
map, the newly unfurled edge,
   To which the sourdough puts his two strong hands,
and pushes ever forward:
   The crisp and northerly edge of the world's map,
where blind men
   In their fear have written down the words: " Here
dwells Chimera!"
   Others, in hope, exalted with extended horizons,
have written: " Here are the Lost Dreams of Youth
Fulfilled!"
   I sing the snow-mobile.   I sing the tractor and the
advancing plow turning the heavy loam.
   I sing advancing steel, iron horse, the whir of
mighty wings over the Last Frontier.
   O Pioneers!   Build well your epic, create your
empire.
   Build it with yellow dust of gold, build with your
golden wheat, build red with copper.
   Weld into it the foot-sore blood stains of old trails.
   Uplift it to the Arctic sky, where now moose-
ptarmigan out-roar the howling husky.
   Write a new message of a new land, a new mean-
ing of new dawn, across your new Aurora of The
North.

XXVII

Grapevine and String Talk

WE have asked "How high is the High North?" and now let us ask how big it really is. Alaska is more than twice the size of huge Texas—the largest of our confederated states and a republic in itself. Alaska is more than three times the size of California, our second largest state below-stairs, and also, in its time, an independent entity. The present area of the Thirteen Original States is 325,065 square miles while that of Alaska is 590,884. Add to these thirteen states the areas of Maine, Vermont, Ohio, Indiana, Tennessee, Kentucky and Michigan, and you are still far short of Alaska's tremendous size. Alaska is an empire in the making, as Underwood truly called it, but it is a dozen times the size of the Empire State.

Cutting up the map of Europe is a pastime for warriors and statesmen, but we can tackle it without bloodshed and perhaps gain another notion of size. Take your sharp shears and cut out Norway, Sweden, Finland, England, Scotland and Ireland, and they will all fit easily, and with a wide area to spare, within the boundaries of Alaska. Or try it another way and cut out Germany, France and Spain, and these, too, will fit within the limits of the Great Country with only a few acres over. The Washington representative of the London *Times* was telling us, recently, that a very great English statesman always advised his bright young men in the British

354

Foreign Office to " use large maps." I thought at the time how fitly this applied to Alaska!

Take a map of Alaska and lay it down upon the map of the United States, drawn to the same scale, and what do you see? Point Barrow will touch the Lake of the Woods, the straight part of the Alaska-Yukon boundary will run from Lake Superior down to the Ohio River, Ketchikan will lie over on Georgia, Seward and Cordova will rest out in Missouri, and Attu Island will touch Santa Barbara, California. Or, in terms of travel, from Attu Island in the Aleutians back to Ketchikan is a greater distance in miles than from San Francisco Bay to New York Harbor. Cape Prince of Wales really reaches as far into the Orient as the Samoans, and San Francisco is less than halfway from New York City to the farthest island in the Aleutian chain. As the Texas cowboy said, after riding half across that state, " If the world is as big the other way as it is the way I've rode, she is some size! "

Do you wonder that all Alaska problems are tied up with distance, or that Alaska's size makes her the Province of Paradox?

Thanks to cable and to wireless we can sometimes receive messages in Fairbanks before they are sent from Washington! This unconsidered miracle is due, of course, to the inexcusably slow-coach roll of our ancient earth, swinging along the old, worn, stellar trail; for when Fifth Avenue is full of luncheon-hurrying shoppers, alarm clocks in Nome are just buzzing their six-o'clock warning for early risers. We humans translate distance in terms of communication, and colonials have especially at heart all matters of intercourse; for your true colonial hungers and thirsts to keep in touch with the mind and thought of Mother Country, and not to lose that precious contact or let himself be lost to the thought of old friends and old ways. Only when that contact is indeed lost does he know true isolation or any sense of desolation in the new land.

I find in a Chicago paper of 1837 this notice: "Highly important: by a foot passenger from the South we learn that the long-expected mail may be looked for in a week." That sounds like the Fairbanks of yesterday, before there was a railroad spread out—a spaced and even path across the great divides, for steam to tread upon. In Fairbanks we have in one decade seen the Frontier push far out beyond us, thanks solely to better means of travel and communication. In the fall of 1918 I sent a Christmas greeting to a friend in Nome. The next August I received this answer, "The post card reached Nome to-day (July 1, 1919). Some mail system!" In May, 1920, we read that "the U. S. Coast Guard cutter *Bear* has sailed for the Arctic to-day taking 25,000 pounds of mail for Nome, the first mail of the season." To-day we hop over to Nome, with our Christmas greetings and Nome's mail, and reach there in time for lunch! Planes, which Interior Indians call "moose-ptarmigan" (large-white-bird) are now replacing dog-sleds in mail service.

And "string talk," as the Indians call radio, is replacing "wire talk" in Alaska. Thirty-five Army radio stations, of which Fairbanks is the center, now serve the Territory, contacting isolated cannery plants and mining camps. Soldiers strung the first telegraph wires along the old Valdez trail, back in the '90's, and have maintained them ever since at great cost and privation. But "string talk" is less subject to interruption by storm; and forest fires, snowbanks

and rock slides don't "put the line out." So the
wire-spell of the telegram is yielding, and a course
in radio is offered at the Alaska college. Alaska is
definitely on the air, and the deaf villages of the
North now listen in to the voice of the world.

A military wireless station was placed last year in
the Chandalár district, the most northerly mining
camp in Alaska. Referring to the value of the station to the residents of that remote section, a miner
from Little Squaw Creek wrote this letter to one of
Uncle Sam's Senators:

> Last winter two of the boys were prospecting on
> Tobin Creek, which is 12 miles from their nearest
> neighbors. They had two borrowed dogs. On the
> night of the 22nd of December, the owner of the
> dogs was awakened by them. He found a note tied
> around one of the dogs' neck. On reading the note,
> he was informed that the men had been blown up in
> an explosion. Every one around that section was
> informed and we rushed over two dog teams and
> succeeded in bringing those boys over to Little
> Squaw. Now here is where the value of the wire-
> less station came in: We were able to wire to Fair-
> banks and get instruction from the doctor, as well
> as a flying machine to take them to a hospital, sav-
> ing their lives.
>
> Now that we have a wireless station and under-
> stand its value in case of an emergency, we wish to
> send our thanks for the care taken of us.

This story was given wide publicity by the Associated Press; but of ten who are healed by the virtue
of this modern miracle, nine are never heard from,
although such instances are daily occurrences in the
Far North. All told (which they are not) the combined accomplishments of air-talk and air-travel in

Alaska, in the last year, would read like high-colored
fiction.   Pleasure as well as business and safety are
served by radio.   Sitting in his cabin on Ester Creek,
Joe McDonald takes in a Pittsburgh show via the
radio route, and Adolph Muller, down-river at far-
away Nulato, picks up his San Francisco, Holly-
wood and a station in Japan.

But " grapevine telegraph " still remains Alaska's
truest source of news, for most real vital news still
travels by word of mouth.   The local papers publish
little or no local gossip, because every one is supposed to know already everything that goes on in
the immediate region.   We read living newspapers,
for every one in Alaska is a reporter and a news
agent.   Wherever you go, here, you know people or
soon get to know them; and although Alaska may
be a fifth the size of the United States, you either
know or know of a large proportion of the white
population, and so, when you travel, you pick up all
the " drift " and relay it.   Like all pioneers, Alaskans
are hungry for news of *people* and listen to tales of
all sorts of people whom they have never met, but
may, on the teasingly converging and diverging trails
of this our North.   It's well to know about all sorts,
everywhere, for you may be running into them at any
time.   *Nil Alaskæ alienum mihi* is our motto.   The
people of the North are neighbors as the people of
the thirteen colonies were, even although the boundaries of the North are far wider.   All whites in
Alaska are shareholders in the same big colonial
job, and this gives us a similar set of interests even
though we live so widely separated in both time and
space.   And do not think the platform of *The Alaska
Fisherman* (a monthly news organ of the Alaska
Native Brotherhood) a strange assortment of ideals,

for they are all very real and equally sought: "Alaska for Alaskans, Full Territorial Government, Abolishment of All Fish Traps, Competent Christian Citizenship."

Out of a wholesome traffic together both in ideas and commodities, one time shall grow a true Alaskan state that shall be a real unit; and added facilities of communication are fast making it possible for all Alaska's towns to get together in place and time, to think and act together, to know themselves one family working for the common good. In the Interior we are getting away from the day of leisurely slow-moving craft on far-reaching rivers, while on the Coast they are realizing the value of business relations with the hinterland and beginning to wonder what up-country products can be brought out through their doors. Once, long ago, Pennsylvania and New York found it hard to understand one another, in those "good old days" when a coach named "The Flying Machine" left Pawles Hook for Philadelphia "every Tuesday and Friday morning at or before sunrise" and reached Penn's little city at the long end of the *second* day—after a night's stop at Princeton! Even these close neighbor colonies could not very well be true neighbors under such conditions of intercommunication, but were actually far apart in heart even though physically touching shoulders. So, too, when the pioneer found the Alleghenies between him and the seaboard, a new set of problems arose as East and West got out of touch with one another's thought—just as our own Interior Alaska people got out of touch with Juneau and Sitka and Valdez, only a short generation ago, before we had adequate means of speaking to and seeing one another frequently.

Once the only trail to the Interior was the musher's trail of tundra and niggerhead, and of this way Lieutenant Allen reported (with his consistent soldierly understatement) : " to walk between them (the hummocky bunch-grass ' nigger-heads ') is to walk continually in water of uncertain depth, which consequently is very tiresome." It is—and was—but now we fly above them and have rolled up space and time within an aviator's luggage-kit. Massachusetts and Connecticut believed themselves independent of one another and self-sufficient, just so long as there was no good road between them; and we in Alaska have just been passing through that period, too, divided by far greater geographical barriers. Before the Alaska Railroad was completed only a few Fairbanksans had ever been to Anchorage or knew or cared a rap about "the Anchorage crowd." Now, with basket ball and baseball teams exchanging frequent friendly games, chambers of commerce visiting back and forth, railroad excursions galore, and planes in constant flight, a different and a most friendly spirit is coming into play. In the early days, the Coast felt quite capable of going it alone, and sometimes wanted to cut loose from the hinterland as the Atlantic Coast sometimes felt an urge to do in its earlier days. But the years, in both cases, have brought a decided change in attitude among all intelligent people.

The width of ocean hasn't changed between Plymouth, England, and Plymouth, Massachusetts; but the time factor has, for the new way is the air way, both in talk and travel, and the airways of our North are unlimited.

XXVIII

Airways—Unlimited

ALASKANS, engrossed in their constant colonial preoccupation with problems of bigness and farness, naturally were very quick to make the plane their own, and Alaska to-day has more fliers and more landing fields in proportion to its population than any other section of the world. Alaska already has double the number of landing fields possessed by the whole United States ten years ago—and more are spreading out their acres throughout the Territory, almost overnight; for we act on the old saying, " Build the bird-house and the birds will come." And they do.

In the winter any lake or river bar is an ice way and snow-levelled savannahs are potential landing fields, making every corner of this space accessible to every other. The Fairbanks airport alone has two runways, each more than 2,000 feet long by 400 feet wide, equipped with a night beacon and flood lights. This is a drastic and swift change of affairs from the day not long ago when Ben Eielson made his first flight with mail, to McGrath on the Kuskokwim. Late that dark winter afternoon we suddenly realized, when we heard that muffled sound of wings above us, that Ben could not possibly see the ball park in that light. We neighbors rushed out and built bonfires, so that when he dropped down from the sky (with only about a pint of gasoline to spare!) he made a perfect landing on his home-improvised

361

skis. Captain Martin, leader of the Army round-the-world air expedition, said of Ben Eielson and his early Alaskan flights: "You can take it from me, that boy has a worse game to play than ours. In the army world flight there are four machines and eight men and we have supply bases scattered all along the route, with accurate maps of the whole course; but Eielson is flying alone, in a strange country, without facilities for repairing his machine. We have to hand it to him; one slip and he's gone."

Aviation in Alaska has followed the pattern of high romance, though in cold fact it is a direct outgrowth of the flight of American army aviators from New York to Nome, now rated as one of the greatest feats of aviation history. That day the army fliers came is marked in indelible red ink, upon any true Alaskan's calendar, for this flight set our Fairbanks business men to thinking. As a former mayor of our town puts it: "We visioned the tremendous economies in time which could be effected by use of the airplane, in travelling over our vast stretches of snow and ice and over the marshy Central Alaska in summer, when other forms of transportation, except by boat, are next to impossible.

"We decided to buy an airplane for ourselves, but first we had to have some one to fly it. Casting about, we found a young science teacher in the Fairbanks High School. His name was Ben Eielson. We found he had been an army flier during the war. He agreed to fly our plane, and so became the father of aviation in Alaska. It was this same Eielson who piloted Sir George Hubert Wilkins on his flight across the Arctic ice from Point Barrow, Alaska, to Spitzbergen, for which he has been awarded the Harmon Trophy.

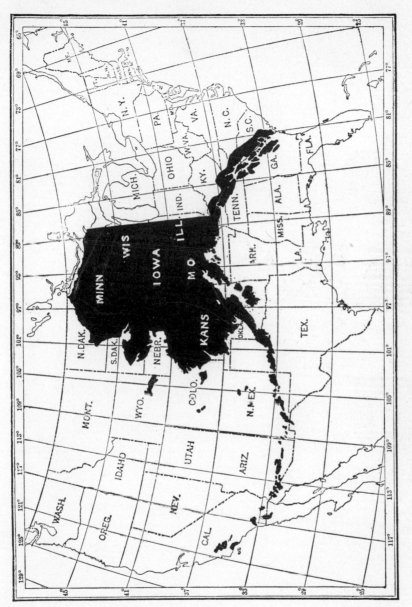

ALASKA WOULD EXTEND FROM GEORGIA TO CALIFORNIA—FROM CANADA TO MEXICO.

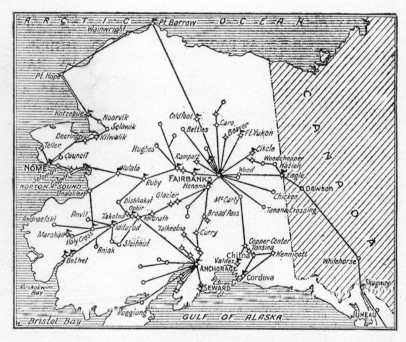

PRESENT AIR ROUTES OF ALASKA TO WHICH NEW FIELDS ARE CON-
STANTLY BEING ADDED.

" Since those first flights of Eielson from the Fairbanks flying field Alaska's interest in aviation has grown rapidly. To-day a network of airways crisscross the country. A veritable fan of lines radiate from Fairbanks. There are 74 graded airports in Alaska for the use of airplanes in summer. In the winter flying with skis, an airplane can land wherever the snow or ice is smooth, and, as Central Alaska is mostly flatlands, such landing places abound."

Eielson's pioneer flights in 1923 with an army Jenny, locally owned, proved conclusively what could be done in making victory of space. The next step was an air-mail contract, under the terms of which Eielson made 600-mile round trips all the late winter of 1924, to McGrath and back. Each round trip was completed the day it started, and he was never once halted by the weather, whereas before this time Kuskokwim mail had taken from 12 to 60 days in transit, with dogs. Eielson flew a total of 4,800 miles in 50 flying hours on this test contract, his regular route being around Mt. McKinley with that great " home of the sun " as his constant air beacon.

When the Eskimos at Point Barrow first saw an airplane, upon the arrival of the Detroit Arctic Expedition, they called it The Devil. When the expedition next returned, Eskimo children were found playing with model planes constructed of the hide and bones of walrus and seal! We old Alaskans, too, are learning swiftly to accommodate ourselves to these new ways and to blaze new trails among the hillocks of the air. The first commercial flying company in Fairbanks had " one small Waco, four poles and a tarpaulin across the top for equipment," as Bennett said. The new hangars are of double-walled lumber with sawdust between the walls, as our house is built, and have furnace heat, a garage and repair shop, apartments for aviators and mechanics, and commercial flights range out to the four points of the compass and for every conceivable purpose. For our airmen of Alaska aren't skylarks or stunters, tumbling about the cloudy billows for the fun of it. Nor are they great war-birds of prey, intent on swooping in a fatal death-pounce upon hapless land victims. They are messengers of trade and mercy and communication, and nothing stays them—nor height nor depth nor tundra waste nor topless peaks nor brittle miles of frost—aloft in the laps of the gods.

We have not overlooked this strategic, economic, commercial, present, actual form of northern space-conquering. We have a new " Company of Gentlemen Adventurers," for airmen of the North are now actually " trading into Hudson Bay." And Alaska herself is a silent partner in the enterprise for, a million years ago or so, she decided to be air-minded and began her patient preparations—laying out landing fields, spreading out rivers and bars and wide winter-smooth, level snow fields, to rest the coming moose-ptarmigan upon their trans-polar flights. Surely, as Adams said in speaking of New England, geographic factors are relative, not absolute: " Countries may be said to be habitable, or uninhabitable, distances to lengthen or shorten, heights to rise or fall, according to the measure of man's control of nature at any given time."

Seven pilots and six mechanics are stationed at Fairbanks alone, and a glance at the opposite map will show you better than any verbal description the air-mesh of commercial aviation in which Alaska's once elusive space is daily being caught and tangled.

The planes used in the Interior are fitted with wheels in summer and skis in winter, while the planes operating on the coast are of the pontoon type. Airways weather service has been extended throughout the Territory, with headquarters at Fairbanks under a forecaster and meteorologist, and weather reports from all radio stations are now coming in twice daily.

Commercial aviation in Alaska has taken such swift leaps and strides because it does not here compete with a web of railroad steel or fine radiating motor roads, but with toiling dog teams, outboard motor boats on meandering, timber-snagged, bar-filled rivers, and tremendous stretches that are for the most part literally trackless. Let the malemutes howl! The old winter mail route to Nome took fifty-six days, but now the dogs may take a vacation. Some Outside people are romantic about the dog teams—when their own mail service does not take fifty-six days—and will perhaps be sorry to hear that we now have actual prospects in Alaska of a proper mail service—by air, which is the reasonable and sensible Alaskan route. Speaking of the proposed new air-mail service, a Fairbanksan says:

Our people cannot understand why it is that, although our airplane companies are eager to perform this service and for the last three years have been equipped to handle it quickly and efficiently and at no greater cost than is now being paid, they have had no opportunity to do so except in emergency cases when all other means of transportation have failed.

As far as I have been able to discover, the Postoffice Department officials who have immediate charge of the Alaska service are to a great extent influenced by the romantic history of the dog teams and the sentimental idea that they must be preserved and fostered. There has always been too much romancing about Alaska. Alaskans are a practical people and are as eager to participate in the advantages of modern scientific developments as people elsewhere.

We will always have dog teams up here. They have played a wonderful and vital part in the pioneering of the Territory and they will be used for years to come in their proper sphere. Their heroic exploits are a part of our intimate history, but from a romantic standpoint they appeal to us in about the same way as I imagine the Indian canoe and paddle of the Potomac and the rolling roads that once brought casks of tobacco to Georgetown appeal to the romantic sensibilities of Washingtonians.

Forward-looking Alaskans rejoice at this new era in communication, for we know what that service will mean. Serum is now carried swiftly in times of epidemic, doctors are fetched in speed to the disabled in far-lying camps, fortunes in furs are brought to Fairbanks almost weekly by the planes in early spring from Arctic posts and from Siberia, and the purr of the air motor is now heard in a land that sounded only to the pat of the wolf-padded husky. Wilkins and Eielson flew to Point Barrow and returned to Fairbanks in the brief space of 34 hours, on the second preliminary flight with base supplies for their Arctic Expedition—a trip that by the tundra route would have taken months. Mountains mapped as 5,000 feet were found to be nearer 10,000, and to verify the course a note was dropped on one little settlement asking the people to spell off the name of the town. "With remarkable perception," Wilkins said, "two persons immediately rushed to the river and stamped out the word ALATNA in the snow." It was on the first trip to Barrow that two Eskimo women fainted from fear and excitement at their first sight of a plane, and suffered hemorrhages of the eyes, nose and mouth; but on the second trip all the natives realized by now that planes were material things and not evil spirits, and gave them a warm welcome.

Passengers are carried to Kantishna now by plane, and Jack Tobin, Kantishna miner, was landed recently within 200 yards of his own cabin. The trip was made in late June, " in the dead of night "—the sun shining brightly all the time since they flew at 3,500 feet. Operating from Sitka, a cannery company is using planes to locate salmon runs. The Gorst Air Transport was the first to cross the Gulf of Alaska from Juneau to Cordova and later to Seward. Flying from Teller, Noel Wien took up a reindeer herder to check the position of a widely-scattered herd, saving two weeks of hard foot-work and obtaining much more exact information. Hunters are locating moose and caribou from the air, and the upper reaches of the Noatuk and Kobuk arc being prospected by Swallow bi-plane. Two, three, four at a time, scattering to all points of the compass, airplanes rise from our Alaskan fields to-day and we think it no more strange to use them than city people do to take a taxi, and don't even stop to watch them go. One trapper runs a 250-mile line by plane. Miners go by plane, get their supplies by plane—including light machinery and drill parts. They reach places the dog teams never even found.

Camps 100 miles from Fairbanks have a standing weekly order for supplies by plane. Many of the dredge crews and cooks for outlying camps are taken out to work by plane—ultra-modern ships with heated cabins—while autos and " cats " do the heavier freighting. Frank Yasuba, Beaver merchant, wires in that ham and eggs are both "all," at the Flats, and Bennett wings away with them, for prospecting is minus without your breakfast ham and eggs! With all other transportation and communication flagrantly inadequate, the planes are heaven-sent chariots—to sailors marooned by ice or wreck, to the wounded and sick far from doctor and hospital, to biological and geological surveyors, to judges, bishops, mining engineers and fur farmers.

Ask any experienced flier to name the essentials of successful flight and what will he say? "Good air conditions, dependable weather, lack of mists and fogs, no violent winds, many natural emergency landing places." What has he described if not Interior Alaska? No wonder airmen are "crazy about it here," for they find air conditions ideal; and it was not in our loved inner land but on fog-ridden Siberian coast, Ben Eielson fatally crashed. Then, too, most Alaskans are mechanics by second nature, instinctively geared, motor-minded, ear-tuned; so, with the Icarus mind already in place, it's not at all hard for them to turn this innate aptitude to flight. It goes with the grain. Airmen, it is said, must think in hundredths-of-a-second speed, but swift decision has been for a generation the a-b-c of all Alaskan schooling. The minds of Alaskan pioneers have been constantly over-leaping—constantly thinking, not in local terms, but in the haunting pull of "what lies behind the ranges." That which was once thought high-flown, can now be over-flown.

Psychologically speaking, there is that "total giving of one's self to the air," as a ski-jumper does—the thing that aviators consider so essential; and total giving of one's self to the environment is, as we know, a notable characteristic of the North. Then, too, the best sea-going races have been found to be, in general, the best air-goers; and a large proportion of Alaska's present population are either Scandinavian and British descended, or they are children and grandchildren of those Yankees who combed the Seven Seas, built and manned their own whaling and trading vessels, and swung around the Horn when California gold fields called. The seaman's pale blue eye, wind-wrinkled at the corner, is typical of the Alaska pioneer—the man with the quiet unruffled head who is apparently a tremendous chance-taker with the elements, but is in reality taking no chances at all, moving with cool and calculated sure control. The air appeals to the eagle-hearted as well as to the eagle-visioned.

Aviation is more appropriate and more necessary to a country like Alaska than to a country like modern New England, already settled and with its many roads and railroads. When the rest of the United States was developing its waterways, Alaska was as yet unknown to us. When the rest of the United States was building its trans-continental railroads, Alaska was the newly bought " Seward's Ice Box "— and that was in the day when men did not connect refrigeration and motors! No one thought of polar bears and walrus as travellers on railroads. So Alaska almost skipped and missed the patient, long-drawn, steamboat age, has had to fight hard to get even a be-grudged sample of the many blessings of the railroad age, and has jumped to-day almost full-panoplied into the airplane age. The trails of the wild quad-rupeds, which after long ages became the trails of toiling bipeds, echo now to the drone of the great man-locust on his homing wings. And almost before

Alaska has become an integral part of national American thinking, it is becoming a very vital part of international thinking, through the agency of this new vehicle that is able to lope past meridians and longitudes as easily as old Dobbin used to make the turns on the soft dirt roads to town. Aviation has made Alaska the real Northwest Passage.

A study of the world's map shows clearly the strategic position Alaska occupies as far as all-land air routes to the Orient from America are concerned. In the last year an overland project has been put forward—the proposed International Highway connecting Mexico, the United States, Canada, Alaska, and eventually Asia—backed by Alaska's Governor and her Delegate to Congress, by Yukon Territory and British Columbia officials, by world-famous road engineers and world-famous aviators. Planned as a motor road that will follow in its northern swing very much the old line of the Western Union International Telegraph trail of long ago, the 2,000 miles from Seattle to Fairbanks need only a few links to make it a reality. Even more important than motors upon it is the fact that the ribbon of this road (set back 200 miles behind the coast range, where the snowfall is light and the way free from the mists and fogs, coastal storms and frequent winter mishaps of the Inside Passage) would be essentially a guide to airmen winging north and Asiaward. If the right of way through forested area should be cut 100 feet wide, this would provide emergency landing fields; necessary gas, oil and equipment supply stations as well as towns would spring up in favorable places; and road houses, farms, and telegraph stations would be established. Seattle, Vancouver, Frazer River, Prince George, Hazleton, Telegraph Creek, Stikine

River, Atlin, Whitehorse, Fairbanks—this international route provides a grandiose summer tourist way and a safe year-round air way.

Only 750 miles of the 4,000 between Mexico and Alaska's Interior remain to be built, of which 200 each lie in Alaska and Yukon Territory and 350 in British Columbia; and while some parts of the United States may look on 750 miles of road as " a considerable," in the broad vision of the North it is a mere " link " soon, we believe, to be welded, for this part of the route is mostly old pioneer trail over which cattle have been driven in the past. Branch roads will undoubtedly be built to several seacoast terminals—Prince Rupert and Ketchikan, down the Stikine to Wrangell and Petersburg, down the Taku Valley to Juneau—and a winter road is already built from Whitehorse to Dawson. The Dominion has been very liberal in the construction of roads to her far northern mining camps, and it is to be hoped that Uncle Sam will follow his northern neighbor's lead in this matter, for Canada is pushing the International Highway project with vigor. And echoes of the old Scotch pioneering days of Hudson Bay still persist in the North, though working now in a new medium. An engineer of the Alaska Road Commission presented the first practical plans for this daring but eminently feasible project, and his name is Donald MacDonald! The plaid of Caledonia is still being thrown upon the lonely ways of the Northwest.

Sturdy Roman roads made Roman law possible in the land of the Angles, wide metalled French roads spread the Code Napoléon into the farthest Pyrenees and Cévennes. The best way I know to make united Americans of this colony of yours, is to give us more

roads and extend by them the circle of American law
and tradition, American commerce and transportation and intercommunication. For The Rule of the
Road is very much more than a mere traffic phrase.
A road *is* a code. It means convention in both senses
of the word, a coming together of people in both
spirit and body. Rubber will roll over these roads,
Alaska farmers and tourists riding in Uncle Sam's
twenty million autos will alike employ them, while
above their guiding threads the motors of the air
will shuttle back and forth to weave that web of
get-togetherness between all people—to-day's ambas-
sadors of actual good will.

The Russians are doing great things in airways
just across the Straits, and Russia's military air force
is said to be as large as England's. She has connected Baku, Teheran and Moscow by air as well
as Kabul. The Soviet Government maintains air
service around the White Sea where, four or five
months of the year, ice is moved by sea currents and
there are fissures through which ships may pass,—if
they can find them,—and airplanes signal these by
radio, and sea-borne traffic is thereby greatly helped.
They also report on seal herds and schools of whales.
In fact, U. S. S. R. is written largely on the northern
air, and over country very similar to ours. There are
Russian airplanes to-day in Samarkand, the capital
of Tamerlane. Asia across the Straits is rising on
red wings. But there is no blood red upon the
fuselage of Alaska's planes, and our mutual air contacts with Asiatic Russia have been those of boon and
not of bane—beneficent rescues or time-and-money-
saving flights between the all-but-touching continents.

The distance from Alaska to Liverpool by present

routes is 9,000 miles, whereas by air it is but 4,000 across the Arctic Sea. In summer it is light here twenty-four hours of the day, when " more heat per square mile is received from the sun within the Polar regions than at the Equator." Certainly low temperatures do not interfere with summer trans-polar air journeys. If you want to know what modern Russia thinks of polar air flight and the strategic position of Arctic lands, then look at her defiance in holding on to little Wrangell Island against the protests of both England and America. Consider here the paradox of history! Russia, which once sold all Alaska for a song, now takes her stand on lonely Wrangell Island in the Arctic—utterly useless *except* as an air-station— and snarls defiance at the world, refusing to be dislodged.

A British naval commander has this to say: " The focus of naval power has moved to the Pacific Ocean, and, owing to the manner in which land and water are distributed over the surface of the earth, the area to be patrolled in the Pacific is three times that which had formerly to be patrolled in the Atlantic and the Mediterranean. The cost of constructing and maintaining sufficient seagoing vessels to cope adequately with this extra work would be likely to impose on this country a greater economic burden than it could bear; but if the development of airships were suitably and promptly undertaken, they could perform at an immensely reduced cost the reconnaissance duties that are necessary to control great ocean spaces."

The present page of history needs readers who think, as did the Yankees of a century ago, in terms of the Pacific—people not afraid to face our world in terms of vast continents and seas. America has been noted in the past for a " bold enterprise in the pursuit of gain and a keen scent for the trails that lead to it," as Admiral Mahan once remarked. But northern-leading trade lanes are being blazed through air to-day, which America will either definitely control or be as definitely debarred from, according to our own immediate generation's appreciation of this Arctic problem.

The sister hemispheres are linked here at the north. Once there was a starry canopy, and an earth that was flat. Columbus negated that when he failed to sail over the rim and plunge into nothingness. The Seven Seas were once thought to be inhabited by fearsome monsters, but at last there remained unknown and unsurveyed only the Sea of the North —and then the *Norge* came and took even that ultimate mystery from us. To-day a U. S. naval officer can say:

" Communities situated on the great trade routes become great hives of human toil. . . . So it will be with Alaska. No other civilized community is so strategically situated to become the pole route's great and only service station. Ice-buried Greenland; Canada blanketed by a vast and barren archipelago; Russia and Siberia with the natural cruelty of their desert steppes—what chance have they to compete with a land of plenty or a people with a will, as marks our own Alaska? Let the Arctic traffic begin to flow and, like Chicago, Alaska must spring to wealth."

XXIX

The Crucible of the North

ONE day I was reading aloud a new book called "The Founding of New England," by James Truslow Adams, which proved so fascinating I was not surprised when later it became famous as a searching analysis of early colonial conditions, treated from their human side. But to us the book is even better remembered for a curious thing which happened while we ourselves were reading it.

Through a slip of the tongue, I read "Alaska" for "New England" in one of the opening sentences. That was an inspired slip, I believe, for it opened up to us from that moment whole vistas—a panorama and a swift impelling insight we have never since lost, which have meant much to us in terms of better understanding of our own intimate Alaskan conditions.

"Alaska!" I exclaimed. "Did I read 'Alaska' just then?"

"You did," my husband said. "But the strange thing is, that statement, as read, is absolutely true."

"It is—and that's a queer thing, too. For New England in the seventeenth century seems a mighty far cry from Alaska in the twentieth. I never thought—I say, let's try something! Let's read this chapter through, and substitute 'Alaska' for 'New England' every time the words occur, and see what happens! That will be interesting."

It was so very interesting that we continued to read it so throughout the entire book, and that's how we came to discover that Alaska to-day is in very much the same estate—politically and socially and economically and all the other "-allys"—as was colonial New England then. You see, we found that practically every statement Adams made about those Englishmen in America then, applied equally well to us Americans in Alaska now. It gave us much food for thought. I never knew a "history book" to seem so mighty real! It read like home-town gossip.

Most people think of New England in the late seventeenth or early eighteenth century as a land without much of a history—but it wasn't, for things had already happened there which were to shape its destiny. And though most people think of Alaska to-day as a land without any history at all, that is not true, either. We have even, I believe, a parallel to the saga of the Northmen's coming and the tale of Leif the Lucky. For if Vitus Bering was Alaska's Columbus, there is at least a possibility that Chinese sailors were our long-ago first touchers on this shore —who came, and stayed a while in this new Vinland, and then returned, leaving only a lost manuscript to tell of that adventure.

One day in 1926 I was speaking to Mrs. Hoover of my interest in early Alaskan history and the many similarities I had found (led by that tongue-slip clue!) between it and the Thirteen Colonies in the East. She said, as I remember: "I must tell you, then, of something which I myself found when we were living in China, for it fits in perfectly with your notion. I think the manuscript was from the since-destroyed Han-Lin Academy, which was in fact a classical library, the storehouse of precious literary treasures. But though I do not now remember clearly the details, I do remember well (and you may quote me as having seen the document) that I heard read and translated to me the old, old story of the members of a fishing party, which I think contained two junks full of people, who had been driven by storm north and east and then south and east— until finally, realizing that they were now too far from home to get back before winter, they deliberately went further south along the coast of the 'pleasant land' they had found and spent two winters and a summer there. They started back the way they had come, early in the second summer, and finally reached their home in China, where of course they had been given up for dead. I have a copy of this manuscript, which I made at the time, and I shall be delighted to let you see it—whenever I get all my things together in one place again, and can find it!"

Like the Icelandic tales of Red Eric's son, this story of Mrs. Hoover takes us back to a land of far away and long ago. It must have been a similar journey, on a similar northern sea—drifting past similar low-eaved earthen huts of similar Eskimo villages, watching the stars slip past their similar carved dragon-crested prows, until they drove upon a similar foggy coast of similar gray flat rocks, porches to similar great plateaus where crowding ice-floes ground—then southward and the landfall of dark tapestry of forest thrown on the islanded shore line, where in calm days they heard the spouting whales, and strange fish leaped upon their similar low decks.

> " So Leif came rowing up the Charles,
> He and his golden-bearded carls."

And so, perhaps, came these dark men from far-off Asia to "the pleasant land" of Portland canal, Tongass or Metlakatla. Both tales are legend—but Legend is the name of History's mother.

"Alaska has no tradition, no legend," cry some who annually seek for these in alien Switzerland and France. Look nearer home, and you will find here in Alaska not only a written history older than that of many of our own forty-eight states, but you will see history in the making, and living people like ourselves as part of this colonial adventuring. You will drop back 200 years into the very heart of colonial America—the Last Frontier, pushed out and up, under the very ridge-pole of the Earth. Here, everyday life is reënacting one of the oldest plots in history—"That unfinished drama," as Wells calls it, "of which our lives are a part." The early story of Alaska is already written by its earliest settlers, who were driven here by the same incentives which have been characteristic of English-speaking enterprise everywhere—substituting placers for puritanism in the robust glittering excitement of early gold-camps! Adventuring cavaliers from the splendid court of Catherine sought out our coast as cavaliers of Elizabeth's day sought out both Virginia and that "North Virginia" which Captain Smith was first to name "New England." Shelikof's colonization of Kodiak antedates the Constitution of the United States. Sitka-cast mission bells reached California when Philadelphia's Liberty Bell was yet young. Russian governors were sending representatives to Japan and Hawaii long before our War of 1812. Some of the stoutest little ships on the Pacific were built from Alaska timber and launched from Alaskan ways long years before our war with Mexico; and the Western

Union began to survey a telegraph line across Alaska before a firm Atlantic cable had been coupled.

Bering came in the early eighteenth century, whereas Columbus and those others came to the East Coast in late fifteenth and early sixteenth centuries; so, to play fair you must give us at least a 200-year handicap! Four hundred years ago Verazzano approached the mouth of Hudson River, and he wrote: "We left the land with much regret, because of its commodiousness and beauty, *thinking it not without some properties of value.*" What price New York real estate, then! Two hundred years later Bering came to the coast of Alaska, and his men also reported it "not without some properties of value." Alaska has but half as old a history as eastern U. S. A. and it has come but relatively half as far upon its path of development.

Two hundred years after Verazzano's discovery of Manhattan, the little town of New York had a population of 5,000—the population of Ketchikan to-day. In 1700, the colony of New York had almost exactly the same population of whites as Alaska has this minute. In 1763 there were dense woods where New York's City Hall now stands, a deep pond on the site of the Tombs. But during the Atlantic colonies' early period Europe was in turmoil politically and economically, and many of Europe's best citizens were glad enough to pick up and strike out for a new land overseas; whereas Alaska was exploited savagely until 1867, ignored from '67 to '98, and since that time no great migration has occurred, because this was a time of unexampled material prosperity and internal industrial development in its Mother Country.

To expect to find a present-day New York in

Alaska would be foolish, as it would have been equally foolish to look for another London in the colonies of 1700. But you may find the colonial *beginnings* of many a thrifty city, here and now, in this new land. In 1700, New England had but one small college, and so have we to-day. In 1740, there were no more newspapers in all the eastern colonies together than Alaska has, now. There was prosperity in the colonies, but little luxury, and the same may be said of Alaska. But there was not a single hospital in all America until 1751, whereas every present-day Alaska town boasts at least one; and enlightened Boston did not light her streets until 1773, whereas every Alaska town of any size at all has electricity. Most of Alaska's communities to-day are more comfortable, more prosperous, more advanced, than those of the Atlantic seaboard in 1730. " A few passable towns were then built—Boston, Philadelphia, New York—but their means were small, their horizon narrow, yet their spirit was large." There are a score of " passable towns " in Alaska—comfortable living places, forward-looking, energetic—which have more immediate raw material of resource lying at their doors this minute than had the " cities " of the Atlantic seaboard in 1700, or even 1750.

If ever you come to Alaska, I beg of you to come with this colonial parallel in mind, because the best preparation for a thoroughly good time in Alaska is a well-informed and richly imaginative historical sense. Any one who knows anything of the founding of New England, or the epic story of the winning of the West, will see through these spectacles the true aspect of America's North to-day. The person who takes the most mental baggage—and the least actual baggage—is your real traveller, and he will best remember that even our most cultured eastern states were considered crude and vulgar, not so very long ago, by visiting tourists from England. " The Great Dickens and the delightful Mrs. Trollope, setting foot on our shores, with diagnostic intentions," as Langdon Mitchell puts it, " glanced hastily at the Yankee patient and, using no very obscure or technical terms, said: ' Coarse, crass, ignorant, impudent, barbarous, green yet corrupt, and strangely embarrassed with a superfluity of spittle! ' " I know of no Alaskan traveller who has reported worse or equal crudities in the northwest colony of to-day! If you bring with you a cargo of sympathetic understanding for the meaning of a colonial job to those who *do* it, you can here drift out and away from a highly speeded-up mechanistic age, away from hurry, herding and unrest and back into another day, another way of life and thinking—" when the world was younger, less exploited, and a more fresh wind blew between the hills of time." To do so " would from many a blunder free us, and selfish notion."

Alaska grows more complex as it grows older, and the larger towns and longer settled regions are remarkably sophisticated for their actual age. There are sections of the country still in the period of exploration and discovery. Other sections are still in the early fur and fish and hand-mining periods of simple trade and barter, pioneer farming and pioneer herding are springing up in other sections, while ports and routes of trade are fast becoming modern beacon lights of commerce in a most modern and amazing fashion, new things and old co-twisted. Every chapter of the colonial story is open here to the wise man's reading, and the enquiring person on

Alaskan journey may truly turn back history, bid time return. Alaskans have the true pioneer mind, thinking little of the past and much of the future, and the true pioneer spirit of the independence of the individual. The traveller saturated in the color and spirit of America's early days will see with delight here a firm grafting upon the spreading tree of Anglo-Saxon colonial tradition—another one of those fresh grafts which insure that the old tree will surely live on, because of the Anglo-Saxon heritage of adaptation to the new while yet keeping the best of the old.

He will see here, too, and will understand for what it is, the hot and headstrong and impulsive qualities of national youth, and will realize that the worst of Alaska's trouble is merely the malaise of pubescence, rapidly being outgrown; for countries have their growing pains of both body and spirit. The wise person does not expect old heads on young shoulders, and he will not expect the sedate qualities of ripe old age to coexist with the exuberance and charm of youth. In 1789, when it took two months for a courier to travel from the new seat of government to the distant frontier, even a Thomas Jefferson could be mistaken in predicting that it would take a thousand years for the country to be thickly settled as far west as the Mississippi. So—do not scoff at empty spaces, in our Alaska.

The wise traveller will not despise the day of small things, for he will recall that in Washington's day it was seriously debated whether New York or Alexandria, Virginia, would grow to be the greater city! No one could then foresee, and so the wise traveller will not turn up his nose at small cities, but will see in them the seedlings of empire. He will know that a Great Country, even as a great man, has an uncertain childhood and times when help and aid and quiet understanding are needed from kin and elders, more than a slap or a scolding. He will remember that Uncle Sam's own early years were spent within the family of the British Lion, and so he will feel kindly toward this unlicked Cub of the Great Bear which has been taken to raise. He will recall that great things have inconsidered origins, and that even the world-famous Kennecott was only a prospect hole—once—until a wizard tamed the wildcat with a drill. For all great mines were wildcats, once, and big capital only comes after small capital has developed possibility into potentiality— mixing time and intelligence, as we do with people, to make them truly " grow up " to usefulness and production.

The wise traveller will understand that people often seek out the Frontier in protest against something in the social life of the old country, and so he will expect to find many a true protest-ant here. The Puritan protest was a fight as well as a creed, and the swords that rang against the pates of cavaliers at Naseby and at Marston Moor were swords of protest, wrought of the selfsame steel that swung in echoing axe-strokes against New England's primeval forests. While not all who came to New England were Puritans, any more than here, yet the essence of the idea was a fight. There was, and is, plenty of chance for Puritan mettle upon any northern frontier. The North, the forest, the new land, the new way of life—these are a crucible, in which the virgin gold of character is assayed by strong reagents. Let no one cast himself unthinking into this crucible. Let no one with weak armor to his spirit enlist as warden of the northern marches, where only strong men hold the thin far line of civilization's self, upon the Last Frontier.

Captain John Smith once wrote a famous prospectus for colonists, that *Description* which will never lose its charm so long as English-speaking people continue to roam and to colonize. In naming New England, at the request of Prince Charles, he said of it:

I would rather liue here than anywhere: & if it did not maintain it selfe, were wee but once indifferently well fitted, let vs starue. . . . The Summer is not so hot & the winter is more colde in these parts . . . than we finde in the same height in Europe or Asia. Yet the Sea there is the strangest fish-pond I euer saw; & those barren Iles so furnished with good woods, springs, fruits, fish and fowls it makes men think though the Coast be rockie & affrightable: the Vallies, Plaines & Interior parts may well (not-withstanding) be verie fertile . . . & New-England is great enough to make many Kingdomes & Countries, were it all inhabited.

When Professor Snodgrass starts out on his tour to interest northern-minded people in Alaska as a colony, backed up by Uncle Sam himself and the Government Railroad in Alaska, I hope he carries Captain John Smith in his pocket as I know he must do in his mind. I hope that he tells people: " Quit envying your colonial ancestors their ' chance.' Take your own chance, to-day, and yourself become—if you have the proper 'makings'—a contemporary ancestor in this new colonial adventure. Here is a land for producers and workers, for those who love to work on a large pattern and see the picture grow —a land not finished, but rather just begun. El

Dorado really exists, but whether you find it or not depends upon the seeker and not upon the land in which you seek it. If you have not the durance of our winter wheat, to lie in patient undevelopment until the new soil works its miracle of life in you, do not come North."

Alaska is not a land of get-rich-quick, any more than was New England. It needs, as New England needed in its youth, both men and time. Alaska doesn't ask for frenzied gold-seekers, to-day. She asks for leaders, for thinkers, and " He who would bring home the wealth of the Indies must carry the wealth of the Indies with him." A cultural background is the very best provision for re-creative mental normalcy, under the stresses of pioneering life. Alaska is not a land for those who delight in compactitude, in the finished thing, the rounded, the exact, the classically composed entity. This is a land prodigious in flux, a land for people who revel in breadth and strangeness, in " beauty touched with strangeness "—rough-edged, unfinished. We need colonists who are, as Roosevelt saw it, " nearest akin to us by blood, belief, speech and law, and that are closest to us by the kindly ties of a former common history and tradition." That need is vitally and doubly true here in the North to-day. Alaska is to the United States what Scandinavia is to Europe, and that is why Colonel Ohlson of the Alaska Railroad is in search of farmers from Finland and the Scandinavian countries—who have long combined fishing in the Gulf with making hay on the salt marshes—as well as Swiss, German and Hollanders. Alaska's Delegate to Congress said to me only the other day: " The most difficult thing, I find, is to get people to think of Alaska as populated with the same racial strains that predominate in the United States. The northern Territory differs from all other American Territories and possessions in respect to its national origins." The North is, and continues to be, the land of the Northmen.

Every pioneer should be a born optimist, for the frontier is a land for the sanguine and not the melancholic disposition. I do not recommend Alaska today to the ordinary tourist, the person who wants things oil-smooth, who expects be-buttoned bell-boys to emerge from Ritzy hotels en route, who is disappointed if he does not see finished cities and finished lands. Such an one forgets that when a city or a land is finished it is dead, and such people should stay away from the Frontier. The North of freedom and friendliness will appeal most to the observant and intelligent real traveller. To my mind, the difference between a tourist and a traveller is that the latter has some notion of what he goes forth to see, while the former has not. Then, as Plato said so long ago, " Either we shall find that which we seek or we shall be less likely to think that we know what we do not know, and this surely is no mean reward." An open and a cheerful mind is an essential to any understanding of Alaska. Written above her gateway, we who know her read constantly this legend: *"Abandon Mope, All Ye Who Enter Here."*

Neither is Alaska a place for those who are saving of their energies or sympathies. Grumps are not wanted or needed, and if either your mind or your heart is all buttoned up neat and tight, then avoid Alaska as you would the plague, for it is not for you. Even if you came and looked, you'd never really see the true Alaska. Many people going to Alaska on a trip take a change of heavy underclothing. What

they really need to bring is a possible change of
mind! Stefansson says, " It is chiefly our unwilling-
ness to change our minds which prevents the North
from changing into a country to be used and lived in
like the rest of the world." Uncle Sam's children
have not until the last generation tried living in the
attic; but those who do, like it immensely. Come on
up, and take a look out of Uncle Sam's attic windows, if you wish to get a new view of the world.
Wasn't it Lowell who said that our ancestors came
to find a new world and found instead a new state
of mind?

Bigness is the dominant note, so take your time if
you go to Alaska, and don't be like the Englishman
who, on reaching Seattle, said, " I think I'll jolly
well run over to Alaska for the week-end! " Men
and mountains are big here, largeness of heart and
broadness of mind match dominoes with largeness of
territory. It is a place of big distance, as well as
big promise. Its beauty is not arranged and formal
like the English landscape, but wide and grand and
crude and open— a wild beauty, untamed, and a
beauty more than artificially skin deep. It is the very
real beauty of inner vigor and health, engendering
strength, promising plenty.

This is an adventure for those who value " peace
and their spiritual comforte above any other riches
whatsoever," as Bradford once wrote of some other
much more famous colonists. But there is no such
thing as salvation by geography. The Pilgrims of
old did what they did, and how, because of what they
brought with them as mental equipment and because
of what they deliberately left behind, much more
than by what they found in a new world. Merely
coming to Alaska won't solve any one's problem, for

it is only the Land of Promise to men of promise. The inexorable Law of the Yukon will reject all others. New England once asked that only colonists of " winnowed seed " be sent to her, and our need here is also for winnowed seed, not chance-blown pollen. Alaska had her one unhappy experience of haphazard unwinnowed sowing, back in the days of '98, and a good part of that hodge-podge planting of ill-adapted people has since been rooted out as unprofitable weeds. To-day she vastly prefers a small working population to a large gambling population. The early New Englanders were but transplanted English, and we Alaskans are but transplanted Americans, not so much founding a new culture as prolonging an old one. We need true pioneer men and we need true pioneer women. To paraphrase Whitman:

" With all thy gifts, Alaska . . .
     What if one gift thou lackest (The ultimate
          human problem never solving)
     The gift of perfect woman fit for thee?
     . . . The measured faiths of other lands,
          the grandeurs of the past,
     Are not for thee, but grandeurs of thine own—
     Deific faiths, and amplitudes."

XXX

Looking to a Long Future

MEN who do not know the facts about Alaska and who do not realize the full implications of Alaska's colonial status, sometimes say, " Uncle Sam saddled himself with a white elephant when he bought Alaska." Did he? This has been said so often, by the unthinking and the unknowing, that perhaps we should not take it as a joke—which it really is—but treat it seriously for a moment. Getting down to solid brass tacks, then, how does the Alaska ledger balance, to date?

Every one has been taught that the United States paid $7,200,000 for the title to Russia's American possessions. Let us leave aside the fact, now recognized through Secretary Lane's researches, that of this sum only $1,400,000 was actually paid *for Alaska,* and that the rest went to reimburse Russia for her friendly naval demonstration during the War between the States. Keeping in mind the larger figure—the "marked up," padded expense account —how much has Alaska actually returned to Uncle Sam's pockets?

Alaska has already produced over a billion and a half dollars in new wealth. In 100 days in 1906 Nome alone produced $7,500,000 in gold—more than the original purchase price of the Territory. In the one month of August, 1929, $787,134 in new gold was shipped from Alaska,—more than one tenth of the purchase price—and the total 1929 gold production is close to $8,000,000. In 1928, California with its millions of population produced 523,429 ounces of gold, and Alaska, with its few scattered thousands, was second with 330,604 ounces; and " only an ingrained pessimistic die-hard would prophesy that there will be no more big gold strikes in this great Territory." Every ten years whales alone, one of the least-considered industries here, pay the "blood money" for the Territory. Silver, merely a by-product as mined in Alaska, had as long ago as 1922 paid $8,104,000—topping the cost price and paying good interest on it. Tin, marble, gypsum, coal, petroleum, lead—resources just scratched in possibility—have already much more than paid for Alaska. Every five years the fur-bearing animals (*not* including seals) more than pay for Alaska. Exports for the one month of April, 1929, were worth a million and a half dollars—20 per cent. of the purchase price.

Alaska's potential water power has yet to be turned on. Thirty years ago the Eskimos had practically no real wealth, and now (at a minimum outlay on Uncle Sam's part) they control reindeer stock worth many millions. Wheat grown near Fairbanks took first prize at the agricultural fair in Minneapolis, in competition with the finest Minnesota and Dakota wheats. Twenty-one million acres of coal lands in Alaska, picked up on the international bargain counter at something like two cents per acre, hold enough coal (as estimated by the U. S. Geological Survey) to keep Uncle Sam's furnace running for full 300 years, at the present national rate of consumption. In round figures, fish and fur have brought in nearly a billion dollars to the United

States, and the metal mines of Alaska another half
billion.[1] One single mine, the Treadwell, paid for

[1] The following statistics were compiled from government reports, by the Alaska Department of the Seattle Chamber of Commerce:

Minerals	1928	1867 to 1929
Gold ....$	6,834,200	$ 372,885,515
Silver	292,115	11,030,913
Copper	6,781,655	206,915,513
Tin	42,595	1,031,139
Lead	130,321	1,428,734
Antimony		237,500
Coal	624,000	5,801,460
Palladium		683,948
Miscellaneous	123,224	4,266,423
Totals ....$	14,828,110	$ 604,281,145
Fish Products		
Salmon ....$	47,542,264	$ 688,252,233
Halibut	1,726,671	28,064,417
Herring	1,674,387	20,656,055
Cod	79,192	11,702,270
Trout		115,990
Shellfish	360,351	4,956,761
Whalebone	6,564	1,139,127
Fertilizer and Meal ..	694,915	4,436,649
Oil	1,327,253	13,222,115
Miscellaneous	105,690	4,814,422
Totals ....$	53,517,287	$ 777,360,039
Furs (including seal)..	4,694,262	116,499,587
Timber	130,579	1,666,152
Miscellaneous	441,515	5,881,549
Grand Totals ...$	73,611,753	$1,505,688,472

These figures include the value of exports only, and to them
should be added the sources of wealth consumed in the Territory
and the value of goods imported by Alaska and used there, if the
gross profits of " Seward's bargain " are fully to be appreciated.

Alaska over and over again in gold; and another, the Kennecott, has done the same in copper. At first, the main export of Alaska was fur; gold came to the front after 1900. During the World War the *relative* value of gold went down while copper prices soared, but after the War salmon supplanted copper as the main item in production value. Maybe, one day, wheat flour and reindeer meat will in turn supplant the " Silver Horde." That would be but a natural industrial development.

Even by the most pared-down official figures Alaska has already returned more than 200 times the purchase. The total cost of the purchase, of improvements that include a mountain-piercing railroad, and all administrative outlay on the attic since 1867, amounts to but 200 million dollars, and Alaska has already paid back over 1500 millions; or, if you accept Franklin K. Lane's statement that only $1,400,000 was actual purchase price, then the original investment has paid, to date, *over a hundred thousand per cent!* Was this " a poor bargain " ? How long must this continue before unthinking men shall cease to cry, " Alaska does not pay " ?

Perhaps Uncle Sam is a little like old Jacob. When his sons told him certain facts about the land of Egypt, he believed them not; but when he saw the Egyptian wagons actually standing before him, the spirit of the patriarch revived and he said, " It is enough! " Of the " Egyptian wagons " Judge Wickersham has stated: " In the Territory of Alaska there is wealth of every variety. There is more coal than there is in Pennsylvania, Ohio and West Virginia; there is more copper than in Michigan, Arizona and Montana; there is more gold than in California and Colorado; there is more agricultural land than in

Sweden, Norway and Finland; and there is more
fish than in all the balance of American waters, together." The truth is that Alaska to-day, if put up
for auction on the international block, would fetch
a thumping fat price on its visible assets and past,
unaided, pioneer production.

Any misconception about Alaska's contribution
arises from the fact that little of this wealth has remained in the land that produced it. Most of it has
" gone Outside," to enrich the rest of the United
States at Alaska's expense—just as many of New
England's colonial profits went back into the pockets
of stay-at-home Englishmen. That is why this Territory, rich beyond belief in natural resource, is
virtually on trial for its economic life whenever
pessimistic Congressmen choose to go on the ram-
page. The producer of these accretions to the national wealth is in the position of a stepchild, a
Cinderella, " an adopted orphan reared with pity
and condescension (as one sourdough put it), scrub-
bing the floors of the nation, like a bound boy at a
shucking "—compelled to accept whatever amount
is doled out from Washington. Alaska has taxation
with misrepresentation.

Alaska was purchased the same year that Canada
was confederated into a Dominion. In the 1840's
British statesmen were very indifferent to the fate of
Canada. Disraeli referred to " these wretched colonies " (Canada) as " a millstone round our necks,"
and Tennyson, official poet of the Crown, sang
lyrically,

" So loyal is too costly! Friends, your love
Is but a burden; break the bonds *and go!* "

But a new order came, and if Alaska had benefited

by a fraction of the development Canada's northwest railroads have given, or by a fraction of the understanding and appreciation showered on the Dominion by the British Government since '67, Alaska's position to-day would be a marvel to the civilized world, and our one, lone, voteless Delegate would not now be seen standing, hat in hand, humbly begging largess of Congress for Alaska's just and modest needs—a sum which is but a fraction of the usufruct of her own inherited natural wealth.

We Alaskans see no problems here unsolvable by time and patience and the least mite of understanding on the part of Mother Country statesmen—and journalists! For if there be an "Alaska problem," it is but the old one of colonial administration without true representation, of employing the outworn and hoary and long-exploded "mercantile theory" of colonial exploitation in this twentieth century, of not heeding the clear-written lessons of history, of not listening to words of Pitt which echo down the years like a Cassandra message: "The colonies have become too great an object to be grasped, *except in the arms of affection.*"

Stefansson remarks, with great truth, that it is merely "human nature to undervalue whatever lands are distant and to consider disagreeable whatever is different." New and undeveloped countries (like new and undeveloped people—children) must depend for the unfolding of their "natural resources" or future greatness, not only upon their own inherent health and vigor but, in good part, upon the patience and the oversight and long-term credits of older, perhaps wiser, but surely more stable and financially able mother countries. Vigorous young provinces must have wise and able parents, if they are to grow to full and safe maturity and not sow too many wild oats en route.

Our own United States, in its youth, was able to develop its great national resources because of the long-term credits extended to it by English and Dutch bankers, who were glad to lend their money to young and ambitious America wishing to build great railroads and great mills. There must be this element of faith—of patience and generosity and understanding of the needs of youth, upon the one hand, and willingness to learn and to do upon the other. When and how did the Louisiana Purchase begin to pay? When and how did the Oregon Tract begin to pay—or California, or Texas? When they were taken in and treated as one of the family, and not as aliens and strangers. Carpers say, " Alaska is a non-contiguous territory." Oregon and California were both made into States while they were yet non-contiguous territory, were not yet touching other States of the Union; and Oregon and California have well repaid this confidence.

Granted that Alaska is a stepchild of the Nation, what is the education a parent gives a child but another name for long-term financing? Development and education are two words with but one meaning —leading out, drawing out from its enwrapping envelope the precious hidden thing—out and up and on. Alaska needs these things now, in her days of youth. It is easy to realize why Service imagined her saying:

" Lofty I stand from each sister land, patient and
        wearily wise,
    With the weight of a world of sadness in my quiet
    passionless eyes,

Dreaming alone of a people, dreaming alone of a
   day,
When men shall not rape my riches, and curse me
   and go away; . . .
Dreaming of men who will bless me, of women
   esteeming me good,
Of children born in my borders of radiant mother-
   hood,
Of cities leaping to stature, of fame like a flag unfurled,
As I pour the tide of my riches in the eager lap of
   the world."

Not long ago I listened to a very well-known gen-
tleman lecture upon Alaska. He talked for an hour
about the scenery, the fish, the foxes, the seals of
Alaska—but he never once mentioned the Alaskans!
In last night's Washington paper I saw a headline,
" Alaska Evening at the Cosmos Club." I read that
eminent scientists had discussed the geology of
Alaska, the prehistoric paleo-Asiatic implications of
Alaska, and the progress of Alaskan fisheries—but
not one word had been uttered to indicate that
Alaska, to-day, has meaning to the United States of
America *chiefly* because it is an overseas colony of
actual American citizens, doing a big pioneer job in
the best way they know.

Uncle Sam's attic is a potential living-room, not
a mere storeroom, and to ignore the human element
in " the Alaska problem " seems to me to be ignor-
ing the problem itself, if problem there be. Which,
I ask you, would have proved more worth while to
England, in the eighteenth century: the fish and fur
and timber trade of the colonies, or the good will of
John and Sam Adams of New England, the respect
of a certain printer-body named Franklin who lived

in Philadelphia, and the confidence and unexasperated loyalty of a quiet Private Gentleman then recently married to a wealthy widow and settled on his comforable plantation at Mt. Vernon? The income from a colony may be golden eggs, but no wise householder kills his goose to get that egg! Rather he feeds the goose and plays silent partner with Time, for his own increased profit.

How much is a colonist worth to a mother country? How can you measure such worth? You can measure it in part by dollars, and in dollars a white man in Alaska to-day is said to be worth $1,302.75 in yearly trade! But the commerce of Alaska is worth about a hundred million dollars a year, in imports and exports. In 1927, the exports were $80,000,000 and the imports $32,000,000. In the one month of August, 1929, the exports were $19,000,000, with half a million in imports. Commerce with Alaska averaged more than trade with the Orient, over a period of several years, and Alaska is the greatest per capita contributor to the national revenues. Alaska's Governor has said, " If taxes collected in the United States from the people, the industries, and the resources, equalled per capita similar collections from Alaska, the yearly national revenues would be roughly five times as much as the Treasury receives at present."—So much for the tangible value of colonists.

But there are other values, intangible but no less real—questions of national honor, prestige, contracted word, given bond. How are these to be rated? How many colonists are equal to a shipload of copper? George III found, to his sorrow, that satisfied colonials might be the best product of a colony, and the British Government have never had

398 Uncle Sam's Attic

to re-learn that lesson, be it said to their great credit.
It was an expensive lesson, but the meaning penetrated and stuck. There is a famous speech which
every schoolboy knows (spoken by one Edmund
Burke, Esq., in the British House of Commons on a
day in March of 1775) in which I'd like to change
but two words and then recall to your memory:

Magnanimity in politics is not seldom the truest wisdom; and a great empire and little minds go ill together.
If we are conscious of our situation and glow with zeal to
fill our place as becomes our station and ourselves, we
ought to auspicate all our public proceedings on *Alaska*
with the old warning of the Church, Sursum corda! We
ought to elevate our minds to the greatness of that trust
to which the order of Providence has called us. By
adverting to the dignity of this high calling, our ancestors
have turned a savage wilderness into a glorious empire,
and have made the most extensive, and the only honorable conquests—not by destroying, but by promoting, the
wealth, the number, the happiness of the human race.
Let us get an *Alaskan* revenue as we have got an *Alaskan*
empire. *American* privileges have made it all it is;
American privileges alone will make it all it can be.

George III never visited America, but the one
American President who has visited Alaska during
his term of office said, as he left the country, that he
now had a suspicion that most of the complaints
which he had heard about Alaska had " come from
those who are commercially disposed, who have a
desire to acquire more than the average share of this
world's goods—and then take it somewhere else!
From this day forth my official as well as my personal interest in Alaskans will be in those who are
trying to make a real empire of Alaska, and who

intend to abide in the empire which they have helped to create."

Who "owns" a colony—the Mother Country or the colonists who go there and live? Neither—both —and partnership often causes bad feeling about responsibility and profit, *unless* there is perfect accord and perfect understanding of one another's points of view. The nation as a whole has a great stake in Uncle Sam's attic, as a storehouse of commodities; but the people who live in Alaska, who have made their homes here, who have invested everything they own in time and money here, are certainly entitled to be heard in matters which affect their destiny. They have not become aliens by coming to Alaska, for this is American soil. Without their coming, the country would nourish only its aboriginal and "savage" population, and a country without a working population is not a country but a waste, a desert, no matter what potential riches lie hidden within it. To let raw materials lie idle seems to Americans absurd, but raw materials are of no value unless and until there are people who know how to produce and use them.

Alaska, a decade after the World War, stands to America as the far West stood a decade after the Civil War. To-day America's citizens have elbow room, but to-morrow they may know crowding. Then these spaces may truly be put to work, to feed, clothe and house American citizens of a new Northwest, and tie them further to a soil that is also truly American. If there be any Alaskan problem, it is not the problem people outside of Alaska are talking about, but one they do not even think about: the problem of absentee government and ownership; the problem of getting an informed and working Federal administration to coöperate with an informed and working group of local colonists. The Alaska problem is not that of getting profitable products *out of* the country, but of getting profitable people *in to* the country. If you must have an "Alaska Problem," here it is in a paper-shelled nut!

Alaska needs the right kind of people, Alaska needs small capital in many industries and large capital in a few, and Alaska needs liberal Federal development of her roads and all other transportation facilities. But more than these things, Alaska needs time, the ally of all youthful projects and lands; and Alaska needs patience and understanding—that last great test of true friendliness. For, more than any material want, Alaska stands in need of friends. "The truth about Alaska is good enough," as Colonel Dick used to say. She needs to be spoken of simply as she is, nothing extenuated and naught set down in malice. Alaska has been called The Ugly Duckling, Cinderella, Orphan Annie, Alaska the Misunderstood. In all these names there lies the hint of need for patient friendliness and quiet intelligent understanding. Aren't friends the people who make us do our best because they believe the best about us, under whose eyes we double our capabilities and possibilities? Alaska needs such friends, to-day.

This colony of Alaska stands as yet, politically, in the early and not in the late eighteenth century. She stands in need of friendly and eloquent Burkes in Congress, but she has not yet reached to 1776 nor has she a formidable list of grievances such as the famous Philadelphia document of that date contained. There have been irritation and petty annoyance, but the cauldron has not yet boiled over;

and there is no good reason why it ever should. But
" he who knows the whence will also know the
whither," and in a democratic country such as the
United States it is essential that every private citizen
should make himself a potential statesman, by considering the past and gaining the perspective which
is seen through historical parallel. As globe circlers
will tell you, through Alaska alone of all American
territory runs the line where yesterday, to-day and to-
morrow actually meet.

There are three classes of people whose questioning about Alaska should be answered freely and
truly by all loyal Alaskans: real colonists seeking a
home here, honest national statesmen seeking a
genuine Alaska policy (something as yet unformu-
lated), and the youth of America's to-day seeking
facts about the new frontier which is their national
right and heritage and which they, to-morrow, will
be called upon to administer. To all three of these
classes I believe the historical parallel between
Alaska now and New England 200 years ago may
prove, as I know it has to me, a touchstone to truth.
With the founding of New England in mind, its
problems and its potentialities, the colonist can
imagine what to expect in present-day Alaska, the
statesman has an index from the past to point out
possible future difficulty, and the youth of America's
to-day can best realize the promise and the future
dormant in this heritage—*provided* it is preserved
for them in honest stewardship, and *provided* a body
of contented colonials grow up on America's last
frontier. If, when reading of Alaska news and doings, you will keep in the background of your mind
this thought—" She is a colony; she is passing now
through phases and experiences that New England

knew 200 years ago, that the West knew 100 years ago "—then and then only, I believe, will any one not himself an Alaskan understand The Great Country.

Think of us as men and women of your own race and breed, holding fast behind our feeble palisade of hope and fear Uncle Sam's last outpost to the not unfriendly North. Think of us as distant colonial kinsmen, as "contemporary ancestors." And think of us as Charles Sumner thought, when with the vision of a true statesman, he rose in the Senate of the United States to beg for the ratification of the cession of Russian America, and concluded with these words:

"Your best work and most important endowment will be the republican government which, *looking to a long future,* you will organize, with schools free to all and with *equal laws,* before which every citizen will stand erect in the consciousness of manhood. *Here* will be a motive power, without which Coal itself will be insufficient. *Here* will be a source of wealth, more inexhaustible than any Fisheries. Bestow such a government, and you will bestow what is better than all you can receive—whether quintals of fish, sands of gold, choicest furs, or most beautiful ivory."